An Excursion
through Chaos

ALSO AVAILABLE FROM BLOOMSBURY

Melancholic Joy: On Life Worth Living, Brian Treanor
Dump Philosophy: A Phenomenology of Devastation, Michael Marder
Art, Politics and the Pamphleteer, ed. Jane Tormey, Gillian Whiteley

An Excursion through Chaos

Disorder under
the Heavens

Stuart Walton

BLOOMSBURY ACADEMIC
LONDON • NEW YORK • OXFORD • NEW DELHI • SYDNEY

BLOOMSBURY ACADEMIC
Bloomsbury Publishing Plc
50 Bedford Square, London, WC1B 3DP, UK
1385 Broadway, New York, NY 10018, USA

BLOOMSBURY, BLOOMSBURY ACADEMIC and the Diana logo
are trademarks of Bloomsbury Publishing Plc

First published in Great Britain 2021

Cover design by Charlotte Daniels
Cover image © BIWA / Getty Images

A catalogue record for this book is available from the British Library.

A catalog record for this book is available from the Library of Congress.

ISBN: HB: 978-1-3501-4409-5
         PB: 978-1-3501-4408-8
         ePDF: 978-1-3501-4410-1
         eBook: 978-1-3501-4411-8

Typeset by Integra Software Services Pvt. Ltd.,
Printed and bound in Great Britain

To find out more about our authors and books visit www.bloomsbury.com
and sign up for our newsletters.

For Ankur Hazarika

Poor naked wretches, wheresoe'er you are,
That bide the pelting of this pitiless storm,
How shall your houseless heads and unfed sides,
Your looped and windowed raggedness, defend you
From seasons such as these?

King Lear, III:iv

'Take care of yourself!' screamed the White Queen, seizing Alice's hair with both her hands. 'Something's going to happen!'

Lewis Carroll, *Through the Looking-Glass*

Contents

Acknowledgements viii

Part One The birth of order from chaotophobia 1

Part Two

    The phenomenology of chaos: A mythical overture 45

1   Displacement 63

2   Simultaneity 99

3   Discordance 137

4   Malevolence 173

5   Hilarity 211

Notes 247
Index 256

Acknowledgements

The repeated, largely unthinking invocation of 'chaos' in the news media, and in the canons of moral debate in our time, seems to leave no room for considering it as anything other than a mess. I hope that the following work proves effective in challenging at least some of the unsuspected ideological presumptions in such a usage, and that far from being invariably the context of debilitating disorder, it might also begin to seem, under some of its aspects at least, an occasion for rethinking, remodelling, or else abandoning altogether, our present habits of mind.

That, certainly, is what has emerged from the many productive conversations and interchanges I have had on this theme with colleagues and friends. I would particularly like to express my gratitude to Liza Thompson, Lisa Goodrum and Lucy Russell at Bloomsbury Academic, to the anonymous assessors and readers of the proposal and the finished text, and to those who have made suggestions for the improvement and clarification of its arguments.

I would also like to thank, in no order other than that parodic approach to order, the alphabetical: Houman Barekat, Rajesh Borborah, Susan Castillo, Oliver Davis, Andrew Gallix, Matthew Scott, Sheila Walton, Susannah Wilson, Tim Winter and John Zerzan. The contribution to the present work by its dedicatee, Ankur Hazarika, far surpasses anything he suspects.

Finally, I was kept afloat during work on this project by a generous, and very gratefully received, grant from the Royal Literary Fund, which God preserve. And by a PPI refund disgorged from the institutional chaos of the banking industry.

Stuart Walton
Torquay
March 2020

Part One

The birth of order from chaotophobia

It is vital to have chaos within oneself, Nietzsche's Zarathustra teaches in his opening remarks to his followers, to be able to give birth to a dancing star. Only if everything within is wrought up into a creative ferment can one hang a lasting, glittering legacy in the benighted sky.

In an epoch rapidly surrendering to forms of disorder unimaginable to any prior generation, a question urges itself upon us: What is chaos? Is it a transitional process or a final state, a matter of Becoming or of Being? Is it possible to see it coming, or does it always take us by surprise? Even if it may be anticipated, does it belong to its nature always to be worse on arrival than everybody had feared? What, after all, does it feel like? Or is it, rather, a place? In which case our inaugural question ought perhaps to be: Where is chaos? Does it have secure or porous borders? How near are we to it at any one time, and does its territory show a definite tendency to expand until it threatens the very edges of the republic of order? How do we extricate ourselves from it once it has annexed the avenues of our own once-peaceable domain? Why do some people actively want to go there?

In Ionian antiquity, where Western culture began, it lay somewhere beyond the Aegean coast, in lands to which the ancient mythic heroes had first ventured, but it also underlay the rushing current of the present everyday life, in which, as Heraclitus of Ephesus taught, everything that lives and moves is subject to change. If war has always represented the most noxious distillate of it in human experience, any place of disorder, or state of confusion, would become, by gradual metaphoric dilution, the placeholder of an original – and possibly originary – chaos. In the globalized and mass-mediatic present, chaos is at once feared and enjoyed. It is the ready epithet for any situation that is not sufficiently subject to, or even only marginally outside, official control, but it is also the delightful transgressive element of postmodernity that reminds us that ossified systems of regulation are not entirely or always at the command of the authorities. Whichever pole of this continuum one oscillates towards, chaos is not something freely adopted, a sudden access of the untrammelled will, but an adventitious state that takes over, in which seemingly anything can happen. If the failure of the traffic signals causes utter chaos on the roads, the double-booking of a lecture hall for two separate audiences might result in hilarious confusion. A power outage at the hospital causes life-threatening turmoil, but the breakdown of the electronic scoreboard at a boring tennis match reduces proceedings to a glorious befuddlement. Its ontological ambivalence as a category of experience is the index of truth of a society that veers between too little functional dependability and all too much.

A narrative of the potential excitements of disorder began and ended in the nineteenth century, bequeathed by the first Romantic generation as a call to free-spiritedness in the face of encroaching industrial urbanism, the confinement of the human soul within the tethers of mechanistic production, but had been comprehensively discredited by the century's end in the discovery by theoretical physics that all systems tended to decay. The seething turbulence of a disintegrative phase was bound to issue in its entropic deceleration and final collapse, a law that was all too easily applicable to societies in the grip of fundamental technological and political change. A steady state could be monotonous enough, but was less menacing to human communion than social fragmentation and spiritual dissolution. The Victorian and Bismarckian eras closed amid threnodies of apocalyptic threat from imaginative writers and philosophers, an autumnal mood that soon turned, as the new century hit its stride, to abysmal winter, as the first continental war since the Napoleonic age engulfed an entire generation in technologized slaughter. Wholesale reconstruction after the devastations of both global conflicts appeared to have put an end to any lingering taste for disorder. In our own day, however, something resembling chaos has returned as the element of chance in late-modernist aesthetic movements, as the barely supervised belligerences and fantasies of online networks, and as a celebration of the stochastic element in mathematics, biology, astrophysics and other disciplinary systems once subject to the circumscription of immutable laws. A climate of uncertainty, once the guilty secret of scientific enquiry, the uncharted terra incognita of outer space and the inner brain alike, always offers the most propitious conditions for the freelance imagination, a jubilee period in which all are free to entertain their own theories until the correct one, or what appears for the time being to be the correct one, is imposed demonstratively. Despite the rationalist ideal, however, the science of the twentieth century was driven by the progressive realization that systems are not immutable and predictable, but that they display unaccountable variations within the same broad parameters. Nothing quite comes out how a fully qualified observer might have expected, for all that the deviations may be on the microscopic scale. Nothing can quite precisely be said, then, about what tomorrow's reprise of the same experiment will produce. We laugh at the nonsense they believed a hundred years ago, Nabokov says somewhere, before replacing it with some nonsense of our own. I want to make it clear at the outset, however, that I do not intend this study to supplement the already voluminous philosophical consideration of mathematical chaos theory, which is not strictly about chaos at all, but rather chance or contingency. In this respect, 'chaos theory' ought to be seen as a contradiction in terms, and many of its exponents indeed have been concerned to demonstrate how many structural or temporal parameters so-called chaotic systems do in fact observe. Chaos itself, which is, to be sure, subject to the random influences of the accidental, just as are the air currents unleashed by the famous butterfly of nonlinear systems theory, is about what happens as a result of such motile contingency, making its study a matter of the effects of its movements, and not simply of the movements themselves.

A widespread sense that the civilized world had fallen apart by the 1940s persisted into the aftermath of the Second World War, made luridly visible by evidence of the extent of Nazi inhumanity, and then of the torturous conditions of paranoid control that obtained in the Soviet East. Reconstruction was not just an economic affair, but a social and cultural one too. The centre of gravity shifted from Europe with its old oppugnances and its clapped-out, crudely exposed gentilities to the unabashed consumer culture of a United States that may still have been in the grip of vicious racial segregation, but at least promised a loosening of social mobility, the unlacing of punctilious manners, and exciting new cultural currents in abstract expressionism, the modern picaresque novel, production-line public catering, Coca-Cola, rock-and-roll. What lay behind the Western renaissance of the years of reconstruction, both in its North American heartlands and financial centres and in the resurgent economies that they begot on Western Europe, was a return to order, something like the social correlative of the *rappel à l'ordre* in the arts of the 1920s that followed the experimental mayhem of wartime Dada. In this perspective, the turbulent decade and a half that extended from the rise of the 1960s counterculture to the vanquishment of Keynesian economics and the social consensus at the end of the 1970s represented what remains for now the final blip in the steamrolling juggernaut of administrative order. The later twentieth century hardly lacked for oppositional currents of thought and ways of life in wider contexts than the counterculture, but it was the moment of the late 1960s that both crystallized dissent across much of the first world and ensured its neutralization.

The reasons for the collapse of the culture of dissidence are readable from both ends of the spectrum. It is a now familiar point that what Thomas Frank has called 'the conquest of cool' had already begun to be prepared during the high-water mark of the festival era.[1] Corporate culture was already appropriating the lineaments of alternative lifestyles – their patois, music, sartorial and sexual styles, even the ecstatic relation to intoxicants, where that remained roughly within the bounds of legal sanction – and not only selling them back to adepts of the counterculture, but incorporating them into their own economic and discursive procedures. It was possible, indeed positively encouraged, to be a risk-taking rebel in the advertising industry and in speculative finance, to practise an intuitive, self-rewarding approach to consumerism instead of heading out every Monday with a shopping list. As such, as Eugene McCarraher has argued, the alternative reality of the dissidents was assimilated more or less whole:

> The Cold War counterculture, so often considered a flamboyant adversary of 'conformity' and virtuous consumerism, was in fact more amenable to pecuniary and technological rationality than it appeared to be … Replacing 'virtuous consumerism' as the quintessence of the American spectacle, the democratization of bohemia represented the final incorporation of Romanticism, the annexation of the modern sacramental consciousness into the empire of corporate iconography.[2]

By the same token, if corporate capitalism was busy drawing lifeblood from the legions of refuseniks, they themselves proved exceptionally porous to the oldest and most powerful tenets of class society. Free love turned out to be as much a provocation of erotic rivalrousness as it was a liberation from it, while it did precisely nothing to rebalance relations of clientage between the sexes. It clung to the definition of anything but heterosexual desire as thrillingly deviant, worth engaging in for its non-normativity, which thereby reinforced normativity itself. Where there was instinctual opposition to the economic structures of post-war capitalism, it was informed by nothing like the fully articulated analysis that might have convicted the economy of its injustice, only a sententious, soppy sense that it wasn't nice. Niceness indeed was the watchword, readily apparent as one garlanded oneself with flowers and subsided into the bestial stupidity of being stoned. The cosmic gibberish of Al Hubbard and Timothy Leary stood in for articulate philosophy, and an amalgam of Hindu and Buddhist ceremonial ambience, carefully shorn of their pensive injunctions to the ascetic life, was as much belief as was required. Despite its revolutionary rhetoric, instead of a combative challenge, it amounted to an indolent accommodation with the way things were, a parallel world running peaceably alongside the predominant one.

There were, to be sure, intelligent critics of the post-war status quo who pointed out the terrible cost in self-alienation that societies forsworn to corporate culture and social obedience were extracting from their clients. People who had experienced corporations from the inside and then dropped out often had cautionary tales to tell about the spiritual effects of such structures on human will, but they rarely counselled outright opposition to the system as a whole. This was very much the tenor of William H Whyte's sociological classic *The Organization Man* (1956) and Alan Harrington's autobiographical fiction *Life in the Crystal Palace* (1959), texts that expressed a professionalized concern over the toll in spontaneous life and the creative faculty that working in Fordist corporate enterprises was taking on their middle managers. Menopausal discontent with the pedestrian time-serving that office life demanded of its officers in return for ample salaries, health insurance and pension plans began to be a durable novelistic theme from this period too, a tendency inaugurated by Sloan Wilson's *The Man in the Gray Flannel Suit* (1955), whose hero Tom Rath is a PR writer for a New York television company. He accepts the system, which in turn accepts his own stifled chafing at its straitened expectations:

> The important thing is to create an island of order in a sea of chaos, and an island of order obviously must be made of money, for one doesn't bring up children in an orderly way without money, and one doesn't even have one's meals in an orderly way, or dress in an orderly way, or think in an orderly way without money. Money is the root of all order, he told himself, and the only trouble with it is, it's so damn hard to get, especially when one has a job which consists of sitting behind a desk all day doing absolutely nothing.[3]

'Order' is the catchword that rings like a passing bell throughout Rath's interior monologues, appearing to him as in a vision in the guise of something devoutly to be wished but forever just tantalizingly out of reach, and at the same time the brutal principle by which his working life is dominated anyway. He takes the sanguine view that while he is powerless to do anything about the state of the world, he can at least set his own life in order, failing to see that the two things are closely imbricated. There would be dissatisfied junior executives all over the cultural show as the American 1950s wore on towards the turning of the decade. Harry Angstrom, antihero of John Updike's most celebrated novel cycle, makes his first appearance in his mid-twenties as the restlessly bored sales operative for a kitchen gadget in *Rabbit, Run* (1960). Richard Yates's Frank Wheeler in *Revolutionary Road* (1961) is seduced by his wife into the fleeting dream of throwing the corporate life over and moving to Paris to begin a new life less trammelled by capitalist conformism. 'At their most penetrating', writes McCarraher of the rat-race critiques of the 1950s, 'they revealed the religious longings that galvanized devotion to corporate life, yet they offered no alternative to the corporate system aside from an innocuous "nonconformity."'[4]

Such nonconformity would eventually be given a nebulous shape in the hippie era, but even then not all dissenting intellectual voices were muffled by the monotonous churn of the conformist rock music. The American historian and sociologist Lewis Mumford's coruscating counterblast to the Woodstock Festival of August 1969 saw in it nothing but a perpetuation of the same degraded consumer culture to which it imagined itself the antithesis. The light-shows and psychotropic intoxicants were nothing other than an exaggerated reflection of the dullness of mainstream society, with which they were thereby indissociably bound. Woodstock itself, apart from producing a massive traffic-jam and a gargantuan heap of trash, was an unbridled context of delusion mounted by the self-emancipated in hopeful escape from a thoroughly technologized culture:

The depressing monotony of megatechnic society, with its standardized environment, its standardized foods, its standardized invitations to commercial amusement, its standardized daily routines, produces a counter-drive in over-stimulation and over-excitement in order to achieve a simulation of life. Hence 'Speed' in all its forms, from drag races to drugs. With its narcotics and hallucinogens, its electrically amplified noise and stroboscopic lights and supersonic flights from nowhere to nowhere, modern technology has helped to create a counter-culture whose very disorder serves admirably to stabilize the power system.[5]

By 1971, the alienated executive of the 1950s had been taught by the dropout culture of the hippie interlude that a freewheeling life of self-invention might just be within reach, as is hoped for by David Bell, the television executive who embarks on a meandering road trip with a movie camera in Don De Lillo's first novel, *Americana*. The trope is still enduring more hardily than the angst-ridden managers themselves in Alan Ball's screenplay for the Sam Mendes film *American Beauty* (1999), in which a mid-life magazine executive, Lester Burnham, signals his own excursion into nonconformity by the time-hallowed, toothless tactic of behaving out of character – pumping weights in the garage, developing a sexual obsession with a teenage cheerleader, his daughter's friend, and smoking cannabis supplied by the teenage boy next door. If nonconformity had to be the indispensable starting-point of any opposition, its performance alone, much satirized in comic films and TV shows in the 1970s – Leonard Rossiter's Reginald Perrin, from a 1975–8 novel sequence by David Nobbs, was the British paradigm – would scarcely be sufficient. What was needed was the critical consciousness that could understand and see through the rationale for conformity mounted by the current dispensation in the first place. Order and hierarchy were firmly enough entrenched that they could withstand parodic onslaughts on their jargon and the pettiness of their bureaucratic procedures, much as they could absorb sudden resignations by executive staff. In the end, there was something cosy about peripheral spasms of discontent. If you chose not to resign, they were what helped get you through.

Although the alternative to regimented order does not indeed have to be what we are calling chaos, exponents of the status quo nonetheless typically insisted – and still do – that without the present order, there would be nothing but chaos. The most fully articulated attempt to resist that simple equation was expressed in the theoretical work of the first generation of the Frankfurt School, exiled to the United States with the ascendancy of the Nazi state in Germany, and bequeathing certain of its leading thinkers, most notably Herbert Marcuse, to American academia, after most of its luminaries returned to the Federal Republic after the war. Established as the Institute for Social Research in 1923, it had begun by constructing a multi-disciplinary Marxist assault on Western capitalism as the latter entered what was widely felt to be its final moribund phase, embracing economic and sociological analysis, as well as dialectical approaches to traditional and avant-garde culture. Translated piecemeal from Frankfurt University to New York and Los Angeles, it responded to its new cultural milieu by formulating a global theory of the progress of Enlightenment rationality towards the technological vapidities of the contemporary day, which it saw cathected in the shape of the narcotized consumerism being prepared in the United States as a modus vivendi for the world at large. Theodor Adorno and Max Horkheimer's *Dialectic of Enlightenment* (1947), which circulated in draft in the period immediately following the war, prior to its issue by an independent Dutch publisher, was the Institute's first fully articulated statement. A complete English translation would not appear until 1972, but the challenging substance and tone of the work made it notorious long before anybody in the Anglophone world had had chance to read it.

A key point of disputation raised by Adorno and Horkheimer was the thesis that society, in its progress from barbarism to civilization according to the narrative of the European Enlightenment, had been cumulatively founded on the principle of reason. Where mythology once held sway, the rationalistic sciences now reigned supreme. Among the Frankfurt School's most provocative contentions was that Western civilization had unwittingly executed a reversal of this narrative. The heroic phase of the eighteenth-century Enlightenment purported to have freed humankind of antique superstition and the demons of the irrational, but the horrors of the twentieth century gave the lie to such brash triumphalism. Far from humane liberation, Europe had plunged into decades of savage barbarism. The Frankfurt School theorists argued that universal rationality had been raised to the status of an idol. At the heart of this was what they called 'instrumental reason', the mechanism by which everything in human affairs was consumed and metabolized. When reason enabled human beings to interpret the natural world around them in ways that ceased to frighten them, it was a liberating faculty of the mind. In the Frankfurt account, however, its fatal flaw was that it depended on domination, on subjecting the external world to the processes of abstract thought. Eventually, by a heuristic process of trial and error, everything in the phenomenal world would be explained by scientific investigation, which would lay bare the previously hidden rules and principles by which it operated, and which could be demonstrated anew any number of times. The rationalizing faculty had thereby become, according to Adorno and Horkheimer, a tyrannical process, through which all human experience of the world was subjected to infinitely repeatable rational explanation, a process in which reason had turned from being liberating to being the instrumental means of categorizing and classifying an infinitely various reality. As the most tangible proof of this thesis, culture itself was subjected to a kind of factory production in the cinema and recording industries. The Frankfurt theorists maintained a deep distrust of what passed as 'popular culture', which neither enlightened nor truly entertained the mass of society, but only kept people in a state of permanently unsatiated demand for the dross with which they were going to be fed anyway. And driving the whole coruscating analysis was a visceral commitment to the Marxist theme of the presentness of the past. History was not just something that happened yesterday, but a dynamic force that remained active in the world of today, which was its material product and its consequence. By contrast, the attitude of instrumental reason produced only a version of the past that ascended towards the triumph of the enlightened and well-ordered democratic societies of the present day.

In the years following the defeat of Hitler, society had coalesced into a state of micrological bureaucratic control that the Frankfurt School referred to as '*die verwaltete Welt*' ('the administered world', often intensified polemically by Adorno to 'the totally administered world'), a milieu in which not just the large organizational structures of human community, such as the provision of public services, a medical system, the arrangement of elections and so on, were the province of the state, but so too were the rhythms and measures of personal existence, the habits of thought and intersubjective response that furnished the contours of day-to-day living. The national electricity grid and the gas pipelines could supply the energy needed to power society, but something less crude than the official nostrums of cultural policy in the Eastern bloc – the unrelieved diet of socialist realism that bureaucratically drearified what had once been the dynamic modes of naturalistic theatre and the realist novel – was required to satiate the recreative spirit. If the answer lay to hand in the pre-existing developments of radio and the cinema, joined after the Second World War by the domestic dissemination of television, this was doing no more than stating the obvious, but the early oppositional potential of these media, in the forms of polemical radio broadcasts and dissonant, socially critical film, would have to be rinsed away, the bulk of their production streamlined instead in accordance with the industrial model of automobile production, their ideological content freighted with potently conformist messages, if they were to be of use in the homogenization of mass consciousness. The culture industry was born partly from the privations of the Depression years and partly from the emergency of the world war, when the unifying potential of mass entertainment media was instrumental in shoring up morale, but its mechanisms survived into the era of affluence and peacetime that followed, making official culture – a broad arc that spanned everything from blockbuster concerts conducted by Arturo Toscanini to the hit-songs of the nascent pop industry, from the earnest existential poetry of the German recovery years to the addled flimflam of the soap operas – one of the principal recruiting agents to an unalloyed faith in the post-war status quo. The second generation of the Frankfurt School, led by Jürgen Habermas, would undertake a thoroughgoing revisionist overhaul of this thesis, beginning from the premise that if the administered world and its culture industry had deluded everybody, which nobody in the first generation had actually argued, it would amount to a performative contradiction to be able to point it out.

An alternative current to the theory of the wholly administered society emerged in the writings and lectures of Michel Foucault, where the concept of 'biopower', occasionally 'biopolitics', carries out much the same conceptual labour. Administrative structures have extended to cover the life-events and daily existence of their clients, through measures such as the public regulation of health, the distribution of welfare benefits, the compulsion to pay national insurance and so forth. Human beings in this conception are not just political citizens, but a biological species too, which must be preserved by the existing order so that it can continue to staff the economic reproduction of capital. Political power, once the arbitrary dispensation of hereditary rulers, was now the preserve of a simultaneously bureaucratic and disciplinary apparatus that extended its panoptical sway over the life-processes of individuals, who were conceived not as individuals but as an agglomerate mass. When the state disposes over nothing less than life itself, either directly in the exorbitant use of judicial killing in polities as officially distinct as the United States and China, or indirectly by the targeting of public health measures on those population sectors likely to be of more productive use to the economy than the less capable, such as the selective availability of reproductive technology and the defrayment (or not) of resources to ensure the safety of residential tower blocks, it has achieved a greater mastery over consciousness and the emotional lives of its clients than even feudal absolutism managed.

What these celebrated, and still widely adopted, critiques implicitly envisaged was some form of inchoate liberation from the bondage of order, a rediscovery of spontaneity and autonomy that could only begin at the level of consciousness. Adorno would argue in the late 1960s that, as a sine qua non of resistance to the entrenched imperatives of administered society, it was necessary to refuse its thought-forms at the individual level. Everything that bureaucracy and the culture industry uttered to their captive audiences should be subjected to reflexively suspicious examination, its presumptions unravelled, its self-contradictions laid bare, if humanity were not to succumb wholesale to that final domination over its inner essence that began with Palaeolithic domination of nature. Even during the years of the Frankfurt diaspora in the United States, the Institute's general staff were kept under official surveillance by the security services, and by the time they returned to the Federal Republic of Germany following the defeat of Hitler, after a period in which their advice on education policy and cultural matters was actively courted by the state, they came to be vilified in conservative circles from the 1970s on for their allegedly nihilistic hatred of the post-war consensus. There were those who held Adorno and his colleagues responsible for emboldening, through their corpus of theoretical dissent, the violent praxis of the Red Army Faction or Baader-Meinhof Group, a ludicrous slur that nonetheless expressed the perceived obligation for universal consent that the reactionary right now considered society's due. Leftist dissension and the counterculture more generally had resulted in calamities such as the homicidal hippies of the Manson gang, mindless sexual anarchy, selfish irresponsibility instead of a sense of collegiate duty, the cult of everyone-for-themselves that capitalism itself had in fact always been, but which looked hideous when translated to the realm of personal morality. As the bitterly simplistic divisions of the Cold War solidified into a neurotic impasse to which citizens were invited to give the name of 'peace', a hegemonic interpretation of democracy on the Western side was drilled into its clients. Even if some malcontents harboured no taste for the pabulum of the culture industry, or persisted in voting for parties that wished to dismantle the capital economy, it was incumbent on them all to remember that the purgatory of repression and enforced conformity on the other side of the Wall represented the only possible alternative. An acceptance of the lesser of two evils was enjoined on post-war societies, principally because anything less savoured of lending encouragement to the enemy, but also because the result of a breakdown of consent would be chaos.

To return to our inaugural question, then: Where is chaos today?

It is decried more or less daily in the tribunes of press opinion every time it is seen as the result of administrative failure, the absence of leadership in what is perceived to be a crisis, when any outbreak of disobedience, including industrial action, demonstrations and occupations, halts the flow of the streamlined bureaucratic state. The worldwide coronavirus pandemic of 2020 brought a constant drip-feed of systems disintegrating into helpless disorder: 'Travellers face airport chaos', 'Chaos for holidaymakers as cruises are cancelled', 'GMB coronavirus chaos as presenter goes into self-isolation', the last an allegedly frantic meltdown at the studios of the *Good Morning Britain* breakfast show because one of its anchors had had to confirm she was putting herself under fourteen days' quarantine. These strident alarums did not have to await the arrival of a global outbreak of disease, but have been the lingua franca of journalistic chastisement whenever a system is perceived to be working at less than full efficiency. They speak to at least two deeply internalized public needs in these contexts – the hyperbolic impulse to condemn the contingent effects of system failures in the strongest terms imaginable and a concomitant perverse pleasure in invoking an atmosphere of absolute exigency. On the first count, the cry of 'chaos', more often than not a childish exaggeration, feels like the best strategy for urging those responsible to take the necessary corrective measures. If a broken-down ticket machine can be said to have caused 'chaos', perhaps somebody will repair it more quickly. In the second sense, taking upon oneself the diagnosis of a state of 'chaos' performs the function of making those uttering it feel superior to the unravelling system, to which they are otherwise impotently subjugated. As it falls apart at the seams, those whom it ought to be serving can now stand above it and call it by its name. It also, at least where one has a chance of not being personally too incommoded by it, creates a vicarious thrill of liberation, precisely because its dishevelment means it is now unpredictable. Anything could happen.

If ever a globally unfolding event deserved the name of 'chaos', the COVID-19 crisis fulfilled all the criteria. Before whatever manifestations of disarray there were in attempts to contain it, the virus itself was a paradigm case of a chaotic system. By the time it had hit its stride outside China, in the early months of 2020, it was impossible to say where it would pop up next, subject as it was not just to the vagaries of international air travel but to the unpredictability of its routes of interpersonal transmission.[6] Even when testing and tracing systems were put in place in various localities, their results were often patchy, and those countries where its probable eradication was prematurely announced – South Korea, New Zealand, China itself – in due course started seeing renewed outbreaks of it. The frantic search for a medical solution in the form of a vaccine, or at least a medication that would mitigate its worst effects in those diagnosed with it, represented the best hope of defeating it, but were repeatedly led up blind alleys by false reports of the efficacy of various existing pharmaceuticals, most notably the antimalarial agent, hydroxychloroquine. In the meantime, the administrative measures put in place to try to limit the spread of the virus, the chief among which was a more or less rigorously enforced quarantine measure widely known in the carceral terminology as 'lockdown', generated often unseen emotional side-effects in the forms of depression, anxiety, paranoia, the distress suffered by separated families, domestic violence in troubled households and an incalculable level of barely suppressed rage at examples of public figures taking it upon themselves to disregard the regulations, sometimes with impunity.

During the reflective period in which everybody was under restriction, theories proliferated. One of the most enduring of these, as Slavoj Zizek noted in a short work on coronavirus and its societal effects published at the height of the crisis, was a kind of pathetic fallacy in which the disease was credited with a consciousness, as one of the teleological forces of history. It was a malevolent agent that had declared war on humanity, or else was the revenge of an affronted Nature against its own worst enemy, humankind:

> We should resist the temptation to treat the ongoing epidemic as something that has a deeper meaning: the cruel but just punishment of humanity for the ruthless exploitation of other forms of life on earth. If we search for such a hidden message, we remain premodern: we treat our universe as a partner in communication … The really difficult thing to accept is the fact that the ongoing epidemic is a result of natural contingency at its purest, that it just happened and hides no deeper meaning. In the larger order of things, we are just a species with no special importance.[7]

Inasmuch as it fails to fit the role of enemy so easily, COVID-19 was purely chaotic. Even a vengeful nature would have suggested a systemic response that could in turn be addressed, but no such dialogic structure presents itself. It is an idiotically mutating pathogen that accidentally destroys many of its weaker hosts in the course of its exponential transmission between populations of potential bearers.

What the crisis did achieve was to throw everybody together in their physical or spiritual apartness, by the simple expedient of making it impossible for them to socialize in the regular way. Virtual communities of solidarity were created, not all of them dragooned into being by organized local care initiatives or TV tutorials in making improvised home decorations. People felt their togetherness precisely through their separation, as though the demarcation of distance between them was enough to demand ways of imaginatively bridging it while they waited for the moment when the reunions could take place in actuality. The lockdowns annihilated the perception of time, which either ran on in the outside world unheeded as the seasons progressed, or slowed to the standstill of permanent domestic isolation. Coronavirus, as many noted, imitated the insidious effects of ideology, the fear of it and the necessity to avoid it becoming a variety of second nature, the face-masks and gloves an acknowledgement that it could be lurking invisibly anywhere, from the handles of recycle boxes to the mail that dropped through the letterbox each day. Its prevalence allowed the more repressive regimes to rehearse that total control of their societies of which they have always dreamed, and yet at the same time, the utmost benevolence was enacted in the form of radical welfare and social provision measures. In the democratic polities, meanwhile, consensus quickly broke down, with currents of dissent surfacing against governments that were improvising desperately. The moves to neutralize rage among those on the social margins with the least to lose – the homeless, the undocumented refugees and migrants – were telling indicators of a level of official concern which both liberal and repressive regimes normally manage without. The continued threat of a reprise of the outbreak, or of something similar arising each winter, is the nearest thing to global catastrophe that anybody born after 1945 has suffered, including those whose memories reach back to the paranoid stasis of the Cold War. Even more than prolonged periods of war, it has left the mass of humanity feeling caught in a state of passivity, cornered in their homes while the habitual operations of society grind to a halt outside.

Another sort of chaos results not from administrative failure, but rather from the administrative provision of disorder. The most pressing example of this facet in everyday life is the global chatter of online networks, where weightless conspiracy theories are assured far-reaching dissemination, the clashing of rhetorical swords is the daily mood-music of media intended to bring people together, and abuse and vicious hostility continue to outwit official oversight. Among its less morbid consequences, the discursive lexicon of social media has produced a presumption of negative intent, under which the most innocent of emollient responses, statements of assent, are read as being reflexively sardonic. Everybody expects to be treated to what is known as a 'takedown', a term from the ambience of professional wrestling, or that another participant will try to 'shut them down', as though they were a failing business enterprise, with a decisively withering retort. These channels of unmoderated anger have resulted in the grotesque phenomenon of cyber-bullying, virtual threats of violence that have sometimes exploded into concrete acts of criminal aggression, the short fuse and the long leash combining to make life a pandemonium of hysterical contestation – nothing like the genteelly orchestrated cadences of rational interchange portrayed in Milton's original Pandaemonium. On the other hand, as many disgruntled customers have discovered, the quickest way to obtain redress of a grievance against a company is not to email them or sit in a phone-queue, but to go public with your complaint on Twitter. That last point raises the question of how – indeed whether – it might be possible to use a chaotic state of affairs to force an institutional system into responding to its participants. If there is an objective chaos, the one into which structures erupt or dissolve, taking their clients with them, there is also a subjective version, deliberately provoked to begin with, as well as an objective chaos that can be subjectively exploited for its possibilities of emancipation.

Before we consider those possibilities, it is necessary to ask what ideology lies behind the assertion that, far from revelling in carnivalesque uproar, we are confirmed creatures of order. One of the classic statements of this in twentieth-century aesthetics was uttered by Wallace Stevens in a poem, 'The Idea of Order at Key West', written in 1934 when economic depression was in spate and the storm-clouds of conflict were massing again. The poet speaks of listening to a wild singer at the sea's edge on a Florida island, and muses on where aesthetic inspiration has its sources. A dialectic of the susurrating sea and the woman's voice reflects the imposition of intent with which the artist or creator encounters the raw materials of the world, as distinct from that raw material itself in the form of the water and its 'meaningless plungings'. As the song ends, the poet addresses his companion, one Ramon Fernandez, and asks him rhetorically why it was that, as the night descended on the scene, the lights of the fishing-boats in the harbour appeared to take on a patterning and regulative function, as they 'mastered the night and portioned out the sea, / Fixing emblazoned zones and fiery poles, / Arranging, deepening, enchanting night'. The insight generates an exclamatory final insight that human perception harbours a 'blessed rage for order':

> The maker's rage to order words of the sea,
> Words of the fragrant portals, dimly-starred,
> And of ourselves and of our origins,
> In ghostlier demarcations, keener sounds.[8]

For all that the instinctual grasp at order is beatified in the poet's address, it is also pathologized as a rage, in that it aims to subdue and incorporate the untamed natural language around it, and by extension tell itself stories of the nature of humankind and its origins. The enigmatic final line seems to hint, though, that the lineaments of form in which the aesthetic capture of the world is disposed ought to be at once less crudely material and sensually sharper than a formalist conception of art is given to allowing. Less rigid formal constraints would free the sensual element to emerge more richly and more immediately. Included in a 1935 collection, *Ideas of Order*, the poem is often seen as strangely antithetical to the sentiments of the poems it accompanies, and yet the 'rage for order' it apostrophizes is not what it might at first appear, but a yearning for an order that will do justice precisely to the resistances to order that the phenomenal world seems to embody.

The post-war intellectual vogue that came to be known as structuralism represented the last attempt in Western thought to put intellectual enquiry on a systematic footing. Applied as it was most notably in the areas of anthropology (by Claude Lévi-Strauss), linguistics (by a host of minor figures working belatedly in the tradition established in the early years of the twentieth century by Ferdinand de Saussure and Roman Jakobson), psychoanalysis (by Jacques Lacan) and in a scientifically elaborated Marxist politics (represented pre-eminently by Louis Althusser), structuralist theory believed implicitly that its objects of study could be fitted into pre-existent parametrical confines. It was a diverse, and often undoubtedly creative, exercise in system-building, its various projects resulting in such intricate theoretical edifices as the psychoanalytic seminars of Lacan, the comparative analysis of archaic mythologies throughout Levi-Strauss's prodigious career, and the totalizing conspectus of literary aesthetics in Northrop Frye's *Anatomy of Criticism* (1957). The more hubristic its towers of intellectual Babel grew, however, the more vulnerable they became to seismic tremors, none more so than the movement of Deconstruction inaugurated by Jacques Derrida, the very name of which indicated its open-ended revisionist approach to all disciplinary structures. Structuralism in the grand manner, which virtually nobody professes now outside the aridities of classical economics, was both mythical in its conception and ahistorical in its practice. How had these putative structures come into being if not through the same human intelligences that could unravel them at a moment's notice, or at least collectively subject them to continuous development? Had Derrida not finished off structuralism's rage for order with his theoretical notations of undecidability and dissemination, the counterculture of the 1960s, which was not overtly hospitable to ready-made systems, would have subjected its appeal to the same obsolescence as the fashion industry's rustication of last season's trouser-width.

Palaeolithic advances in human culture depended on early communities developing the classifying principles of definition and explanation. Observations of changes in weather patterns, the life-cycles of the flora and fauna on which they subsisted, the development of weaponry, the systematic use of fire and – out of the formation of mythical consciousness – the conception of enchanted interpretations of the world around them: all contributed to the survival and sociocultural success of the proto-human race. The Frankfurt School narrative argued that because the accumulation of knowledge became a means of taming and dominating natural conditions, this archetypal scene prepared the ground for the historical development of human affairs as a progress in the subjugation not just of the earth itself, but of each other, and finally of their own inner beings. Michel Foucault's account in *The Order of Things* (1966), to which we shall return in more detail later, shows that, probably from the sixteenth century on, the taxonomic urge invades consciousness itself and refashions it in its own image. What these theories therefore insist on is that, if there is ever to be a way out of the instrumental and technological rationality under which the greater part of life is now subsumed, it can only come about through solving the riddle of how the human species can understand and accommodate itself to objective reality without simultaneously remoulding itself in accordance with the very methods that it brings to the task.

The abandonment of axiomatic Cartesian certainty as an assumption of scientific investigation has been its prevalent trend over the last century. Incalculability, unpredictability and the observation of an apparently random factor in the most elementary physical systems have been the defining breakthroughs of what one might call the post-relativity era. While science has, however, for its own hyperbolic purposes, chosen to define this as 'chaos', two divergent stances have emerged within these parameters. As Katherine Hayles has pointed out, one current insists that chaos is the precursor of order, into which it inevitably resolves, while the other proposes that there are structures of inherent order within chaos, observable only when previously orderly systems transmute into the chaotic state. According to the former, entropic systems that are in a decisive condition of decay exhibit strong tendencies to self-organization, as was demonstrated by Ilya Prigogine and Isabelle Stengers in their touchstone work, *Order out of Chaos: Man's New Dialogue with Nature* (1984). In the case of the second branch, deeply encoded structures known as 'strange attractors' give evidence of the inherent tendency to order that is to be discovered in systems that remain chaotic, not merely random but genuinely, durably chaotic, a finding that is replicated across an extraordinarily disparate field of phenomena. To put it brutally simply, the first paradigm is interested in what emerges from chaos, while the second concentrates on how systems descend into chaos, if that is the correct spatial metaphor, in the first place.[9]

From the political point of view, these two variants of chaos theory can be characterized, respectively, as the conservative and radical paradigms. In the first, there is a teleological need to believe that all disordered situations are yearning to be brought back into order, which licenses the state's intervention to help them back to an equilibrium to which they would theoretically be tending anyway. In the second theory, though, what matters is what happens within the state of chaos, how it came about through dissipative tendencies within the pre-existing order, to be sure, but predominantly what potentials and hidden possibilities it now manifests.[10] The two variants perfectly encapsulate the age-old dilemma faced by all sudden moments of historical emancipation, whether the new situation generated then succumbs to the same forms of deadening bureaucratic control from which they have just wrested society, or whether they continue to be productive, imaginative and unsettling to normative order. David Graeber has argued that the sense of liberation prompted by insurrectionary episodes in history helps explain 'why revolutionary moments always seem to be followed by an outpouring of social, artistic, and intellectual creativity. Normally unequal structures of imaginative identification are disrupted; everyone is experimenting with trying to see the world from unfamiliar points of view; everyone feels not only the right, but usually the immediate practical need to re-create and reimagine everything around them'. Then again, the imperative is 'how to ensure that those who go through this experience are not immediately reorganized under some new rubric … that then gives way to the construction of a new set of rules, regulations, and bureaucratic institutions around it, which will inevitably come to be enforced by new categories of police'.[11] In other words, how does one prevent the second chaos paradigm from mutating regressively into the first? In Graeber's case, that experiment took the form of the Occupy movement in New York in autumn 2011, the same year that had begun with the convulsions of the Arab Spring in Tunisia and Egypt. The latter resulted in governments that were at least as oppressive, authoritarian and corrupt, if not even more so, than the moribund regimes they overthrew, while Occupy ended not with the bang of the abolition of capitalism but with the whimper of a ludic pantomime of protest that was fascinated by its own aptitude for formulating new discursive forms, but which had nothing concrete to demand of state authorities, which tolerated it until the coming of the cold weather persuaded everybody to go home. The earnest attempt to change the way politics was done cannot be faulted in either case, but both bequeathed to their participants, and to libertarian strategists in the world around, that nothing substitutes in insurrectionary circumstances for a coherent set of demands. Be these ever so impossible for the ruling polity to concede, their focused intensity can begin to burn a hole in it.

At the most basic personal level, life urges an order on us in the form of agendas, lists and priorities, and friction often results from encounters with people who manage to live without these structures. A non-familial shared house cannot, at least in theory, function without everybody doing their bit, although the others all secretly harbour a resentment against the one who pins up the rota. What very often happens is that the more conscientious take up the slack created by the less willing, which breeds its own atmosphere of repressed confrontation. People who drift to the front of queues without noticing that other people are waiting, or – as the others suspect – pretending not to notice, occasion particularly virulent indignation. A shopping list is not only a good way to avoid forgetting what you need, but also a route-map for the most efficient way around the hypermarket, but many people are happy to keep doubling back and going around in circles as they keep chancing to remember things at random. The truth, however, about people's relation to order reveals itself when they experience sudden irruptions of chaos as deeply satisfying. A disruption to the sway of appointed and self-appointed officialdom, in workplaces, schools, political procedures, sport and other institutional contexts, sustains its subjects through many a dull afternoon of the soul. The mere unexpectedness is enjoyable, but at a deeper stratum of sensibility, it becomes an ecstasy at the prospect of regimentation coming unstuck, failing to live up to its own measure. It assures us, in short, that the exception precisely does not prove the rule: it suspends it.

What is crucial to the dialectic of order and chaos is not to oppose them as two halves of a worldview between which it is incumbent to choose, thereby resulting in the mythical formation of social tribes, so that devotees of the former are recast as brutal authoritarians and the latter connoisseurs of a jejune anarchism, but to ask what it is that each aspect of the duality is being asked to do. As to the principle of order, there is, as I readily acknowledge, nothing implicitly objectionable about the impulse to measure and classify. The question is more what that means for human conduct and the ordering of society. Lewis Mumford addressed these questions with exhaustive diligence over the course of a long career, most productively during the interwar period, in such works as *Technics and Civilization* (1934). Dividing the progress of technological development into three great eras – the eotechnic (i.e. the dawn of technology) from 1300 to 1700, the palaeotechnic from 1700 to 1900, and the neotechnic beginning in 1900 and progressing inexorably to the cybernetic nightmare Mumford's longevity permitted him to see – the book argues that the first of these eras was characterized by a sense of wonder that possessed humans when they discovered what artisanal craft and the power of fire and hydraulics could help them achieve. Such power intensified the sensual experience of life, rather than being pursued for its own sake. Mumford identified this delight in the structure of medieval guilds and universities, and the transparent relationship Christian societies had with an all-providing God. The rot sets in with mechanization, the coming of industrial processes, factory labour that reduces the human operator of the machine to one of its appendages, work that was organized not for the satisfaction of craftsmanship and skill but for the reproduction and reign of capital. As a good historical materialist, Mumford did not disdain to see the origins of the mechanistic palaeotechnic orientation in the medieval world that preceded it. Benedictine monastic communities, after all, lived under their famous Rule, their days sliced into precisely timed observances, their conduct regulated practically to the level of the individual breath of prayer. Measuring time in this way would be exactly the principle on which the urban factories would be run. The problem lay not with the notion of clock-time itself, but of applying it to human beings' daily affairs. Everything thereafter, from the productivity ratios of mechanized industry to the length of the breaks that workers were permitted, would be subject to the weighing of hours and minutes – 'time is money!' in the obsessive-compulsive expostulation of managerial slavedrivers. The more he raked back through history, though, the more Mumford detected the mechanizing impulse in the human soul, back to the military rule in Rome's conquered territories, further back to the hieroglyphs of Egypt's court bureaucracy, and further still to the cuneiform tablets of Mesopotamian record-keeping. As he puts it in the preamble to the book, 'Men became mechanical before they perfected complicated machines to express their new bent and interest [i.e. in the palaeotechnic turn]; and the will-to-order had appeared once more in the monastery and the army and the counting-house before it finally manifested itself in the factory.'[12] The whole process would result in the sacralization of the machine, the miraculous power of automation replacing the mysterious ways of God. The question was, whether the social evolution of humanity could ever have produced anything different, and if it could have, what were the chances of being able to retrace our steps, recover the organic relation to work and a non-alienated rapport with the natural world, even in the midst of the delusive techno-paradise of the machine age?

History's most recent example of the attempt to ordain the refusal of bureaucratic order on a gigantic national scale was the so-called Proletarian Cultural Revolution of Maoist China, an incandescent decade of carnivalesque subversion and homicidal destruction launched under the homiletic simplicity, 'It is right to rebel!' Mao himself, increasingly marginalized by the early 1960s after the titanic disaster of the Great Leap Forward, the combined collectivizing of land and catalysing of industry that had issued in atrocious mass starvation, launched the new initiative as a means of holding the new oligarchy in the Politburo to account, not least for adopting quasi-capitalist economic innovations. As so often in China's modern history, the issue of bureaucratic corruption loomed large, and the movement for national renewal triggered in 1966 was darkened with the atmosphere of retribution from the outset. Students began by staging tribunals of popular justice, in which their lecturers and college principals were tried for crimes against the people. The same ideological language of cleansing and purification that had marked the pre-war Nazi pogroms in Germany and the contemporaneous Moscow show trials returned in unbridled force. After the teachers, local officials and party secretaries became the next target of the ardent loathing of the Red Guards. They were treated like brutalized animals, beaten and tormented, with shaming placards hung about their necks before they were publicly put to death. Schools and colleges closed down, transport systems ground to a halt. The cultural side of the revolution involved the brainless obliteration of the splendours of China's antiquity – temples, scrolls, monuments, paintings, ceramics. Rival factions, all claiming with grimly comic inevitability to be the only true devotees of Maoist doctrine, fought each other to the death. Army barracks were raided for their ammunition. Amid the catastrophic violence were manifestations of what would be progressive political consciousness in less rapacious circumstances, the questioning of bureaucratic rule, demonstrations against the megalithic party state, strikes for better working conditions – the last resulting in stoppages in virtually every workplace across the city of Shanghai by early 1967. When Mao sent battalions of the People's Liberation Army throughout China's provinces to disperse the rebellious Red Guards, the latter assumed that the soldiers too must have succumbed to counter-revolutionary bourgeois thinking and began sustained campaigns of guerrilla warfare against them, in some cases rolling back the centuries as they retreated to remote mountain regions to set up hostile encampments. Reports of cannibalism, not in extremis but as a retributive technique against captured soldiers, circulated. When factions of the army and navy themselves began to debate whether they were under any political obligation to obey the orders of their officers, and as hordes of hysterical Red Guards massed on the Soviet border to taunt the Russian troops with imprecations from the Red Book, Mao's faction finally decided in March 1969 that enough had now been enough. It took at least another two years for the situation to be brought under widespread national control, and the legacy of what is now referred to in Chinese official history as the period of 'turbulence' was decisively snuffed out only with Mao's own death in 1976.[13]

Quite apart from its exorbitant humanitarian cost, the Cultural Revolution fits very uneasily into the theorizing of later generations of radical political philosophy. Alain Badiou elaborated a tripartite theory of popular uprisings in the wake of the largely unproductive events of the Arab Spring of 2011. In this model, what he calls an 'immediate riot' is an unfocused expression of momentary resentment, sometimes nothing more than a day or two of orgiastic lashing out accompanied by opportunistic looting, such as the riots that erupted in British cities in the summer of the same year. The second type of disturbance is what Badiou calls a 'latent riot', manifestations of potential unrest in countries, pre-eminently the Western parliamentary democracies that have not experienced a genuine popular upheaval since the 1970s. These phenomena are often relatively quickly bought off with the amendment of an unpopular public policy, or the resignation of a detested public official. The direction in which all revolutionary situations should ideally be tending is the 'historical riot', so named because it inaugurates a new phase of historical development, in which the established system yields to the power of impregnable collective will. Under this last head, Badiou distinguishes three indispensable characteristics: intensification, by which the demands of the crowd become cathected into an intoxicating mass passion, what Kant called 'enthusiasm' with reference to the French Revolution; contraction, the process by which the general will of a mass insurgency becomes concentrated in a small emblematic cadre of its activists, who can be trusted to express the will of the movement; and localization, whereby the movement occupies a single representative site – Tahrir Square in Cairo, for example – which becomes the venue of a potential historical event. The alignment of localized Site and intensified Idea is the key to successful resistance. In Badiou's equation, 'A political event occurring everywhere is something that does not exist. The site is the thing whereby the Idea, still fluid, encounters popular genericity. A non-localized Idea is impotent; a site without an Idea is merely an immediate riot, a nihilistic spurt.'[14] In this theoretical framework, it is hard to see the events of the Cultural Revolution, especially the reckless early years of 1966–9, as anything other than a series of unconnected immediate riots. Clearly, the intermediate concept of the latent riot is inapplicable, but where Mao's faction within the Chinese Communist Party intended these events to amount to a historical riot, the reawakening of history in the context of a gelidly bureaucratic party-state, they signally failed. On Badiou's definition, they were 'a political event occurring everywhere', 'a non-localized Idea' in the sense that they were an encouragement to communities all over the nation to begin taking their own local initiatives and, where they were cathected in individual actions against local functionaries or particularly despised families, 'a site without an Idea'. Badiou has long argued, with persuasive force, that the party framework, at least to all radical intents and purposes, is dead. Tracing its lineage from the Jacobin Club of the 1790s through the First and Second

Internationals of the communist movement to the institutional Communist Parties of the twentieth century, which both Lenin and Mao attempted to revolutionize, Badiou concludes that the failure of the latter in the form of the Cultural Revolution lay in the fact that it 'was not able to realise the desire of Mao and the revolutionaries, students and workers, to transform the Party of the socialist dictatorship into a Party of the communist movement'.[15] The point Badiou leaves hanging is that the attempt ended in failure because it was not a genuinely spontaneous popular uprising, not a 'historical riot' according to his own typology, but a largely cynical manoeuvre to try to outflank the reformist wing of the Politburo, which had begun to sideline him. The evidence, quite apart from the murderous rampages, lies in the fact that Mao himself toured the country on an increasingly desperate rabble-rousing mission, exhorting crowds by screaming at them, 'Don't you want to overthrow state authority?', where he was not actively demanding that they involve themselves in the affairs of the very state they ought simultaneously to be capsizing. For all that it produced a state of self-consuming terror throughout the country, the effect was barely more rhetorically dignified than Bart Simpson's dream of Principal Skinner exhorting the classes of Springfield Elementary on the last day of the school year to rise up and demolish the building – 'I trust you all remembered to bring in your implements of destruction. Now let's trash this dump!'[16]

What Badiou has been far less interested in is the Tiananmen Square demonstrations of 1989, a prolonged standoff between revolutionary students and an implacable state edifice that began, at least initially, to bend in the face of their demands. This event fulfils all the criteria for a historical riot, and if it was ultimately crushed by the homicidal reflex of a party-state in fear of its own life, that does not in itself distinguish it from the authentically promising event of Tahrir Square in 2011, which failed in a different way. The Chinese students' sit-in was initially motivated by distaste at the neoliberal economic direction of the state capitalism being pursued in China, and which was then just beginning to create the grossly stratified society that now obtains in the People's Republic. As the demonstration came up against the sclerotic refusal of the state to engage in mutually respectful dialogue, it evolved into a classic act of anti-authoritarian defiance, in which the participants began to voice increasingly daring demands for political reform. The fact that they had little or no chance of achieving these represented an impeccable example of a grassroots radical movement issuing unfulfillable commands to an embattled state apparatus. For many weeks, the state had no idea how to respond to a scene not witnessed in China since the last days of a soi-disant Cultural Revolution which it in no way resembled. Tiananmen was an intensified, contracted, localized historical riot in Badiou's paradigm, but remains entirely absent from his systematic theory.[17]

In terms of the definitions of chaotic situations outlined above, where we contrasted the conservative impulse to see order emerge from chaos with the radical tradition of seeing the outlines of order in chaotic situations themselves, the event of Tiananmen Square very precisely conforms to the latter. Within the theoretical enunciations that the episode produced, a vision of a more responsive, participatory state appeared to be emerging, the whole process taking on the lineaments of the extended self-education of a generation, one too young to recall the manipulative orchestrations of Mao's last days as an expiring force. The physical and political logjam that the students created opened a space for another reality, and a path that China could have followed without imploding. From the viewpoint of the self-perpetuating oligarchy that runs the country, the events of 4 June represented the blessed resumption of order from several months of chaos, even a blessing in disguise in that many of the most articulate spokespersons of the resistance were among those massacred. The occupation was termed a 'counter-revolutionary riot' in the official nomenclature, as though there were anything revolutionary remaining in the operations of the ossified state bureaucracy. A nascent activist legacy was erased from official memory, its sporadic residual trace elements in the consciousness of the generation that followed perhaps personified by the symbolically gagged teenage student who, having refused to be budged from his cross-legged solo sit-in on the north side of the Square in October 2008, was manhandled into a police van right in front of me. He might have been Tiananmen's last martyr. Our exchange of glances could have expressed a world-historical complicity, or else a chasm of myopic incomprehension.

These magnified visions of social chaos, mostly viewed from afar in foreign lands of which even now, despite global connectivity, we know little, present us with the spectacle of a distilled essence of disorder, a spectacle sufficiently powerful to provoke fascinated horror. In these circumstances, it is all too evident that a chaotic breakdown is the end of an era, the decrepit collapse written in the mingled puzzlement and panic on Nicolae Ceaușescu's face at his last appearance on an official Bucharest balcony, the panoramic view from which, fastidiously unseen by the TV cameras, of crowds erupting into jeers and catcalls, followed by obscene gestures and minor acts of destruction, afforded him a ringside vantage point on his own demise. Whether they will also herald the arrival of the new is always a wager, but at many historical moments, the new is inconceivable without such a prelude, as it was in Romania, and as it shall be in North Korea. The destruction in the Philippines in February 1986 of the regime of Ferdinand Marcos, a demented kleptocrat who had rigged an election following the assassination of his chief political opponent, Benigno Aquino, unfolded over a period of days of mass demonstrations in Manila, culminating in the retreat of an armoured tank brigade sent in to liquidate them. At such moments, nobody knows what will happen next, but the uncertainty of that scarcely matters beside the urgent imperative, and the precious opportunity, to be rid of what there is. As I shall argue later, the disruptive, disintegrative power of the 'not this' is all that keeps hope alive in such circumstances.

Where we are not living in a world-changing historical epoch, however, but only milling through what Walter Benjamin referred to as the 'empty, homogeneous time' that precedes the unforeseen irruptions of history, chaos takes on instead the ludic character of inversion that is the last faint historical echo of the Carnival tradition anatomized so diligently by Mikhail Bakhtin, the festivals of misrule, the masquerade, the charivari. And from this emerges an important anthropological lesson still. Inasmuch as it would be impossible to live in a permanently chaotic society, the beguilement of chaos is precisely an index, and an indictment, of the overwhelming order that bureaucratic systems, the racket of consumerism and the strictures of socio-economic reality, including the specific moral demands they make on subjectivity, have delivered to the atomized collectivities of the present day. If there is something properly unsettling about the prospect of destruction for its own sake, in the form of nihilistic vandalism for example, there is nonetheless an impulse of liberation that has not been quite driven out of members of the wholly administered society that can still see what a release of possibilities, what a disinfectant blast of fresh air, there would be in seeing the edifice of constraint blown down. The painstaking dismantling of dysfunctional systems, and their replacement with something more responsive, more successful at recruiting consent, is in the purview of parliamentary inquiries, community task-forces and sociological surveys, but there are many instances when only the wholesale collapse of such a system, even with all the disorder and confusion that ensue, will suit the moment. This is what, on an apocalyptically broader canvas, Nietzsche meant in the *Zarathustra* when he said that what was already falling should also be pushed.

Nietzsche's aperçu already anticipates modern theories of entropy, the notion that all living things are tending paradoxically to a more complex state, but one in which their energies will have dissipated. This vision would enter the imaginative nightmares of the turn of the twentieth century, most pungently perhaps in the exotically scented poetry and prose of the decadent era,[18] and unites the two poles of chaos as traditionally conceived – multiplicity and nothingness. The gradual abandonment of a rigid concept of causality in Victorian science, which caused a dichotomy within interpretations of the laws of thermodynamics, reflected the dichotomous world itself. On the one hand, it responded to human will, but was also demonstrably everywhere recalcitrant to it. By the dawn of the era of information theory, in 1948, Claude Shannon of Bell Laboratories equated entropy in a paper of 1948 with the inexorable build-up of information within a system until it overwhelms our ability to understand it, a conception of chaos as excessively fertile in semantics rather than deficient in order, a point that recalls Erasmus's sixteenth-century worry that while books might be useful one at a time, the mass of printed literature had become a positive obstacle to understanding.[19] Indeed, it was precisely the voluminous nature of accumulated learning that led directly to increasing academic specialization within the universities, what Eugene McCarraher has defined as 'an enclosure movement of knowledge'.[20] Between the bewilderment originally registered by Erasmus and the onset of entropy, a shift that occurred roughly between the mid-eighteenth and mid-nineteenth centuries, chaos became the symbol of a transformative energy, a liberating principle rather than a disruptive one. Society itself and its political forms, the gathering impetus of the Industrial Revolution, came to seem thrillingly at odds with the ordained natural order of things. A shift in the mental construction of chaos emerged, as Martin Meisel has outlined:

> Energetic chaos could be felt as valuable and liberating, could be embraced as potentiality, as freedom, as the condition of progress, as life, while order could be resented as oppressive and inhibiting, as confinement, deprivation, a reduced semblance of life. The difference lay between life as a protean energy transcending the many forms into which it might flow and – perhaps paradoxically – the pseudolife of the perfect machine.[21]

It is that last point that prefigures the withering of a dynamic notion of chaotic energy into its lethal parody in the modern world. Schopenhauer had ridiculed the impulse to find order in meaningless chaos merely because of a perceived requirement for it, a notion to which Tolstoy would attempt to do honour in his depiction of the unbridled mayhem of the Battle of Borodino. If the happier antipode of war, though, was to be located in the unfettered spontaneity of life in the big cities, the pastiche of life that the actuality of economic relations delivered to the mass of their inhabitants sold the pass on the liberating potentials of modern energy.

Writing at the end of the Second World War from exile in the United States, Adorno already diagnosed a factor in modern life that would become its controlling temperament in the years of peace and prosperity that followed. A bustling air of preoccupation infected everybody, the need to appear extremely busy and with so many competing demands on one's time and attention that they could not all be satisfied, leading to difficult prioritizing decisions having to be made. A nervous, restless flurry indicated that there was a permanent agenda awaiting fulfilment. Adorno notes that the same frenzied air now also imbued intellectual work, militating against its own principle of patient reflection. The tasks of thinking and writing were gradually being relegated to the inessential margins of thought, only to be resorted to when all the other exigencies and urgencies of business and practical life had been undertaken. Appearing constantly in demand, flitting breathlessly from one seeming duty to another, gave everybody else the impression of one's great importance and, at least for some of the time, performed the function of deluding oneself along the same lines. In this way, what ought to have been unmolested private life, or the moments of privacy within the working day, was subjected to the same conveyor-belt mentality that work itself obeyed. The same spirit stained all leisure activities with the character of chores as well. In a psychological analysis of this tendency, Adorno argues that what individuals are doing, as the administered society extends its tentacular grasp to all its members, is preparing themselves spiritually for the inevitable:

> Doing things and going places is an attempt by the sensorium to set up a kind of counter-irritant against a threatening collectivization, to get in training for it by using the hours apparently left to freedom to coach oneself as a member of the mass. The technique is try to outdo the danger. One lives in a sense even worse, that is, with even less self, than one expects to have to live. At the same time, one learns through this playful excess of self-loss that to live in earnest without a self could be easier, not more difficult.[22]

The constant dance of pseudo-activity, immensely more pervasive and frenzied now than it was in the mid-1940s, offers the simulacrum of a dynamically eventful existence, the sort of creative chaos that the apostles of energy among the early Victorians took to be the driving force of life. If you stopped, you might succumb to boredom. 'The boredom that people are running away from,' says Adorno, 'merely mirrors the process of running away that started long before.'[23] A complex dialectical insight, what this intends is not just that escapism resembles the boredom it is trying to escape, but that boredom itself imitates the act of escape, so that as fast as one tries to flee from tedium, the tedium conforms itself to the fugitive act of running from it. There is a formal analogy beyond mere moralizing to be made with the lives of substance addicts, whose own flight from the ennui of a return to reality remakes the ennui itself in its own image. At the end of this aphorism, Adorno's scope broadens to take in the vast historical calamities unfolding in Europe, where mass displacements of the homeless and other uprooted people will also be circulating aimlessly from one inadequate refuge to another. 'The countless people who suddenly succumb to their own quantity and mobility, to the swarming getaway as to a drug [i.e. the superficially busy], are recruits to the migration of nations, in whose desolated territories bourgeois history is preparing to meet its end.'[24]

As it is, while order is enthroned as the supreme principle of daily existence, as the configuration into which everybody will happily resolve life where it is not already present, an ideologically conceptualized chaos has been made to stand as its minatory opposite, the only and unavoidable consequence of the breakdown of smoothly functioning regularity. That view does not quite cohere with what we have called the conservative theory of chaos, as expounded by Prigogine and Stengers and encapsulated by Katherine Hayles: 'to see chaos as that which makes order possible. Life arises not in spite but because of dissipative processes that are rich in entropy production. Chaos is the womb of life, not its tomb.'[25] If chaos were always to be feared as the calamitous result of the end of order, it could not also be the productive element that in turn makes a new order possible – other than by a process of Hegelian sublation, which tends not to be within the logical compass of rigid conformism. It should not take much exercise of the imagination to deduce ways in which official procedures, the operations of society and culture, the events and dispositions of individual lives, could be freed from ironbound order, without their subsiding into the simplistic version of anarchy. A fertilizing orientation towards flexibility can enrich human experience immeasurably. If variety, spontaneity and an openness to contingency will be among its hallmarks, one should also concede that in the consumer economy, despite its self-advertisement as a cornucopia of choices, there is only a limited range of types of experience available. There are just not enough different things to do over the course of an active lifetime without establishing regular patterns of enjoyment, and accepting stoically that it is in the character of regular patterns that their enjoyment will steadily diminish. Journalistic features that suggest a range of possible activities for the newly retired, or of things to do with the kids during the long summer holiday, and which always have the air of a minutely detailed sentence of cruel and unusual punishments, are repellent less for the activities themselves than for the fact that somebody else is trying to talk you into doing them, as though life were one long summer camp run by imperious organizers with clipboards and stop-watches. Accidentally stumbling on something that restores the glow to life is incomparably better than having had it recommended, but either way, this flight from the daily round is hardly chaotic.

Real chaos, the swirling, burbling, nihilistic type conceived as what happens when all order and reason are put to flight by events out of the control of rational minds, has its own literature and demonology, and a long-honoured place in the imaginary of historians and philosophers of the Enlightenment. Thomas Carlyle, in his mammoth epic history of *The French Revolution* (1837), resorts repeatedly to the concept, an insight announced in his earlier essay 'On History', in which the raw material of history itself is a Chaos, in the sense of being without dimensions, boundless and fathomless, inevitably so since it is the record of the actions and influence of humankind itself, which has shown no respect for boundaries either in the extent of its physical habitations or the spiritual reaches of its soul. In surveying the great panorama of the Revolution, to be sure, its preamble and its extravagant effects, he invokes the homiletic view that 'in all vital Chaos, there is new Order shaping itself free', but emphasizes that the order that supervenes is not necessarily what anybody would have prescribed or desired. And it is through Chaos that a revolutionary movement such as the Girondins will propagate, precisely because no external force is present or strong enough to stop it. Who can doubt

> Whatsoever man or men can best interpret the inward tendencies it has, and give them voice and activity, will obtain the lead of it? For the rest, that as a thing *without* order, a thing proceeding from beyond and beneath the region of order, it must work and welter, not as a Regularity but as a Chaos; destructive and self-destructive; always till something that *has* order arise, strong enough to bind it into subjection again? Which something, we may further conjecture, will not be a Formula, with philosophical propositions and forensic eloquence; but a Reality, probably with a sword in its hand!

This is qualitatively quite a different thought from the notion that order will struggle free from a chaotic turn of events. It states the fearful case that chaos obeys no logic other than its own, and that its eventual vanquishment will be just that, an extraneous force that subdues it according to its resources and in its own terms. There is no rational disputation with chaos, only the strength of arms that can quell it into submission or destroy it utterly, which leaves open the permanent historical possibility that the currents that animated the ferocity of the chaotic insurrection have not been resolved or addressed, only put to flight for the time being. Many is the war that has been won by the side with moral right just happening to have the superior firepower and the luck to prevail, but whether the argument has been settled forever remains impossible to say. Arguments, in any case, are part of the armoury of Chaos for Carlyle, as witness the disputations in the revolutionary *Parlement* of 1791, where 'they go on, debating, denouncing, objurgating: loud weltering Chaos, which devours *itself*'. In the coffeehouses, as he tells it, reverting to the epic Miltonic vein, the roar of contumely reigns unchecked: 'there, in the ancient pigtail mode, or with modern Brutus' heads, do well-frizzed logicians hold hubbub, and Chaos umpire sits', its confusion extending to the very tonsorial styles of the disputants. As we shall see when we turn to *Paradise Lost*, Milton's Pandaemonium is a realm of decorous deliberation, but the intermediary realm between it and Heaven, over which Chaos presides, is where all the obstreperous uproar takes place. Just so is the public fractiousness of Paris in the Bastille years an intermediate time of contestation and disorder between the fall of an overstuffed absolute monarchy and the nationalistic arrogance of the Napoleonic Empire. Carlyle's Chaos is not the Hesiodic chaos of the thing before the first things, but authentic mayhem, the fermentation of war, the unleashed furore of Mahler's symphonic death-shrieks.[26]

In the chapters that follow, after an outline of the mythical origins and later elaboration of the concept, we shall consider a series of qualitative aspects of this latter version of chaos. There will be the chaos that spontaneously erupts and that which is intentionally provoked by malign – and occasionally benign – forces. There will be representations of chaos in the visual and literary arts and in music, and reflections on its occurrence as a philosophical category. Historical episodes conventionally given the name of chaos will show us something of the resources and possibilities that chaotic situations engender, and the role of chaos in prompting laughter in satire and nihilistic confusion will raise the question of whether, and to what end, we could ever live without it. Might it be that the most readily present self-administrations of chaos come to the great mass of humanity through the use of intoxicants in their refulgent intensity and variety? What chaos, or more specifically the imperative urge to forestall it, does to societies, and the individuals they have increasingly subsumed under their systems, is a pertinent question that only assumes greater acuity in the era of online self-expression. What potentials it still harbours as an aesthetic or theoretical strategy press themselves on an age more saturated with the official nostrums of the global culture industries than ever before. Is chaos a land of fertility, or is it the desert dead-zone of blasted hope? Will it ever be overcome in the present world, or must humankind await deliverance from it in some version of the post-political or imaginative or devotional Kingdom of Heaven?

And again, insistently: What is it?

Part Two

The phenomenology of chaos: A mythical overture

In the beginning, there is nothing. That is what chaos is, an unformed, undifferentiated, inconceivable absence. It is not conceivable as such, because there would be nothing to conceive it. Indeed, even to posit that this state is what exists 'in the beginning' is, properly speaking, inaccurate, since a beginning would have to be the beginning of something. The original chaos cannot be the prelude to anything, or it would itself be a matter of inherent potentials, and would thereby already contain some ordering principle. The void is not creative. It does not promise. It existed in a non-time before causality. Even the postulate of its existence implies that it is in itself a something, and therefore not nothing.

Philosophical traditions have only been able to conceive of a state of primordial nothingness by a conceptual process of subtraction.

Take away all phenomenal objects. Take away their surroundings. Take away light. Take away all physical laws, even the notion of the physical itself. What is left must be nothing, but the intellect still yearns to conceive this void as a space, an existent entity with extension and borders. Alternatively, in a *reductio ad hominem*, it attempted to imagine the void as what would be left of it after its own death, or – since one's own existence might be preserved in physical legacies, documentary traces, memories – what there was of it before its birth. Its own subjective nullity, however, is beside the point. Everything else will go on after, and did go on before, its own contingent appearance in the great world. The nothingness, or nihilation, or negation, of twentieth-century existentialism, from Heidegger to Sartre, is only such a subjective apprehension on the part of each being of its own insertion, or 'thrownness', into a reality that means strictly nothing to it. It is a nothingness that is formed relatively to the very world that nihilates it, not an autonomous condition.

The origin myths of the world religions, by contrast, utterly depend on the self-contradictory notion of a figuration of nothingness. In the Hebrew tradition, a plenipotentiary Supreme Being must begin with nothing, not the blank slate or the empty page, but literally nothing, the *nihilo* from which the creation will be fashioned. Nobody mortal has ever created anything out of nothing. Even the speculations of abstract thought must be moulded from pre-existent concepts, the thoughts of minds antecedent to itself solidified, objectified, into intellectual forms. The *creatio ex nihilo* works only in accordance with its own creative urge, not knowing concepts or laws any more than it has substances, technical paraphernalia, morphological principles or scientific languages at its disposal. These are, along with the heavens and the earth, just what it creates. From then on, the story of creation can be told, or imagined, itself created. What came before the day of creation, though, was uncreated Chaos. Chaos is, then, precisely the absence or lack of creation, the state before a transcendent intentionality began to fill it in with a fecund mass of somethings.

Joseph Haydn's oratorio, *The Creation* (1799), opens with a prefatory movement entitled 'The Representation [*Vorstellung*] of Chaos', the earliest attempt in the classical tradition to imagine the original void in sonic terms, prior to the beginning of God's creative labours on Day One. The opening sound is a single chord that is not a chord, since nearly every instrument in the sizeable orchestra is playing a unison C. Beginning at forte, the sound diminishes through a decrescendo to a fermata, an indefinite pause at the discretion of the conductor, an unprecedented occurrence at the very beginning of a work. The music seems to insist that there is this one uniform piece of stuff, a mass of malleable clay from which everything will be fashioned. Lawrence Kramer characterizes this effect as an auditory 'fade to black', a reminder that although there is some form of primordial material, it exists in a contextless void, awaiting its artisan.[1] What follows, in stately largo, are a series of sudden forte chords interspersed with drifting embellishments in the strings and woodwinds, which may seem hardly to conform to either of the conventional definitions of chaos – unruly disorder, or stark emptiness. The clue to the musical conception, however, is given in the remark Haydn himself made when playing the movement at the piano for the Swedish chargé d'affaires in Vienna: 'You have certainly noticed how I avoided the resolutions that you would most readily expect. The reason is, that there is no form in anything in the universe yet.'[2] The aptly tutored classical ear would search in vain for the anticipated direction of the harmonic progression it conventionally expected. An abrupt A-flat major triad has a dissonant effect in the context of the implied tonic key of C minor, and is left obstinately unresolved as the music continues. If modern conceptual sensibilities might figure John Cage's four-and-a-half minutes of silence as more nearly representing the originary nothingness, Haydn's attempt effectively postulates that there has to be a something in the nothing from which everything is made. As the movement continues, the accumulating detail takes the listener inexorably further away from the idea of nothing at all, as though by ramifying the original bare materials the clay is being tempered and readied for its first transmutations into formed matter, but the oratorio's opening at least is a bold approximation of what might have preceded them.

The cosmological grandeur of the great nothing informed a host of metaphorical flights in the literature of the late Victorian and Edwardian eras. It became the controlling figuration of the contemplative mood confronted by the chasms of the post-Romantic sublime. Where Burke had seen plunging gorges and ravines, the early modernist generation trained their sights on the primordial empty firmament, at rest and benighted before motion and daytime had been conceived. Drowsing through his maths lesson, the schoolboy Stephen Dedalus imagines the unfolding of equations on the page before him as figuring the ramifications of his own soul into a vast fathomless space, 'going forth to experience, unfolding itself sin by sin, spreading abroad the balefire of its burning stars and folding back upon itself, fading slowly, quenching its own lights and fires. They were quenched: and the cold darkness filled chaos'. If everything emerged from nothing, it is all too easy for the wanton boy to imagine the return of everything to the nothing from whence it issued. 'The chaos in which his ardour extinguished itself was a cold indifferent knowledge of himself.'[3] A progression towards the self-awareness of maturity is a kind of kenosis, an emptying of subjectivity into something like the sterile facticity of mathematical reason.

In the Babylonian religion, according to the tablets recovered at the ancient library of Ashurbanipal at Nineveh (now Mosul in Iraq) in the mid-nineteenth century, what existed at the origin were two deities, Apsu and Tiamat, male and female personifications respectively of fresh and salt water. The creative mingling of their two principles eventually begets further deities, and before long they are at war with each other, but at the outset, as described in the opening lines of the antique scripture, the Enûma Eliš, there is nothing, because the primordial elements have not received their nomenclature:

> When on high the heaven had not been named,
> Firm ground below had not been called by name,
> Naught but primordial Apsu, their begetter,
> (And) Mummu-Tiamat, she who bore them all,
> Their waters commingling as a single body;
> No reed hut had been matted, no marsh land had appeared,
> When no gods whatever had been brought into being,
> Uncalled by name, their destinies undetermined –
> Then it was that the gods were formed within them.[4]

Here too the subtraction principle is at work. The great absence before the present world came into being is given material force by its conspicuous lack of those features with which the societies were familiar – the marshy land dotted with grass-woven huts. There is an ether and there is a notional firm ground beneath it, but because it has not been named, it has no ontic existence. If the aqueous chaos from which the earth was generated bears obvious affinities with the Hebraic creation myth, the differences are not to be elided. A plethora of deities representing various natural forces are at variance with the notion of a single God apodictically willing the Creation into being from nothing whatever. The once-canonical theory that the biblical creation story was inherited from Mesopotamian cultures by the

Israelites has now yielded ground to the suggestion that they are both derived from a common, even more ancient set of lost source beliefs, in which nonetheless, if they were ever to be recovered, it may be confidently expected that the primal scene would turn out to have been one of watery formlessness.

The same principle of determinate negation in describing the pre-existent, cognate with the absence of reed huts in the Babylonian myth and the formless void of the Genesis story, also structures the Sanskrit foundation hymn of the Rig Veda (*c.* 1400 BC), supplementing its negative assertions with the rhetorical questions that such negation calls forth: 'There was no nonexistent; and there [was] no existent at that time. There was neither the mid-space nor the heaven beyond. What stirred? And in whose control? Was there water? The abyss was deep.' Not merely the expected absences of a non-ontological state obtain, but that too is subject to negation: 'Neither death nor deathlessness was there then. There was no sign of night or day.' There is no night in the sense of an obverse of day, but there is a perpetual murk that, at some point in a time that only began with its occurrence, ceases to be a steady state: 'Darkness there was, hidden by darkness, in the beginning. A signless ocean was everything here.' So, in answer to the earlier question, there was water, the whole void replete with what the text then calls 'the potential that was hidden by emptiness', a potential activated by the internal generation of heat.[5] As with the other myths, the amorphousness symbolized by water is the very condition in which the first forms came to be generated. Today's extraterrestrial probes, scanning space, so far fruitlessly, for the evidence of life on other worlds are searching for any geological formation suggestive of the long-vanished presence of water, a medium in which the same protozoa that made the Earth fertile might once have bred microorganisms out of the unpromising barren desertion to which the other planets have returned.

In the *Theogony* of Hesiod, composed around 700 BC, the origin of all, of the gods themselves, of night and day and of the earth, is Chaos, which is not, as in the Sanskrit, Babylonian and Hebraic texts, a primal default state but was in itself borne into being. 'First of all, Chaos came into being [l 116, *êtoi men prôtista Khaos genet'*].' The verb in the Greek hovers suggestively between the senses of an originary state that simply is and the denotation of an event in itself, something that happens within whatever condition preceded Chaos. In its etymology, the word is derived from the verb stem *Ka*, to gape open, fixing Chaos in the image of the yawning chasm that it also lexically generates. Chaos is not just an empty space, but one that stretches wide, a dimensionless gaping void into which the teeming matter of the creation will be poured. It has, in that sense, a physical property, prior to the begetting of any other entities with physical attributes. Chaos has a beginning like everything else.

In its personification, it is female, and duly gives birth to the elements of Darkness (Erebus) and Night (Nyx). Because the more minatory aspects of existence were in turn generated out of Nyx, most obviously War and Famine, Chaos took on a negative aspect, which harmonized with the derogation of the feminine present in virtually all antique cosmogonies. It is also conceived as a dwelling place, either the bottomless abyss of the underworld, Tartarus – 'There is great Chaos. A whole year would not be enough / to find its floor' (ll 740–1), or the space between the Earth (Gaia) and the Heavens (Uranus) that opens up following a primal war between the Titan and Olympian deities. In the later Orphic hymns, Chaos contracts through a process of fecundation brought about by Eros into the great cosmic egg from which the world and its phenomena are hatched. The connecting threads in this shifting mythical morphology are the principles of the female, of ethereal formlessness, of creativity and of the generation of the darker, negative aspects of existence.

What is quite as striking as the mythical homologies among these narratives, the persistence of water and atmosphere as the preparatory media before the grand fabrication begins, is the ontological status of these elements. This is given its highest level of subtlety in the Vedic poem, which insists minutely on the primal condition of neutrality in which the nothingness rests. There is neither existence nor non-existence, neither death nor deathlessness. In an almost Hegelian echo, there is darkness, but it is hidden under darkness, as though the pre-ontological state were hidden from, or alien to, itself. All arcana must be self-opaque, in the sense that Hegel points out that, before they were mysteries to later societies investigating them, the ancient Egyptian myths were mysteries to the Egyptians themselves. Only when the light is created, and night and day become distinguishable entities, does the darkness truly become darkness, paradoxically illuminated to itself. In the obvious sense, it becomes darkness by means of its distinction from the light, as the land will be distinguished from the sea, or the male from the female, but it also attains a new ontological status in itself. It fully becomes what it is, instead of lying obscured to itself. The same impulse appears in the Hebraic story, but in attenuated form. There is an earth prior to the Creation, albeit a shapeless absence, and an elemental, implicitly infinite body of water over which the spirit of the Creator moves, but they only become the land and the sea with the divine fiat. The conjuration of light produces the first day, the induction of a six-day schedule, and thereby gives a name to the pre-existent gloom, which is now more than gloom, having become night. In other words, the inauguration of order, the principle that displaces the inert formlessness that precedes it, has the dual character of a shaping, a morphology that creates bounded entities, and a naming, that classifying system of conceptual taxonomy in which everything there is has its own nomenclature. Not for nothing is the first man given the task of naming all the other creatures that pre-exist him. He brings order to the unclassified multiplicity into which he emerges supreme, ruler over all except his Creator. The birds and fishes and land animals exist in a state of unconscious self-ignorance both before and after Man comes on the scene, but they exist for him henceforth as something else, the context of boundless otherness into which he himself has now been, if not 'thrown' in the Heideggerian sense, at least carefully inserted. His own name is derived by the Creator from the ground on which the man stands, and from which he is ordained to feed, *adamah*. There are discrete entities, but there is relational dependence among them. With the creation of multiplicity comes relativity, comparativity, the subject–object relation, from which all ordering systems derive their intrinsic meaning.

In quantum physics' version of the foundation myth, the Big Bang, the question of what there was before the cosmic explosion remains a mystery, but what is generally agreed is that the fabric from which the present universe was suddenly detonated into being was of infinitely denser texture and hotter temperature than what exists now. Like all explosions, it resulted in a dispersion of volatile material that has persisted over fourteen billion years, expanding but simultaneously cooling. This is in an evident sense an inverse construction to the Creation myths, in the sense that the universe and what it contains is thinner and more diffused than what came before it, but it echoes Creationism in that it has produced heterogeneity from a notional singularity. It has generated a system of internal elements that are interdependent in their motions and subject to the variant forces and energies at work in them. Only in the last hundred years has it come to be posited that this model does not amount to a system, or a state of natural order, but is subject to entirely contingent influences that may or may not be readily scrutable.

The most profound conceptual transformation Chaos underwent in the Classical era was marked by its reconfiguration from Nothing into Everything. It is as though the notion of an original void of emptiness and absence collapses under its own logical insufficiency. How can things have emerged from nothing? What they must have emerged from, rather, is an unformed mass of potential somethings. The watery and the ethereal elements, even the pitch-darkness, in the foundation myths already acknowledge that even the void is not wholly void. What it is instead is formless. The act of creation, howsoever conceived, is what introduces differentiation within the formlessness, the moulding into separate entities of what already potentially exists within the Chaos, its liberation into being from a non-being defined as the antithesis of order. Just this is what is figured in the overture, 'The Creation of the World', to Book I of the first-century *Metamorphoses* of Ovid:

> Before the seas, and this terrestrial ball,
> And Heav'n's high canopy, that covers all,
> One was the face of Nature; if a face:
> Rather a rude and indigested mass:
> A lifeless lump, unfashion'd, and unfram'd,
> Of jarring seeds; and justly Chaos nam'd.
> No sun was lighted up, the world to view;
> No moon did yet her blunted horns renew:
> Nor yet was Earth suspended in the sky,
> Nor pois'd, did on her own foundations lye:
> Nor seas about the shores their arms had thrown;
> But earth, and air, and water, were in one.
> Thus air was void of light, and earth unstable,
> And water's dark abyss unnavigable.
> No certain form on any was imprest;

All were confus'd, and each disturb'd the rest.
For hot and cold were in one body fixt;
And soft with hard, and light with heavy mixt.[6]

The Creation is a disembroiling of one element from another, the resolution of discord into the harmony of nature. While things are unshaped, they are in a state of strife, as though yearning to be made whole, given finitude through their release from indeterminacy, their inchoate rudeness transformed into sophisticated perfection. It is not that there were no qualities prior to the creation, only that that was all there was, but bound in unproductive melanges of hot and cold, soft and hard, light and heavy. These attributes come into their own by their being sundered from each other so that they become the defining aspects of the world's entities rather than existing in unpredicated static mixtures. In this prolusive state, they are raw (*rudis*), unordered (*indigestaque*), inert (*iners*), piled up anyhow (*congestaque*), homogeneous (*eodem*), not properly articulated (*non bene iunctarum*), in a state of discordance (*discordia*), the mere seeds of things (*semina rerum*) rather than the things themselves.

The separation of night from day in all the myths indicates that the other ordering principle, the companion to spatial extension and boundedness, is time. In one version of the Greek cosmogony, Chaos is one of the daughters of the progenitor god Cronos, but in the majority of the foundation myths, time cannot precede the creation since it would itself be an empty element. If there is Time, it has to be made of events, which mandate the existence of things in causal relations with each other. Time is the medium in which things are deposited, the diurnal and mortal cycles to which all creatures are then subjected. 'The golden age was first,' Ovid continues, the time in which human beings are bound to no external laws other than those that operate instinctually within them, and nobody wishes for anything more than the protean plenty of the world as it is. From then on, matters progressively decline until enmity, war and destruction rule the earth.

In English, the transitional point at which Chaos is transmuted from negation to repletion is the Elizabethan era. In the earlier sixteenth century, it had still been the formless void of Genesis, but by around the 1570s, it had started to take on also the aspect of confusion and disorder. Not unexpectedly, both usages are to be found in the half-dozen occurrences of the term in Shakespeare. In its earliest appearance, in the forensically detailed anatomical self-examination of the Duke of Gloucester (the future Richard III), it has what we have seen to be the intermediate sense of unformed matter, the amorphous lump, fit to metaphorize the congenital abnormalities of the deformed body:

> Why, love forswore me in my mother's womb:
> And, for I should not deal in her soft laws,
> She did corrupt frail nature with some bribe,
> To shrink mine arm up like a wither'd shrub;
> To make an envious mountain on my back,
> Where sits deformity to mock my body;
> To shape my legs of an unequal size;
> To disproportion me in every part,
> Like to a chaos, or an unlick'd bear-whelp
> That carries no impression like the dam. (*3 Henry VI*, III:ii)

The asymmetry of the malformed physique recalls the unmoulded matter of the primordial state, in which nothing suggests the harmonious shapes that will emerge from it, which in Richard's case, owing to a conspiracy between Eros and Nature itself, have left his body in the unlovable, imperfectly formed state of uncreated, or half-created, matter. Its nearest natural analogue is the newborn cub, not yet released by licking from its amniotic sac by a mother it therefore does not yet resemble, not yet, as we say, licked into shape, but neglected by its own mother as by Mother Nature.

In the narrative poem 'Venus and Adonis', the goddess of love bewails the death of her paradigmatically handsome mortal man, whose beauty guaranteed the orderliness and harmony of the world in which he disported himself: 'For he being dead, with him is beauty slain, / And beauty dead, black chaos comes again' (ll 1019–20). This retrograde return of creation to its unformed, unilluminated state is probably derived by Shakespeare from the cosmogony of Spenser's Garden of Adonis in *The Faerie Queene*, where the multiform perfection of the world is generated out of its inner kernel of formlessness:

For in the wide womb of the earth there lies,
In hateful darkness and in deep horror,
An huge eternal Chaos, which supplies
The substances of Nature's fruitful progenies. (3.6.36)

Chaos here is eternally prolific, but is in itself detestable, dingy, profoundly horrifying. The world, being born from it, is simultaneously liberated from it, so that a retrogression to it, as Venus sees in the death of Adonis in the jaws of the wild boar, is a nightmare reversal both of the generation of order and of the order of time. In the slightly later 'Rape of Lucrece', the violated Lucrece addresses the night in which foul deeds, including her own sexual assault by Sextus Tarquinius, the Roman king's son, are typically committed: 'Black stage for tragedies and murders fell, / Vast sin-concealing chaos, nurse of blame' (ll 766–7). Here too, as in the Spenserian conception, the darkness of chaos is what makes it so hateful when seen from the vantage of the virtuous daylight of the world of innocence. The tenebrous gloom of night, eventually the friend of lovers in the romantic optic, is here still the element that offers putative malefactors their chance.

When Romeo enters the recent scene of interfamilial street violence in Verona, he is subject torturously to his own internal strife, that which accompanies the anguish of unfulfilled love and its riot of contradictions. The paradox of a blind love yet being able to see the imaginative way to its requital, the fever-dream of Romeo's suffering soul, yields a harvest of oxymorons:

> O heavy lightness, serious vanity,
> Misshapen chaos of well-seeming forms,
> Feather of lead, bright smoke, cold fire, sick health,
> Still-waking sleep, that is not what it is! (*Romeo and Juliet*, I:i)

Everything is wrong, turned back on itself, inverted into its antithesis, so that it 'is not what it is', or, more precisely, is what it is not. Things are not disfigured into meaningless shapes, but into the forms of their exact inverse in each case, forms that in themselves are perfectly recognizable and familiar, 'well-seeming'. They are 'misshapen' not because they are shapeless, but because they have been formed into their opposites, so that Chaos has performed its work of generating order, but has performed in a kind of mirror-image of what the natural world requires, quite as though it had made a beautiful girl whom one could love unconditionally, but who appears blithely disregardful of oneself.

Around seven years later, in the famous speech on order and degree by Ulysses in *Troilus and Cressida*, a modulation in the conception of Chaos has crept in. When proportion and right attunement are allowed to fall away, the world falls prey to universal internecine hostility, 'mere oppugnancy'. Everything is overturned, as in Romeo's vision, but with more baleful destructive consequences, releasing not logical conundrums but actual ruination. Sons rise murderously against fathers, the seas flood the land, brute force is uncoupled from any sense of right and wrong, and the law of the primeval swamp

– appetite, magnified by unchecked will and the facility of power – reigns over all, at the ultimate cost of self-annihilation. 'This chaos, when degree is suffocate, / Follows the choking,' Ulysses warns Agamemnon (I:iii). The principle of inversion is supreme, but the result is febrile disorder, something like Hobbes's war of all against all. This is a long stretch from the idea of Chaos as a yawning featureless abyss. Instead, its lack of form has become the lack of order, the condition in which destructive confusion holds sway.

The last and most famous of the references in Shakespeare comes in *Othello*, when the Venetian general is already well under the spell of Iago's scheme to convince him that his wife, Desdemona, is being unfaithful to him. As she departs, having just over-pleaded the case with him of his lieutenant, Michael Cassio, whom he has supposedly slighted, Othello utters an exclamation of his love for her, the unalloyed perfection of which is just beginning to be tinted with suspicion, a distemper that already opens up a prevision of its doleful outcome: 'Perdition catch my soul, / But I do love thee! and when I love thee not, / Chaos is come again' (III:iii). The precise character of this Chaos seems uncertain. Is it wild disorder, mayhem, the subversion of all harmonious existence? Or does it figure a dreary return to a primordial state, before the beginning of love, when nothing that was going to be made had yet been made, and everything repined in darkness? Its phraseology precisely echoes the lament, ten years earlier, of Venus over the dead Adonis, 'black chaos comes again', suggesting that the antecedent state of the world, a benighted featurelessness, is what Othello intends, the barely remembered wilderness on which the lover has the privilege of looking back from his present state of fulfilment, 'The Day Before You Came' in the Andersson / Ulvaeus ABBA lyric of 1982. And yet, what will actually happen as the marriage of Othello and Desdemona unravels is the chaos of savage destruction, a conflicted amalgam of enraged love and sorrowful hatred, emotional cruelty, uxoricide, suicide, all for nothing.

The question is: what habits of thought, what philosophical conceptions, what political presumptions and social attitudes have been generated through human history by the transmutation of the postulate of Chaos from an originating neutral nothingness, via an amorphous undifferentiated mass, to a state of internally riven confusion? Are these three conceptualizations in any sense compatible with each other? In the first model, there is no inherent necessity for the world to come about. It is a purely gratuitous act on the part of the Creator, or the contingent outcome of a war between races of deities. It need not have happened. By the intermediate stage, as formulated by Ovid, the shapeless heap contains all that will become the created world, but it awaits resolution like the musical chords in the early passages of Haydn's oratorio. In a move from ontology to deontology, the jumble that precedes the ordered world is implicitly awaiting intervention to make it what it ought to be. By the final contemporary stage, familiar to Western cultural sensibility for the past five hundred years, it is a post-creative state, the perfectly formed existent having somehow become embroiled in itself, entangled, convoluted, thrown into a state of self-embattlement and derangement, a condition that is crying out to be resolved, disencumbered, reorganized or, in the plain everyday lexicon, sorted. These three successive stages represent and enact the passage from an animist or polytheistic stage of belief, in which elemental forces bring about the world and its ephemera, its accidents and stories, its contentions and calamities, to the monotheistic postulate of a single Creator fabricating everything from his own beneficent genius, the crowning achievement of which is humanity itself, made in the Creator's own image, the better to reflect the glory of it all to itself, and finally the secular Enlightenment, in which human beings themselves, whatever the disposition of their beliefs or the lack of such, are responsible for reconstituting disordered and benighted Chaos, wherever it flares up, into something like the same principle of order to which the entire natural world has been subjected in the classifying projects of scientific endeavour.

What is needed now is a further, post-secular conception of Chaos, one that allows that it is one of the states into which reality sometimes pivots in spite of human intention, a condition in which surprising developments may occur, the medium of a fertile eventfulness that ordering systems frequently suppress. To investigate the potentialities of such a conception, we need to address five of the most fundamental characteristics of the tertiary version of chaos, and the determinations that they have put to human lives at the social, political, cultural and personal levels, enquiring into how their evolution into less rigid rubrics of definition might have an emancipating effect on societies at a critical point of transition, for a species advancing towards its greatest historical crisis.

1

Displacement

In the worldview of European natural philosophy in the seventeenth century, the organization of inert matter into a world of differentiated entities presumed and required a natural order. This order could be perceived through the principle of resemblance. Things of like nature belonged together, and the first evidence of their similitude was adjacency, physical juxtaposition, spatial proximity or, in the classical Latin, *convenientia*. From the verb *convenire*, to come together, the principle of 'convenience' denotes a coming into alignment precisely of entities that in some sense belong together, their adjacency bearing witness to their homology. The effect extends outwards in a graduated chain, so that an object at two removes from its near neighbour bears its similitude to a lesser degree than does one that is directly contiguous with it. Summarizing this proto-Enlightenment construction, Michel Foucault writes in *The Order of Things* (1966) that the resemblance created by adjacency has two modalities. Firstly, the spatial conjunction creates the order of place, 'for in this natural container, the world, adjacency is not an exterior relation between things, but the sign of a relationship, obscure though it may be'. That in turn generates a further qualitative similitude, by which the one phenomenon influences the other in its very being: 'from this contact, by exchange, there arise new resemblances; a common regimen becomes necessary; upon the similitude that was the hidden reason for their propinquity is superimposed a resemblance that is the visible effect of that proximity'.[1] He gives the theological example of the body and soul: the soul is housed in a physical body, but the two elements then reciprocally determine one another, in that the soul receives the physical actions of the body such as movement, while the body itself is in turn subject to the passions of the soul – spiritual devotion, love and the other emotions.

What this creates is a universal context of symmetry, the other meaning of *convenientia*. Seventeenth-century natural science held that there were precisely balanced numbers of fishes in the sea, birds in the air, and animals on land, all reflecting the internal numerical harmony of the Creator himself. 'Thus,' writes Foucault, 'by this linking of resemblance with space, this "convenience" that brings things together and makes adjacent things similar, the world is linked together like a chain.'[2] This chain is nothing other than the Great Chain of Being that had been conceived in the Elizabethan era, with the Supreme Being at its summit, disposing over a vast rope-like structure that connected humans to animals to plants to rocks and minerals, a descending regression from pure spirit all the way down to pure matter. As significant as the contiguities themselves are the links that respectively bind each stage to the one above it and the one below it. According to the *Magia Naturalis* of Giambattista della Porta (1558), the plants are linked to animals through the principle of vegetal growth, the animals to humans by their capacity for physical sensation, humans to the higher powers by their intelligence and consciousness. The overall structure is so finely tuned in its interdependence that if it were to be touched at any point, the whole chain would vibrate sympathetically in response to the contact. Contemporary holistic versions of ecologism, while objecting to the implied hierarchy in the Chain of Being, and often keen to replace the figure of God with a depersonalized creative force typically addressed as the Universe, are otherwise in wholesale agreement with this cosmological conception. Everything is linked, with gradations of similitude forming the connecting links in the chain.

The Chain of Being acknowledges that the phenomena of the world that emerged from the amorphous lump of confused stuff that preceded it represent, in the internal kinships among them, their common derivation from primal matter. Creation is not a matter of heterogeneity, but of comparative differences, in morphology and quality, between entities that are essentially fashioned from the same fundamental ingredient in greater or less proportions, whether that be something like the divine spark or the carbon on which all life is based. The world is predicated on a perceptible order of resemblances, both explicit and hidden, among its elements, rather than being comprised of an assorted miscellany. How else, the implication goes, would the only stage of the Creation that is endowed with consciousness of it, namely humans, be able to make sense of it?

The origins of the European Enlightenment would consign this view to science's attic. For the Descartes of the unfinished *Regulae* (*Rules for the Direction of the Mind, c.* 1619–28), resemblances are not the point at all. There are only two standards of comparison among the things of the world: that of measurement and that of order. One thing can be considered in the light of another by reference to their respective dimensions, in length, width, depth, capacity, volume, temperature and so on, or by applying the principle of order, establishing which is the simplest element before us, which the less simple, and so forth, up to the most complex. Measurement requires the application of an external principle in the form of a measuring system to which objects can be referred, but order requires nothing outside itself, only an analysis of the inherent properties of the objects themselves. 'In this way,' as Foucault summarizes it, 'we establish series in which the first term is a nature that we may intuit independently of any other nature; and in which the other terms are established according to increasing differences.'[3] From then on, the science of order, which works through establishing identities and differences, supersedes the doctrine of resemblances of the sixteenth century, replacing a theoretical infinitude of variable aspects of knowledge with the potential for a finite progressive apprehension, ultimately, of the whole of each field. The axial turn in epistemology is from the exploration of similarities and towards the identification of differences, which alone are what establish the phenomena in their order. Their differences place them in a set of linear relations with each other. 'The activity of the mind,' Foucault writes, 'will therefore no longer consist in *drawing things together*, in setting out on a quest for everything that might reveal some sort of kinship, attraction, or secretly shared nature within them, but, on the contrary, in *discriminating*, that is, in establishing their identities, then the inevitability of the connections with all the successive degrees of a series.'[4] This results effectively in the separation from each other of history and science, the former confined to the written accounts and opinions of the past, the latter to what can be tangibly, demonstrably asserted with confidence about the world. The printed word, language itself, now belongs to the realm of the indeterminate, rather than having a proposed direct relation to intramundane things, as in the Adamic myth of nomination.

In the closing years of the nineteenth century, at the culmination of a dynamic period of scientific investigation and speculation, the psychologist William James subjects the Cartesian formal taxonomy of the world to the version of it that presents itself to subjective consciousness.

The reality *exists* as a *plenum*. All its parts are contemporaneous, each is as real as any other and each essential for making the whole just what it is and nothing else. But we can neither experience nor think this *plenum*. What we experience, what *comes before us*, is a chaos of fragmentary impressions interrupting each other; what we *think* is an abstract system of data and laws.[5]

The two elements, the entire reality and our conception of it, are strictly heterogeneous, the latter being a set of extraneous ordering principles that have no necessary homology with what there is. No longer does the world need to yield its essence, as in the Cartesian conception, to the enquiring mind, which assesses and orders its attributes by the measure of successive differences, but what matters more is the subjective interpretation of them, which may or may not accord with the subjective interpretations entertained by others. 'Is not the sum of your actual experience taken at this moment and added together an utter chaos?' James asks.[6] The rhetorical echo is of the *System of Logic* of John Stuart Mill (1843), who states: 'The order of nature, as perceived at a first glance, presents at every instant a chaos followed by another chaos. We must decompose each chaos into single facts … [W]e must endeavour to effect a separation of the facts from one another, not in our minds only, but in nature.' If that seems to recall the method of Descartes, though, beware. 'The mental analysis, however, must take place first. And everyone knows that in the mode of performing it, one intellect differs immensely from another.'[7] If the individual consciousness, according to James, sorts out for itself what laws and principles it can observe in the world before it, disregarding the remainder, what is particularly unfathomable about the plenum of reality is that it lends itself without apparent obstruction to so many variant conceptions and re-imaginings. It is almost as though there were no order at all, if it can prove so topologically fluid without surrendering its coherence. Is there an objective, ordered reality, or is there not?

What is missing from these observations by Mill and James is precisely the self-constitution of the subject by means of what it sees and feels. It is not that there is a stable subject perceiving an amorphous mass of phenomena, on to which it then maps its own signifying and classifying operations, a transcendentally constituting subject in the Kantian sense. The more accurate picture is that the subject itself is constituted by its differential relations with what it encounters in objective reality, as in the Hegelian definition of Absolute Knowing, not in the sense of a cognition that is omniscient, but of one that is aware of its own position in relation to what it cognizes. When the creation, or the physical universe, or the world we inhabit, emerged from the pre-ontological chaos, it produced a potentially infinite number of beings. There could not just have been one Something, or it would have had the same undifferentiated status as the Void. There had to be a multitude, or at least in the first place, a pair, in oppositional contradistinction to each other – the light and the dark, hot and cold, solid and liquid, masculine and feminine and so forth – each continuum in turn ramifying into ever more finely divided gradations. What happens as it ramifies, however, is that it becomes characterized by disorder, imbalance, self-subversion, the concrete evidence that there is no longer just one universal (non-)medium. One of the imbalances generated by nature, eventually, is human consciousness, which first understands the manifold world and then begins to subject it to the principle of reason. The natural world generates the very agent that will subject it to its own conceptualizing, but one of its corollaries is that that very conceptuality, the ordering principle, is a ruse of subjectivity, and it is the failure of external reality to conform to the subject's conceptualization of it that constitutes the subject itself. Its own imbalances and internal antagonisms, which become second nature to it at the psychic, ethical, sexual and other levels, are the products of a first nature that is riven in the same way. The world is certainly not the unified whole of the Jamesian subject, but nor, the point that James misses, is the subject itself.

This is where radical ecology so often misses the mark: in its critique of the human species as the ultimately destructive, wasteful and selfish life-form that biology has generated, it obscures the fact that nature itself, the nature from which *Homo sapiens sapiens* emerged, embodies the self-same principles, albeit to nothing like the same degree. A piece of cynical conservative wisdom similarly insists that humanity is a kind of cancer, the wildly self-propagating tissue that has become injurious to all other life in the ecosystem, nature's biggest mistake. What are earthquakes and tsunamis compared to human rapacity? Not the least problem with this view is that it posits the natural world as an internally harmonious organism, in which all the various components cohabit and co-function in a state of sublime homeostasis, a view that Darwinian biology already put to flight in the 1850s. The model of a well-ordered machine, in which every component knows its place, cannot help but be a hierarchical system – while all functions are necessary, some are inevitably more crucial than others, so that the extirpation of an ant colony is not of the same order of magnitude as the killing of an indigenous human ethnic group – and the reckoning of hierarchies as unassailable is what leads in human societies to rigid conformism and its *ne plus ultra*, fascism. As Slavoj Zizek has argued, what is chiefly wrong with the restorationist view of cosmic order is precisely that it depends on the supposedly arrogant human species resuming its place in the Chain of Being, but the very position of enunciation of such a sentiment, the transcendent authority reconfiguring the whole structure on behalf of the universe, remaking it in accordance with its own disavowed subjectivity, involves it in a self-negating vanity. 'True arrogance is thus the very opposite of the acceptance of the hubris of subjectivity:

it resides in false humility, i.e. it emerges when the subject pretends to speak and act on behalf of the Global Cosmic Order, posing as its humble instrument.'[8]

Contemporary investigations of the functionalities of the brain have now thrown another perspective on the Victorian interface between philosophy and the empirical sciences in William James and his cohort. The current postulate is that what the physical and internal senses register about the world is not a direct unmediated impression of it, but is transformed into a hypothetical picture constructed by the brain in accord with a repertoire of expectations based on prior experience. The things we see and hear and feel 'are virtual realities conjured by the brain using the same neural machinery that it uses to make your dreams ... [R]ather than passively building a faithful, inner representation of the external world, the brain is constantly trying to stay one step ahead of the game, drawing on its past experiences to *predict* what's happening. Sensory information is not disregarded, but is relegated to the role of reality-testing the brain's guesswork.'[9]

Not only does this have implications for the ways in which perception, and with it whole registers of emotional and philosophical response, might be manipulated, or at least therapeutically remodelled, but it also raises the question as to what intersubjective consequences it entails. If my version of the room in which we are sitting and talking is predicated on a very different prior experience of this environment to yours, and it is that version that my brain is currently delivering to me, while you are comfortably settled in yours, in what concrete sense are we inhabiting the same space? And does it matter?

It matters to the degree that we need not just to interpret external reality, but to put it into some sort of order. Simply knowing what everything is, and being able to make safe, reasonable predictions about what it is likely to do, and in particular what it may do to us, as primarily important as that is, would not suffice to build our inner picture of reality. Its contents need to be placed in conceptual relations with each other, and with us and what we already know about them. For the theorists of the Chain of Being, there was an unmediated relation between the existent and human perception of it, even if that perception was not yet in anything like full knowledge of it all. Cartesian speculation introduces the element of doubt that would henceforth be proper to all scientific investigation. Only those conclusions about physical reality that could be readily tested and established, or by contrast eliminated through empirical falsification, could be admitted into the province of human knowledge. By the time of the nineteenth century, the mediations between objective reality and its perception have grown so thickly numerous as to cast doubt on the nature of doubt itself. Kant had proposed, in the most notoriously opaque section of the first Critique, a bridging faculty termed Schematism that linked external objects with subjective cognition of them. There was a human capability for classifying sense impressions into the conceptual apparatus of the understanding, a link between the empirical and the abstract intuition of it that makes of it a mental principle, a concept. What John Stuart Mill and William James were arguing, half a century apart, is that there is nothing so tangible even as the Kantian schematism to link the two elements, but that they are quite discrepant to each other, a fundamental heterogeneity for which the formulation of an abstract system of understanding can only partially compensate. At the same time, the young HG Wells, in a speculative essay entitled 'The Rediscovery of the Unique' (1891), argued that all scientific measurement, and the postulate of invariable principles that flowed from it, was illusory. Only recently trained in precisely that discipline, Wells abjures it as being in essence contradictory of its own paradigm. If everything shades into everything else by taxonomic contiguity, whether these shadings be the sedimentary layers of geology or the evolutionary developments of organic life, the notion of fixed classes of phenomena must be as fictive in their intellectual function as the foundation myths once were. Put crudely, a group of five baboons in a forest, categorized as such, has been subjected not just to the unstable biological signifier, 'baboon', in terms of which we presume to conform the five of them to exactly the same epistemic standard, but even to the delusive fiction of the concept 'five', a random human construction that, by its imperious totalizing force, subjects these individual creatures to the category of number. 'When we teach a child to count', Wells states in an asseveration worthy of the Victorian pulpit, 'we poison its mind almost irrevocably.'[10] Whatever eccentricity may appear to attach to such a conception, Wells was doing nothing other than anticipating unwittingly the mathematical chaos theory of the twentieth century. If everything is different from everything else, whether hugely and obviously or minutely and subtly, how can we apply principles of classification to it, and then expect those principles to explain and predict everything?

The passage from idealism to materialism in nineteenth-century philosophy ought to have elevated the 'infinity of small differences' that Wells observes in empirical reality into an inviolable axiom, but only succeeded in ratifying the Cartesian view that where abstract mythical forces once possessed the minds of uncomprehending beings, concrete physical laws would now reign supreme, the unbreakable link between them, however, being the panoptical classificatory impulse. Newtonian science was predicated on the notion that a physical law could be infinitely demonstrated, the same mechanism of cause and effect evidenced consistently, no matter how many times an experiment was repeated. Only by repeating it did the law become a law as such in the first place. The discovery that events are in fact random is one of the great breakthroughs of the last century, a finding that has both circumscribed and liberated classical science. In the former sense, science has found the limits of its knowledge, its inability to know what it cannot know, in what it has preferred to call 'chaos', but in the latter sense, this discovery illuminates the insight expressed by the quantum theoretician Anton Zeilinger that 'for the individual event in quantum physics, not only do we not know the cause, there is no cause ... There is nothing in the Universe that determines the way an individual event will happen ... the Universe is fundamentally unpredictable and open, not causally closed'.[11] It is important to see, though, that the fundamental block, structurally analogous to the Kantian block that prevents the individual consciousness from becoming fully aware of the Thing-in-itself, is reflected on both sides of the equation. As the polymath Martin Meisel puts it, 'There are some things we simply can't know, or know in the way we would like to, because of features inherent both in the structure of knowledge and in what is out there to be known.'[12]

The old bourgeois adage that, in the well-ordered home, there is a place for everything and everything is in its place, extols the virtue not merely of having an ordered system, but – just as importantly – of maintaining it by returning things to their proper places after use. 'In a well-conducted man-of-war,' writes the author of nautical romances, Captain Frederick Marryat, inverting the standard formula into a tautology, 'every thing is in its place, and there is a place for every thing' (*Masterman Ready; or The Wreck of the Pacific*, II:1, 1842). A story published by the Religious Tract Society in 1799, 'The Naughty Girl Won', its possible first usage in the familiar verbatim, has its principal character putting the proverbial guideline into brisk practical effect: 'Before ... Lucy had been an hour in the house she had contrived a place for everything and put everything in its place.' Places do not have to have been designed or authorized in advance, but can be decreed by fiat like the divine Creation. Only when they have been so decreed, that is henceforth where each respective thing will belong. A domestic order can be changed with the redecoration or redesign of the room, but the new order will have quite as adamantine an authority as its predecessor. George Herbert's 1640 collection, *Outlandish Proverbs*, a digest of over one thousand adages and epigrams, includes the wistfully subjunctive sentiment, 'All things have their place, knew wee how to place them', which retains a note of pious humility as to the vanity of human endeavour, a note quite vanished by the time the observation has become nothing more than the guarantee of finely tuned domestic organization. Isabella Beeton, in the second chapter of her *Book of Household Management* (1861), entitled 'Duties and Responsibilities', puts the proverb in quote-marks as the piece of unarguable wisdom that it has become.

When the same principle of bureaucratic ordering is applied to people, it underwrites the immovability of social hierarchy, whether it be conceived in the brutally simple pyramidal structures of ancient societies, or their ramification into complex, horizontally expanding layers with the advent of early modern bureaucracy. The conception of the estates comprising society – a hereditary monarchy disposing over a clergy, a nobility (themselves both ordered by internal hierarchies) and the middling and plebeian classes – relied on everybody knowing, understanding and accepting their place within the stratification. In time, the emergence of a literate clerisy of the learned and leisured permitted an audacious degree of mobility from the higher reaches of the third estate, but ultimately the structure held firm through war and adversity until the era of the bourgeois revolutions from 1830 and after began to destabilize its foundations. The notion of mobility is enshrined in the Christian parable of the wedding feast (Luke 14: 7–11), in which Jesus, observing an unseemly scramble for the best seats at the table, cautions the guests that those who jostle for the prime positions risk the humiliation of being moved down if a more esteemed guest turns up. The shrewd way to approach it is to sit at the bottom end among the hoi polloi, an avowal of modesty that could well be rewarded by one's being invited to move up. A bit of etiquette advice with potential benefits for those suffering from status anxiety thereby reflects the great levelling in the forthcoming Kingdom, when the principle of inversion forewarned in the Magnificat will prepare the ground for the celestial equality of God's realm. 'For all those who exalt themselves will be humbled, and those who humble themselves will be exalted.' George Herbert's compendium also includes the adjuration, 'Sit in your place, and none can make you rise', the homiletic force behind every minutely engineered seating-plan and its attendant place-cards, and which, while it contains nothing of the revolutionary undertow of the Christian teaching, nonetheless aims at an assurance that if you are where you are supposed to be, no power on earth can uproot you, at least not righteously.

The ontological problem with the principle that everything belongs in an assigned place is that the whole of human history and, alongside it, even biological evolution have been about things moving away from where they were at the start. It was a cosmic explosion that touched everything off to begin with, from which the celestial objects are still reeling and whirling. If nothing had moved, there would have been no development. In this sense, the only 'places' are where things happen to be, or where they happen to have been put, now. The impulse to return things to the same places enacts thus both a restorationist instinct, which may be psychologically quite comprehensible, and a desire to put an end to movement and to development as far as possible. Reflecting on this notion in the context of those sci-fi films in which reality is thrown out of joint through time travel, or the interface between two incompatible dimensions, Zizek states:

This brings us to the definition of ontological catastrophe, ie. of a disintegration of reality: it occurs not when some key element is out of place but, on the contrary, if the key element whose dislocation opens up and sustains the space of reality returns to its 'proper' place, ie. when the deontological tension that defines reality is overcome. Therein resides the dark message of the stories about an element finally returning to its place: they are really stories about the end of the world.[13]

Even without the element of time travel, it is possible for objects that have been semantically relocated as a result of transpiring events to redetermine the reality around them, and Zizek gives the paradigmatic example of the investigation of crime scenes, in cinematic works such as Francis Ford Coppola's *The Conversation* (1974) and Alfred Hitchcock's *Psycho* (1960). In related scenes from these two films, an empty hotel/motel room is inspected after a murder, particular attention being paid to a bathroom with a shower and toilet. The silence in which the investigative gaze takes in these mises-en-scène, looking for the one element that will be potentially incriminating, is the medium in which an object, while remaining the same object as it was before the crime, might bear witness to the changed reality it now inhabits. In the published screenplay of *Psycho*, its writer Joseph Stefano has indicated, at the moment when Marion's lover and sister enter the cabin at the Bates Motel where she was murdered, 'For a moment they just gaze at the room, as if willing it to tell them some satisfactory story.'[14] In the toilet, a fragment of paper is floating, waiting to bear witness to Marion's having been there, and been in possession of the money she has stolen, for which she might have been killed. Similarly, in the scene in *The Conversation* when the investigator silently examines the vacated hotel room in San Francisco where a murder has taken place, everything devolves on the toilet, which has a band placed across the lowered seat, indicating that housekeeping staff have cleaned it. There is nothing floating in the toilet initially, but on an impulse the investigator flushes it and, to his evident revulsion, a surge of blood and waste matter comes gurgling up from the outlet pipe, overflowing on to the floor. In Zizek's analysis, it is when the respective toilets in the two films return to being apparently ordinary toilets that the normal order of reality is disrupted. Once things have been removed from their habitual contexts, they can only rupture a deceptively seamless reality by being returned to them.

The return to a primal state is not a retrograde progress back to an Edenic innocence, but the cataclysm that puts paid to the present world. At the opening of his first novel, *Tropic of Cancer* (1934), Henry Miller muses, 'When into the womb of time everything is again withdrawn chaos will be restored and chaos is the score upon which reality is written ... It is why I sing. It is not even I, it is the world dying, shedding the skin of time.'[15] If the state of chaos is the musical score on which the composition of reality, with its continually changing time signatures, is written, it can only be by the reverse ingestion of everything back into its uterine origin that a reality congealed into the state of order by history's disaster could begin anew. It is as though the emergence of Cronos, the elemental figure of Time with his castrating sickle and his homicidal readiness to devour his own children, as the grandson of Chaos in the Hesiodic legend, were to be revoked. Meanwhile, what appears to be Miller's own voice in the succeeding text is not his, he insists, but the objective voice of a moribund world, shedding its temporal integument so that something like human experience can start afresh. The present world can only pass away if it is returned, apocalyptically, to its point of origin. This is the same obliterative vision presented in the early dramatic works of Samuel Beckett, of a world inspiring its corrupted biota back into itself, to put an end to history by a wholesale reabsorption. In *Endgame* (1957), the blind domestic tyrant Hamm anxiously insists that his servant Clov keep scanning the world outside through a telescope to ensure that nothing remains. Surprisingly, the odd flea is still living on Clov, obstinately surviving periodic sprinklings with insecticide powder, representing the appalling prospect that life might start again from the same humble beginnings from which it once emerged. The sight of a small boy outdoors prompts a similar urge in Clov to kill him, for fear that the child might eventually become another procreator. In *Happy Days* (1961), the monologist Winnie is shown, over the play's two acts, being subjected to a progressive inhumation, subsiding into the earth in the conventional interpretation, initially waist-deep and then up to the neck, but at least equally plausibly being sucked back into it, in the gigantic act of terrene remorse that reverses the whole project of creation.

If retrogression seems the best strategy, in light of the barely alloyed catastrophe that the world in its historical development turned out to be, the impulse stems from a realization that things have now gone far enough, which is to say, too far. The millenarian temper, habituated to discerning signs of the end-times since immemorial time began, is at one with Beckett's nihilists, even where, perhaps especially where, it is enframed by conventional theology. To the devout of monotheistic eschatology, it is a constant astonishment that God continues to tolerate the extremities of both the created world itself and human depravity without choosing his promised moment to bring down the curtain on it. Not the Black Death, not the earthquake of Lisbon, not the slave trade, nor Auschwitz have yet proved sufficiently atrocious to interrupt the drama with his *deus ex machina*. Instead the whole show blunders on, and humanity finds ways of ameliorating nature's disasters, and some at least of the consequences of its own idiocy. If the principle of suffering nonetheless continues unabated, advances in medicine, agricultural practices, the geological sciences, population management, contribute to the notion of progress as ideology, a forward trajectory to set against the Hegelian political narrative of history as a journey towards humanity's consciousness of its own freedom. The actual unimaginability of regression to a pre-ontological primal state is what conforms such legends as Beckett's, and many of the scenarios of sci-fi films, to the imaginary habitus of the end-times. There can only be an end by means of a retrogressive return to the beginning. Human history is no more rattling along the tracks towards an obvious final act that will represent its structural culmination than is biological evolution. Even those sci-fi stories that envision the wholesale destruction of the world through a nuclear or ecological cataclysm always picture something of it surviving. A familiar trope is the hero who has been unconscious – fast asleep, or under general anaesthetic – while the apocalypse has taken place, and who awakens to find the world transformed unrecognizably into a post-millennial inferno. Having had his eyes treated after an encounter with a plant toxin, research biologist Bill Masen removes his own blindfold at the opening of John Wyndham's *The Day of the Triffids* (1951) to find that the rest of London has gone blind during the course of what was taken to be a spectacular meteor shower, and is now at the mercy of a horde of carnivorous mobile plants. Danny Boyle's 2002 film *28 Days Later*, which explicitly references the narrative structures of Wyndham's novel, has its central character, a bicycle courier called Jim (Cillian Murphy), coming out of a coma in St Thomas's Hospital, London, and discovering that Britain has been overtaken by predatory packs of sub-humans infected by murderous bloodlust, victims of a rage-inducing virus that has been accidentally released from a research laboratory by animal rights activists. If the apocalypse were truly the apocalypse, these awakening Rip Van Winkle figures would be killed by the triffids or the viral marauders within hours of their venturing outside, but they are instead the means by which the apocalypse might, even in extremis, be thwarted, or at least survived. Precisely because they have not witnessed the moment at which society plunged into the abyss, they have not been subjectively remoulded by it. For them, matters could still go either way. 'The worst is not,' says Edgar, confronted with the figure of a king unhinged from the frame of the social order, and thrown to the mercy of the turbulent natural elements, 'so long as we can say "This is the worst"' (*King Lear*, IV: i). But this is a double-edged wisdom, if ever there was. In one sense, it seems to suggest that hope springs eternal, as it still does for Beckett's half-buried Winnie, the mere persistence of objectifying consciousness guaranteeing that this cannot therefore be the worst that could happen, since that would surely bury such consciousness altogether. On the other hand, it cheerily acknowledges, in defiance of the popular axiom that things can only get better, that things can in fact always get worse. Its unspoken third implication is that, if you have to put the question in the first place, things are not likely to be going with a swing.

A venerable and perduring tradition in both Western and Eastern conceptions of the harmoniously ordered cosmos insists that naturally occurring disorder is an integral part of the overall harmony, guaranteeing its organic unity. It is what makes systems of order, and perception, and sensation, dynamic in the first place. Leibniz says as much in the *Theodicy* (1710):

A little acid, sharpness or bitterness is often more pleasing than sugar; shadows enhance colours; and even a dissonance in the right place gives relief to harmony. We wish to be terrified by rope-dancers on the point of falling and we wish that tragedies shall well-nigh cause us to weep. Do men relish health enough, or thank God enough for it, without having ever been sick? And is it not most often necessary that a little evil render the good more discernible, that is to say, greater?[16]

If there appears to be disorder in the world, and the human species appears to be the chief author of it, it is partly because we are only looking at one small aspect of the creation and not the bigger picture: 'the human kind ... is only a fragment, only a small portion of the City of God or of the republic of Spirits, which has an extent too great for us, and whereof we know too little, to be able to observe the wonderful order therein'. Moreover, humans have been endowed by God with free will, in fractional imitation of his own, with the result that they often fall into error, for which they are then, in one way or another, punished by the Creator, as a father chastises his children in the interest of their ultimate moral growth. That divine system of correction is itself then evidence of the supreme order undergirding all. Viewed from the right optical stance, the divine genius of a worldly government in which the teleology of evil is the greater good discloses itself. 'It is as in those devices of perspective, where certain beautiful designs look like mere confusion until one restores them to the right angle of vision or one views them by means of a certain glass or mirror'. It is as though order is only truly order if it is in a continual state of becoming-order, or returning-to-order, so that, as Leibniz asserts, 'there are cases where some disorder in the part is necessary for producing the greatest order in the whole'.[17] This is hardly a mechanical view of the universe in the Newtonian sense, but one that depends on a self-correcting, or rather divinely correcting, action to insure the maintenance of stability, rather as if the pendulum clock ought to stumble in its swing every now and then in order to preserve the integrity of time. It is a regulative conception, and thereby an ethical one, that regards disorder not merely as an unfortunate contingency, but as an essential comparative principle by which order can be all the more admired, an early harbinger of the dingy conformism that sees only the proving of the rule in every exception.

An infinitely expanding universe is one of cosmogony's foundational principles in the modern era, in which chaos is the name of the additive effect of continuous enlargement. Long before Einstein and Edwin Hubble, Kant proposed, in a work of his early career that was instantly suppressed on publication, only seeing the light of day ten years later, that chaos is not just the original state of the diversification of matter, but also underwrites the perpetual development of the physical universe through its limitless elaboration. Written in 1755, the same year that Lisbon would be reduced to rubble, flames and flooding by a colossal earthquake on All Saints' Day, tearing to shreds many of the survivors' faith in a beneficent God, Kant's cosmogony, for all that it builds up to a straight-faced account of the various extraterrestrial beings who inhabit the planets of the solar system, is an early anticipation of the expanding universe theory that was only ratified in the 1920s. Writing from the perspective of a notional central point in the cosmos, Kant states that 'as a consequence of the ordering of nature in this system of ours, creation or, rather, the development of nature, first begins with this central point and with constantly progressive steps extends itself gradually out into all the further distances, in order to fill limitless space with worlds and order in the progress of eternity'. Our own knowledge is confined to the island of order that we presently inhabit, but the further outward the nebular development proceeds, the more likely things are to be in a state of disorder. 'The remaining infinite part will ... still be combating confusion and chaos and will be that much further from a condition of complete development, the further away it is located from the sphere of already developed nature.' There is nothing to invoke terror in the notion that we are surrounded by fathomless tracts of elemental chaos, for the very reason that the development of nature will gradually, inexorably encompass all the present chaotic expanses. There is an unmistakably eighteenth-century frisson of the sublime in the insight that 'the sphere of developed nature is always only an infinitely small part of that being which has in it the seeds of future worlds and strives to develop itself out of the raw condition of chaos in long or short periods of time. Creation is never complete'.[18] The universe is not a structure so much as a process, and even though the ordering principle that governs our own natural world will eventually be functional in worlds that are currently in a state of inchoate disarray, there will never be an end of inchoate disarray. It is generated, in fact, by the continuous expansion of an order that then restyles it in its own image. As Martin Meisel puts it, 'in place of a cosmos that was all system with nothing left over [the stable mechanics of Newtonian science], whose present inertial/ gravitational condition was homeostatic and self-perpetuating, Kant envisaged a universe that incorporated the chaotic principle not simply as antecedent ground but as a constant, inherent in the play of forces and productive of endless, linear change'.[19]

What cannot help but strike modern ears like a disguised melody in the interstices of Kant's grand cosmogonic system is that it also resembles an account of the economic dynamics of capitalism. Although the picture of the market economy that would be painted by Adam Smith in *The Wealth of Nations* (1776) owes more to a Newtonian conception of stability in the money system, and in the access to markets of each sector of the economic edifice, the driving force of capitalism, in its entrepreneurial stage particularly, was the principle of expansion. Manufacturing concerns were always on the lookout for new markets, as well as being perpetually preoccupied with reducing their own costs through automation, ergonomic efficiency and an unspoken reliance on unrewarded overtime. Moreover, the economy itself, as long as it relied on a structure of loans, interest-bearing debts and the continued gamble of new investments, was predicated, as it still is, on the impetus of unimpeded growth. Its alleged self-regulation, in accordance with Smith's enduring postulate that the mass of individual self-interest that comprises the economic system results in collective benefit to the whole of society, rests on the existence of competition. Each company strives to outdo its immediate rivals by lowering its production costs and obtaining its labour more cheaply, with the ultimate aim not of healthy coexistence with other companies but of eliminating the competition altogether if it can. In the era of monopoly capitalism, this tendency became all the more virulent, and in the present globalized economy, it has achieved its most ruthless manifestation yet. By a flawless inverse logic, the desire for infinitely expanding profit is paid for by an infinitely contracting market. When it has torn the throats of all its rivals at the Cretaceous pool, the giganotosaurus has the water to itself. Infinite expansion, the majesty of which in the cosmos causes the young Kant a shiver of the Burkean sublime, takes on the character of depredation when it is applied to the exchange society. Just as cosmic chaos is benevolently transformed by the extension of order, so immiserated populations ought to have been blessed with prosperity at being drawn into the international market system, and yet the price they paid was eternal serfdom to the profit motive in which they barely shared. In this respect, the chaos of the markets, which they jealously guarded against every attempt to encroach on them through restrictions of trade, strictures against unfair competition and a slow but steady accumulation of labour laws, was not to be subjected to rational order, but allowed to reign unchecked. The expansion of profitability comes at the cost of the progressive relative impoverishment of those who generate it. As Marx puts it in 1844, 'The worker becomes all the poorer the more wealth he produces, the more his production increases in power and size. The worker becomes an ever cheaper commodity the more commodities he creates. The *devaluation* of the world of men is in direct proportion to the *increasing value* of the world of things.'[20] If the Kantian cosmos acted in accordance with the principle that order progressively spread into the constantly renewed generation of the provinces of chaos, in free-market economics, by contrast, the principle was that chaos, the anarchy of capital accumulation, would colonize whatever existing outposts of traditional order it came upon in pre-capitalist societies and among those whose lives had not yet been entirely disrupted by its thirst for expansion.

Why should displacement – in culture, society or the self – be a positive value? At the most banal quotidian level, when everything is in the wrong place and not where we expect to find it, the result is frustrated searches and wasted time. The miscellaneous muddle in an untidied cupboard, the dispersal of belongings among boxes during a house move, the piles of unsorted papers on a desk, the racks of CDs that nobody has thought to arrange in order, the unpaired socks that emerge from the washing-machine are paradigms of matter turning chaotic. At the origin of this process are items – the car keys, the mobile phone, the corkscrew – that have simply got lost, and for which one hunts in vain. A mislaid possession is an involuntary sacrifice to the principle of chaos, having slipped its moorings in a concretely policeable spatial realm, for which somebody, perhaps even oneself, may be held to blame. Lost and jumbled objects were once candidates for secure ordering like everything else, but have been allowed to drift into an indeterminate state in which their utility is compromised. Only when they are tracked down, or brought back into some sort of manageable system, is their dignity as objects restored to them. In the meantime, they may well have taken on a life of their own, an idiom to which people often resort when confronted with the uncontrolled behaviour of malfunctioning machinery. An objective world with a life of its own is both magical and malevolent, its functions liberated from human control and turned precisely into autonomous purposes. Nothing else explains the eerie phenomenon whereby lost items appear to be playing cat-and-mouse with the seeker, there one minute, not there the next, or else finally found in an obvious place in which one had already looked several times. The bourgeois domestic paradigm of order, the well-regulated home in which, to recall Mrs Beeton and her predecessors, everything when not in use is in its allotted place, represents not the tranquil idyll to which it aspires, but a hard-won battle over the natural tendency of things to resist secure location.

If things are in their proper places, not only do we know where they are, but we also know what kinds of things they are. A classifying order brings sense to the world, by subsuming its phenomena under the concepts to which they pertain. This principle, which can be seen precipitating into institutional form in the scholarly divisions of the works of Aristotle, who already found Plato's doctrines too precariously founded, undergirds the progress of scientific knowledge according to its various disciplines, which would in turn be reflected in the departmentalization of the modern academy, and in everything in daily life down to the storage system in operation in the kitchen cupboards. When all else fails, an alphabetical arrangement cloaks arbitrariness and contingency in the guise of rational order, drawing apparent disparities under a unifying mechanism, as is discovered by the small child who finds that the lion, the lemon and the ladder are not evidences of the heterogeneity of the world after all, but are joined in a single category by their initial letter. The absence of such ordering systems creates chaos as a condition of directionlessness in which nobody can find their way, something like the garden maze that sought to turn thwarted purpose into a form of amusement.

Ordering systems, by contrast, offer ease and immediacy of access to their constituent elements. What they have also been very good at, however, is demarcating themselves from each other in discrete fields, so that attempts to connect them look eccentric. Creating porosity between zones such as music and mathematics, between theology and the material body, or between astronomy and psychology, leads to epistemological enterprises that are fraught with risk and appear to lack the untroubled stable grounding on which any of these disciplines, considered individually, ought to rest.

Strategies of displacement lie at the heart of the symbolic inversions of the social order that became traditional in medieval societies. Revelries presided over by the Lord of Misrule in the English tradition, the Abbot of Unreason in the Scottish, the Prince des Sots (Prince of Drunkards) in the French marked the Christmas festivities with temporary reversals of the feudal hierarchy, in which lords and ladies waited on their domestic servants and farm labourers. In the Christian church, the three-week December period from the saint's day of St Nicholas through to the Feast of the Holy Innocents was celebrated by the election of a boy bishop, usually a chorister who, garbed in outsize cope and mitre and ineptly wielding the crozier, imitated the gravity of his elder, in fulfilment of the assurance of the Magnificat that the Lord God will put down the mighty from their seats and exalt the humble and meek in their places. These carnivalesque practices have their likely origins in the Roman Saturnalia that took place at roughly the same point in the calendar, in which masters served their slaves at the banqueting, and a comic master of ceremonies satirized the autocracy of the state *princeps* by issuing capricious slapstick commands that had to be obeyed. The salient feature of both the Saturnalia and the Christian Feast of Fools is not that they simply turned the normal order upside-down – a mirror-image reversal of order is still an order –

but that they led to disordered ribaldry, an unpredictable anarchic unruliness founded as much on the choirboy's simple ignorance of what it was that real bishops did as on deliberate mischief-making. Without the unruly element, they would have been too imitative of the official feasts of the ecclesiastical and civic calendar, the function of which was to celebrate, as Mikhail Bakhtin outlines in his study of the European medieval carnival tradition, the continuity of the past and the unbreakable steadfastness of hierarchy. Besides which, there was no jollity at the official celebration: 'It was the triumph of a truth already established, the predominant truth that was put forward as eternal and indisputable. This is why the tone of the official feast was monolithically serious and why the element of laughter was alien to it'.[21] The twin dissolvents of hierarchy at the Carnival, by contrast – the retroversion of the social order, and a general moral levelling, by means of which the upper and lower registers of society, travelling towards their respective antipodes, came into a halfway position of horizontal balance – ensure that hierarchy is eroded from every angle. It is the obscene secret of hierarchies that everybody subjected to them has to participate in the charade of taking them seriously, a secret that the irruption of Carnival is permitted temporarily to lay bare.

The conventional theory of such licensed enactments is that they exercised a socially cathartic function, forestalling the outbreak of real and enduring revolutionary movements by allowing the populace to express the negativity inherent in the established order, precisely through a negative reflection of it. There are numerous periods, however, in which such expressions are inadequate to the social reality, or when prolonged historical calamities demand more than burlesque. Ruinous conflicts, especially those resulting in defeat, often produce a hunger for radical transformation. Even a population on the winning side can turn against its political masters, as did the

British in the 1945 general election, held barely two months after VE Day, but a people reduced to enforced national humiliation, as was Germany in 1919 following the Treaty of Versailles, has nowhere to turn but against the structures of power that have so reduced it. A political situation becomes chaotic when the structures of authority no longer dictate the course or the pace of events, but are subject to the prevailing winds of popular pressure. At what point chaos may be deemed to have set in is generally difficult to determine. Where it is not triggered by a single moment, such as the decision of a government spokesman of the German Democratic Republic, speaking on national television in November 1989, to declare the Berlin checkpoint open, prompting a flood of people with axes and hammers to rush to begin the demolition of the Wall, it is generally the steady transmogrification of a troubled relative stability into uncoordinated turmoil that gives birth to chaos. Nobody can say, in such a process, where a state of chaos has, finally and decisively, come into being, but everybody recognizes it when it is upon them. Even within this developmental scenario, there may be a pivotal moment, brought about by the collective implementation of Nietzsche's advice that that which is falling should also be pushed, but part of the reason chaos is so resistant to the re-imposition of control is that it is hard to say where it began. By definition, it is a condition that has leaked into and filled up every crevice of the polity, so that like a progressive pathological condition that has invaded the whole organism, it defeats any attempt at localized treatment. It may not necessarily be that catastrophes then occur more frequently, but the fact that a state authority cast adrift is helplessly susceptible to everything that happens creates the impression of one damned thing after another, or – more likely – many damned things at once.

The imperative of order is so organically imprinted into the consciousness of modern humans that everybody can readily admit that they have no wish to live in chaotic times. A weather pattern that leaves homes flooded and power cut off, with essential supplies unable to get through, dissolves the normal social order to chaos until a concerted relief effort can be mounted by defence forces and local volunteers. Nobody wants to live in such conditions, or would wish them on anybody else, but the calamitous breakdown of everyday systems of provision has become the unquestioned paradigm of disruptions to the orderly functioning of the state apparatus, and of the hierarchical energies of society at the workplace, in the council chamber and in the upper echelons of national government. A military junta taking power in a country riven by social unrest typically styles itself an interim institution for the restoration of order, as was the case, for over two murderous decades, with the State Law and Order Restoration Council in Myanmar. In the constitutional democracies, the establishment of a parliamentary committee, such as the UK's Committee on Standards in Public Life, founded in 1994 in the wake of a series of financial scandals engulfing the Conservative government of the day, might give the appearance that uncontrolled corruption can be brought in harness by the symbolic constitution of an internal regulative body, the existence of which creates the imaginary guarantee that corruption must henceforth hide its head, even if nobody believes it has thereby been vanquished. A single cancelled train can lead to platforms choked with people treated to nothing but piped apologies over the PA system, the arrival of trains on other platforms that are going at least part of the way to the original destination, and whose operators might not reject a rival company's ticket, creating surges of snarled-up wheelie-bags as passengers run for the footbridge steps. This is the kind of chaos that results from inherent weaknesses in systems officially consecrated to minutely intricate administrative order. There is nothing to recommend it. Where a system is ossified into a rigid structure that serves only itself, however, the subversion of it ought not to be anathematized with the name of chaos.

A countervailing current in scientific thought is that chaos is not in itself disorder, only an unrecognized alternative system of order. In this vein, a philosopher of medical science, Alan Garfinkel, declared in 1983, 'Chaos is *not* disorder. It is a higher form of order.'[22] What this statement evokes, though, is the commitment of contemporary science to the reinterpretation of nonlinear systems, for which meteorology serves as the perennial example, as higher order regulative models. The economist Michael Rothschild enunciates this distinction clearly:

> The nonlinear world occupies a middle ground between perfect Newtonian predictability and utter randomness. Although the terminology is still somewhat fluid, most scientists refer to this nonlinear middle ground as 'chaos'. For nonscientists, this is an unfortunate choice of words [*sic*], because chaotic phenomena are not 'chaotic' in the vernacular sense of total disorder.[23]

Indeed not. What mathematical and physical chaos theory mean by 'chaos' is in fact chance, the aleatoric, Rothschild's 'utter randomness', a usage that fails to leave conceptual space for what would be truly disordered, in the sense of being unhinged from any regulative principle whatsoever, including that of mere chance. This hermeneutic twist has not been confined to scientific axioms, but was already present in dissident modernist culture long before chaos theory saw the light of day. 'Confusion,' suggests Henry Miller in 1939, 'is a word we have invented for an order which is not understood.'[24] The determination to see order everywhere, especially where it appears to be conspicuously lacking, is the mind's imperialism over the contingent, its habituated refusal to see any element of the objective as lying outside the purview of its own conceptualizing impulse. If it fails in bringing order to a disordered state of affairs, it recasts what appears before it as a disguised order. Viewed from another angle, or through an exercise of the comparative faculty, it may well yield up the unnoticed principle it surely obeys. This effort is easiest when the chaotic manifold is purely one of displacement. An arrangement of objects in space, or in (apparent lack of) relation to each other, invites a spatial reinterpretation, in which the movement of only one item to a different position might instantly suggest a pattern. It will be more of an insuperable challenge when it comes to the temporal aspects of chaos, as we shall see in the following chapter.

A more progressive instinct sees the potential chaos in every order, a principle that began to gain traction in aesthetics in the Romantic era. Novalis has the hero of his *Heinrich von Ofterdingen* (1802) hear a daring hypothesis in the course of an aesthetic debate with his teacher, Klingsohr: 'Ich möchte fast sagen, das Chaos mus in jeder Dichtung durch den regelmässigen Flor der Ordnung schimmern [I would almost say that Chaos has to gleam through the regular surface of order in every artwork]'. In the pedagogic context, however, Klingsohr teaches that with maturity the poet comes to understand how to fit the matter of poetry to his technical capacities, aiming at encapsulating the simplest and highest themes, rather than the exuberant 'debaucheries' that appeal to the young, the attempted expression of which results only in 'leeres täuschendes Unding [empty deceptive absurdity]'.[25] The lesson is that Chaos, shimmering through the veil (*Flor*, literally the nap or pile on the surface of a garment) of the finished work, emphasizes the layer of Order that has been imposed on it, like well-fitting clothes that, in outlining the body through its concealment, bestow an integument of decency on the outrage of nakedness. A century and a half and two world wars later, Adorno, in one of the sections of short epigrams in *Minima Moralia*, counters this conservative thought by insisting that 'the task of art today is to bring chaos into order'.[26] The slight ambiguity of the

English translation leaves open the possibility of a false interpretation, that chaos is to be transformed into order, resolved, set right. The German construction – 'Aufgabe von Kunst heute ist es, Chaos in die Ordnung zu bringen' – permits no such uncertainty. Chaos is to be brought into the realm of aesthetic order, introduced into it as a foreign body, where it did not exist before. The old aesthetic categories are forms that, as the sedimented content of earlier eras of artistic expression, are hopelessly insufficient to articulate the truth about the present world of compound catastrophes, which the very same aesthetic categories had proved incapable of forestalling. Only if the glib certitudes of the well-made play and the well-wrought urn are shattered can art stay true to its redemptive mission of confronting a faulty world with its failings. Nothing about today's chaos deserves its sublimation into order, an impulse that, in the same post-war period, led Adorno to the unforgotten notoriety of stating that to write poetry after Auschwitz was barbaric, which is to say, that it did nothing other than further the barbarism to which it fancied itself the antidote.

In the argument of the *Dialectic of Enlightenment*, Adorno and Max Horkheimer claim that not just artforms but the entire epistemology of the human sciences stands in need of liberation from the spell of instrumental reason, the tendency to classify all phenomena into categories, of which they become merely exemplary, thereby reifying thought into a purely tautological operation. Nothing is what it is in itself, but is only ever a genus of an overarching species. As the Enlightenment progressed, it eclipsed the insight that these categories and species themselves were historical constructs, assembled and prioritized in accordance with the predilections of their day. What Adorno would later call 'identity thinking' submits the objective realm to a classificatory principle that permits little or no genuine perception of its affective, symbolic or ideological aspects in contemporary society. The primary aperçu of dynamic dialectics, that everything is connected by intricate associational threads with everything else, is precisely what every ordering principle since Linnaean taxonomy tended to resist. Categories would not be categories unless they were distinguishable from each other, however contiguous they might be in the grand system of knowledge. In the opening section of the *Negative Dialectics* (1966), Adorno makes a counter-intuitive case against thinking in such categorial, factually determined parameters:

> The power of the status quo puts up the façades into which our consciousness crashes. It must seek to crash through them. This alone would strip the postulate of depth from ideology. Surviving in such resistance is the speculative moment: what will not have its law prescribed for it by given facts transcends them even in the closest contact with the objects, and in repudiating a sacrosanct transcendence. Wherever thought overcomes that, by binding itself in resistance, lies its freedom.[27]

The impulse of identity thinking is to be heard whenever an argument is opposed with the sentiment that it is not fair to compare disparate entities, that their disparity renders the consideration invidious. Such a refusal might seem to be preserving the ontological dignity of individual objects, but in actuality only does them a disservice by suggesting that the categories in which they are confined are, as Adorno puts it, 'sacrosanct'. On this view, everything has its own inherent nature, which, for all that transcendental subjectivity may not have final access to it, is nonetheless, and for just that reason, an impermeable given. It both subsumes the objects under their concepts and sets up their facticity as a monstrous golden calf. A consciousness that truly wished to do justice to the object-world would need to trust its own immersive proximity to the objective, and articulate the things the objective makes it feel, rather than standing before facticity in a helpless state of petition, like Kafka's man from the countryside forbidden entry at the Door of the Law.

Objects slotted into their contexts have been subjected to a double law of possession. In one sense, they have been allocated to the intellectual categories to which they belong, but simultaneously they become the conceptual property of whoever does the classifying. Ordering one's belongings into a system in the home confirms their subjection to one's own categorizing will, by which the natural anarchy into which they readily fall if left unordered is abrogated. An alphabetically arranged shelf is the shining illusion of mastery. Even the haphazard order that was frozen in its disarray, and must be maintained undisturbed by its owner, who puts individual items back in the places into which they originally fell, radiates the marks of its possession. These are the ordinary means by which people save time. Just so, however, do ideas, the particles of knowledge without which nobody could conceive of anything, occupy the places that their proprietors, beginning with Plato, first assigned them. When everything becomes an indicative marker of its category, by occupying an unchanging place in the structures of thought, the intellect ceases to respect the objects' integrity. Congealed into each element of the object-world is its history, the uses to which it has been put and the potentials it might release if viewed anew, but they petrify through becoming the inert components of a system, and the whole order, classically conceived, becomes the foundation of history itself. 'During the Classical age,' writes Foucault, 'the constant, fundamental relation of knowledge, even empirical knowledge, to a universal mathesis justified the project ... of a finally unified *corpus* of learning.' By conforming the investigations of the human sciences to an encyclopaedic structure, 'the universal possibility of tabulated order [became] the archaeological basis of knowledge.'[28] It is precisely the consciousness of its historicity, though, that might set it in motion once more.

The true nightmare, to be set against those that science fiction has imagined, is not the apocalyptic disorder of the world, but its immovability, the degree to which emancipatory possibility is blocked from ever becoming actuality. Visions of utopia, by contrast, fail by being static, and by promoting a concrete vision of a postulated reality whose faults are plain for all to see, and which can only be a product of the consciousness produced by present circumstances anyway. Sixteenth-century peasants lying engorged amid a world of surfeit and readily accessible plenty, supremely contented though they look, express nothing more revolutionary than does the grumbling stomach in a time of scarcity. The materials of the established human sciences – for Foucault, the eternal trinity of biology, philology and economics, as organized into systems of organic life, languages and the behaviour of money – now reveal the world to be not merely what we perceive of it, but as having an objective anterior existence external to human beings, which establishes its own relations to them. They are no longer representative of human understanding, but become the ontologies of it. Instead, the intimation of what would be different is better realized negatively, through critical insight into the present, by means of a disruptive, disintegrative 'not-this', which alone could shield hope's flame. Rigidly binary gender definitions, linguistic codes that span a gargantuan arc from the alienated discourses of bureaucracy to the impoverished, instantly referential colloquies of online chat, the unmanageable doom of figures on the bank statement, fractious laws that set injustice in tablets of stone generations ago, commercial music produced to the unvarying templates of an industrial technocracy, the sclerotic narrative procedures of television drama, even the patterns of dissension and damage in brittle personal relationships: all have the character of the heteronomous force of fate, of something that impinges on human experience, descends on it and induces its conformity through habits of thinking that humbly accept that everything has its place.

The antique theologies of both West and East contain moments that offset the baleful counsel to be patient, quiescent, accepting of all that is, which underpins the adept's encounter with the present world. Christianity developed an eschatology of negation, in which everything about the sublunary social order will be stood on its head in a universal righting of wrongs, prior to a celestial equilibrium in the Kingdom of God. The dissidence of the faith consists in its acknowledgement that the created world has gone wrong, and the credence it enjoins in its communities is nothing less than that the present order will irrevocably pass away, which nothing else about the present order encourages its subjects to imagine. Similarly, in the non-theistic world of Zen, the koan – a form of logical verbal conundrum to be pondered by novice monks on the path to enlightenment – is an ancient strategy for training the conceptual intelligence in the ways of suppleness and liberty. In the famous riddle of the goose in a bottle, the apprentice is asked to imagine a gosling that has been raised, for unspecified reasons, inside a large glass receptacle. How, when it is fully grown, can it be freed without either killing the bird or breaking the bottle? The instructive answer of the celebrated ninth-century Zen master Nansen Fugan (Nanquan Puyuan) is, 'See! The goose is out of the bottle.' To think outside the prescribed parameters of what is after all only a thought experiment is the only way to solve an insoluble puzzle. The same exercise of imagination that put the goose in the bottle in the first place can also free it. Not the imaginary goose but the mind itself needs to be liberated from its incarceration within the objective world which, while it retains the character of a wholly classified external objectivity only, is the mind's glass prison.

2

Simultaneity

Even more than the notion that everything is in the wrong place, the vernacular conception of chaos is of everything happening at once. This is the temporal counterpart to its spatial aspect. As with displacement, simultaneity undermines priority. Nobody knows where to look, or what ought to take precedence over what. The effect is of a crowd of people all trying to push their way through a narrow doorway at the same time, or of everybody talking at once as all of them try to make themselves heard. Simultaneity offends temporal logic, which decrees that there is an appropriate order in which to look at, attend to and act on events. Where there is no obvious order, the imposition of a random one serves to tease out the conflicting strands of a tangled mass. One can, with due perseverance, moderate a rowdy public meeting in this way, but history pays no such attention to the principle of predicative succession.

The idea of a temporal logic is reflected in classical grammar and its clausal structures. Rhetoric stipulates the succession of statements of predication, the parentheses by which they make way for subordinate supplementary data, and the larger order to which those statements themselves are articulated together to structure a coherent thought or series of thoughts. A literate culture relying on verbal expressiveness in oratory and in the written word, which acquired decisive significance during the Athenian period, generated normative rules for presenting cases at law, providing legitimacy for political rule and constructing philosophical argument. The edifice of grammar makes propositions consequent on one another, establishing the impetus of deductive relation among their various elements. Its foundational principle is the irresistible force of conclusive predication: if A, then B. If you want A to happen, then you must be prepared for B. The only route to Y is via X. The Greek conception of dialectic permits a series of opposing points to be considered against an initiatory proposition, but the overall tendency of the exchange is to establish what must be the case, so that a Socratic dialogue – so many of which, in Plato's writings, are hardly dialogues at all – unfolds in pursuit of a finally unchallengeable conclusion. By contrast, the moment at which everybody at a symposium abandoned the pre-stipulated rules relating to the quantity of drink and the length of each man's respective contributions to the debate, and all started talking at once, would be the moment that it descended, if not into chaos – which was still figured as a fathomless empty chasm in Athenian thought – then into licentious and unproductive disorder. As the younger members spilled on to the streets in the middle of the night in that partly sanctioned act of class-based lawlessness known as the *komos* (of which more in Chapter 5), creating a din and committing acts of vandalism, the serenity of cerebral order had decisively collapsed.

A sentence, Jan Mieszkowski points out, is a paradigm of coherently informed structure. It 'holds out hope of some order and stability, since it marks a crucial frontier in the hierarchy of verbal units. The borders of the sentence are the points at which grammar's stipulations for how we should arrange words and phrases reach, or nearly reach, their limit'.[1] It was for this reason that Nietzsche suggested that modern human beings needed to rise above their entrapment in grammatical structures, a malady of the Western soul that he characterized as 'the seduction of language (and the fundamental errors of reasoning petrified within it), which construes and misconstrues all actions as conditional upon an agency, a "subject".[2] When everything appears to be aligned in theory with the mechanism of subject–predicate–object, whether the sentence in question is performing the function of stating, commanding, querying or wishing, thought has surrendered too much of its inherent topographical suppleness to a rule-bound conformity, which then determines the parameters of experience and what it might be possible to say or do with it. Rhetorical textbooks from classical antiquity onwards prescribe the optimal use of sentences in both speech and writing, with the emphasis placed on an unequivocal precision derived from the correct ordering of their elements. In most Western linguistic practices, the semantic freight of a sentence tends to be loaded towards or at the sentence's rear end, in narratological fashion, making the labour of following and understanding it a linear progression towards a conclusion, like a piece of tonal music arriving back at the tonic note. That there are many sentences in individual usage that do not obey this structure does nothing to undermine the suggestion that a piece of prose composed entirely in sentences that each opened with their substantive proposition, before allowing the subordinate grammatical material to follow in its wake, would have an eerily unbalanced, and ultimately unsatisfying, rhetorical effect, the lexical equivalent of the east Asian gastronomic habit, incomprehensible to occidental taste, of eating a little of the principal savoury dishes first, to gratify the palate, before satiating the stomach by filling up on plain rice.

Arnold Toynbee may despairingly have summarized the nightmare of history as one damned thing after another, but that is one of the many laws it signally fails to obey. Philosophies of history of all tendential stripes have characterized it as an ontological context, an immaterial entity that gains strikingly material attributes in the theorizing of it, a medium in which events unfold as much as one constituted by those events themselves. Distinguishing between history as just the open-ended sum of what people do, or what happens to them, and the varied historiographies in which they might be written or related remains a vexed enterprise. The latter, after all, are a heterogeneous and scarcely reconcilable multiplicity that would have to include the wayward progress of the Hegelian World Spirit, Whig theories of slow but incremental social amelioration, the Spenglerian tale of slow but incremental decline, Marxist and vulgar-Marxist determinisms of one sort or another, the many eschatologies of the Judeo-Christian tradition from the proleptic currents of Mosaic Judaism to Calvinist predestination, and the simple but remarkably hardy belief in something like fate, as it dawns on its clients in moments of déjà vu, expertly divined numerological patterns or the insights of astrological prognosis. What we call history is the attempt to impose a structure on human affairs, to subject their tendencies to paradigms from which the course of future events might be predicted, or by which they might somehow be influenced. In one sense, if we did not do that, there would be hardly any point in thinking about it at all. History is nothing if not didactic, a resource from which lessons may be drawn, the reservoir of prior (and present) experience that ought to point the way out of the prison of eternal repetition. When Marx stated that history progresses by its bad side, he meant nothing other than that its good side, where it has one, has nothing to teach us. A finally reconciled state of humanity would not require a pedagogic or moral history, despite the millenarian Marxist notion that its arrival would mark history's true beginning, after the prolonged series of false starts humanity has hitherto made. Meanwhile, since history is a narrative, it cannot help being didactic in the Aesopian sense, in which every *longue durée*, as much as every vignette, offers a moral conclusion.

If history, on one all too obvious definition, is what has already happened, there are nonetheless moments when people begin to feel it as a living current, a momentous time that they are actively living through, as when a sudden lurch around a bend in the track reminds the travellers that they are hurtling along in the train. At these points, events seem sufficiently propitious or significant – unprecedented, crucially – that they earn the name of History. Even these episodes are likely to be happening elsewhere, assiduously followed by the daily news bulletins. A single occurrence, such as an election result or the impeachment of a president, might well seem historic, but actual history, in the sense intended by an unfolding process, requires a sequence, an epoch, something that unfurls from day to day. The radical democracy movement that originated among university students in Hong Kong in 2014 as a protest over education policy, to develop eventually into a tide of mass resistance among the general populace, its fervour only intensified by barely veiled threats from Beijing, translated locally into levels of exorbitant violence by a police force that once prided itself on the maintenance of order by consent, more nearly resembled the march of history than contemporaneous larger-than-life events in the European Union and the United States. An explanation for that would have to start from the idea that when whole populations begin to challenge the existing structures of governance and their public figureheads, including their ownership of the exclusive rights of interpretation of what is taking place, things are changing fundamentally. In Europe and North America in the early years of the twenty-first century, demagogic politicians and the party machines that had defied their own convention by producing them became the intrinsic challenges to the status quo, bewitching their client populations into imagining that the systems were generating their own internal insurrectionary currents, so that the people themselves need not trouble to do so. The refusal of official bureaucratic nicety, the short-circuiting of parliamentary procedure, the targeting of establishment figures in politics and the judiciary as only frustrating the will of the people are all tactics once reserved for the disaffected left that, in being co-opted to serve the interests of the radical right at the moment of its most insolent entrenchment in power, have also further neutralized them as tools of leftist opposition. A British conservative tabloid that in November 2016 ran pictures of a trio of high court judges above the headline 'ENEMIES OF THE PEOPLE', after they had made a ruling in favour of parliamentary consent over the will of the executive, was for a day at least indistinguishable from the front page of a communist paper of the 1930s. These events, while extraordinary enough, constitute only an ersatz version of history for the precise reason that they are empty emblems of radical change standing in for the absence of any such change. Where the European and American worlds have managed to foment momentary spasms of defiance, they have failed either through being unabashedly contentless, as in the case of the long-vanished Occupy movement, through confining themselves to the kinds of symbolic actions with which an over-mighty state can happily rub along, such as the burning of heads of state in effigy, or through civil unrest degraded to the level of opportunistic crime, Alain Badiou's lowliest category of the 'immediate riot'. Those who suggested that Occupy represented the unfolding of history in the midst of the New York financial district had confused the mere gathering of people with a reconstructive oppositional force, the chanting of rhyming couplets with political discourse and the absence of a formulated set of demands with creative open-mindedness. In Hong Kong, the protest movement's list of demands multiplied as the tipping-point year of 2019 progressed, cornering a beleaguered and helpless chief executive, despairing at the hideous violence over which she was presiding but forbidden to resign by Beijing, into futile efforts at belated compromise. The democracy movement has achieved the first objective of all insurrections, which is to force the existing power into revealing its true nature. An ossified oligarchy in Beijing, haunted still by the international revulsion that followed the events in Tiananmen Square of thirty years earlier, is being pushed towards acting once more against its own interests in the realpolitik of the day. If the economic cost of brutal repression is likely to be minimal enough amid the global reign of capital, a regime in which China itself is now a major linchpin, the political fallout is less calculable. Even the West's less scrupulous heads of government have little desire to be filmed breaking bread with mass murderers, and if they are not to be mass murderers after all, the democracy movement genuinely will be in the ascendant as a historical force.

Most citizens of the Western world born after the end of the Second World War can fairly say they have never lived through anything resembling history, except vicariously where they saw it happening to other people. They have not participated in mass movements, have not succeeded in altering the conditions in which the courses of their lives are prescribed, and will live with circumstances as they are, despite chafing under more or less daily injustices. The British referendum on leaving the European Union in 2016 produced a profound and irreconcilable split within the populace, but the political upheaval it generated was in due course neutered by the decisive general election result of December 2019, and although it led the country out of an international organization, much against the run of Britain's record of involvement in such alliances, was at least as remarkable for its being the first national or regional referendum in which the British had not voted in accordance with the advice of the governing body, or voted to do anything other than maintain the status quo. There was a case to be made from the anti-capitalist left for all countries – not just the UK – abandoning the EU's present institutional structures, but not a squeak of it was heard amid the indignation about European migrant workers and the expensive foreign muck of laws imposed from outside. This, although it will pass into the historical record, and despite the fact that various events unparalleled in British history took place while the crisis continued, was not history as it was lived, but only pseudo-history, the *plus ça change* impression of things being transformed while, beneath them, the forces of reaction were only being all the more firmly entrenched.

It is my contention, in other words, that to a populace, whether contemporary nation-state or small organic community, that senses it is living through history, events do not simply unfold in a temporal sequence. That is the structure of the dreariest day-to-day reality, whether it actually obeys such a structure in practice or not. The daily tasks one has to accomplish proceed in an order that one has either determined oneself, or had prescribed for one, while the content of what transpires on any given day, assuming anything does, also inherently displays – and if it does not, it is readily given – the linear order of a narrative. There literally is no other way available for the rational cognition of experience to make sense of human affairs, in which the phrase 'make sense of' connotes precisely the manufacturing of a semantic value out of initially formless or only partly formed experiential data. A series of frustrations and fuckups that have antagonized a well-meaning morning into a minor tragedy of thwarted hope are best rationalized into the form of a narrative account that lends itself to the kind of embellishment that makes it all the more worth the telling. As one indeed tells it to each successive auditor, the epithets and phrases precipitate into reiterated emphasis, until something like a canonical version of it has accrued, its diegetic integrity more or less suitable for recounting in a court of law – or, at the least, in an official complaint. By contrast, during a series of properly historical events, everything happens in timeframes that slip against each other and superimpose themselves on one another, making a fluid current of temporality once again, reliquefying time indeed back into what ought to be its properly unsteady state, a rushing and eddying fluvial stream that carries us along, rather than the dry sedimented bedload over which we clamber in the seasons of historical drought. To elaborate, we might look afresh at one of the most richly historicized and scrutinized chaotic periods in twentieth-century European culture and politics. I refer to the fourteen-year historical epic that was the Weimar Republic.

Weimar represents a paradigm case of chaos from a history that, especially in light of recent convulsions in the democratic politics of Europe, seems to be in the process of becoming more recent than of receding into the historically narrativized past. During the precarious decade and a half of its existence, the German Republic given the name of Weimar was marked by profound structural instability. Particularly during its first phase from 1919 to 1924, it was beset by one crisis after another, each one of them mounting another explicit challenge to its constitutional legitimacy, all of which helped undermine it as a political entity when ultimately prevailing hostile forces finally organized themselves sufficiently to destroy it. In a scene of national chaos, the executive authority that should be the still centre of swirling events is repeatedly shown to be weaker than those events themselves, as is famously expressed by Yeats's contemporaneous lyric, 'The Second Coming' (1919):

> Things fall apart; the centre cannot hold;
> Mere anarchy is loosed upon the world,
> The blood-dimmed tide is loosed, and everywhere
> The ceremony of innocence is drowned

When the centre cannot hold – hold everything in place around it, but also hold fast in itself – things will disintegrate into a state of mere (i.e. total, from the Latin *merum,* pure) anarchy. With that comes a tide of minatory violence, its waters dimmed or darkened with spilled blood, ready to engulf an innocence traditionally encapsulated in the sacrament of baptism, in which the stain of original sin is washed away, but which is itself now drowned in the surging waters of the further blood-ocean that history is preparing. Yeats was writing in the aftermath of the Great War and the Easter Rising in Dublin, but these words would turn out to be a night-watchman's horn for the three decades to follow. Everything stems from the unstable centre. In the context of Weimar, the fragile Republic that was born from the elections of January 1919 was subject to the entire set of attributes that marks a chaotic state. Of these, six in particular stand out.

1. From its very inception, the Republic was subject to currents of polarized dissension about its constitutional status. The radical Spartacist left considered that it had betrayed the promise of workers' liberation that the revolutionary movement had begun to envisage and enact even before the German surrender in 1918. It was a centrist political entity dominated by the mainstream Social Democratic Party (SPD), which had become progressively less radical in its orientation since its improbable emergence as a mass party before the war. On the far right, the mood was entirely against any form of parliamentary democracy, and in favour of an authoritarian imperial polity of Bismarckian stamp. Elements of the demobilized officers' corps of the army held the left responsible for Germany's defeat to the Allied powers. By fomenting popular disgruntlement, it was claimed, they had turned the tide of public opinion against the war effort, sabotaging the will of soldiers to go on fighting, and making common cause with the forces of Bolshevism. Both of these

entrenched positions made themselves irreconcilable with the central government, which they were prepared to take practical measures to overthrow.

2. Those measures included the proclamation of the Bavarian Soviet Republic by Leninist forces in Munich in April 1919. The very fact that the national capital, Berlin, had been deemed too unstable to risk holding the January negotiations over the composition of the new state parliament there was itself indicative of the likely frailty of the executive authority that would emerge from them. The Bavarian secession from Weimar was the first significant attempt to create a rival political entity to it. In the event, after only a month, the Munich Soviet was besieged by divisions of the Freikorps, German volunteer units originating in the eighteenth century, which had become by the late imperial era the unofficial mercenary army of the most reactionary forces in national politics, and which did the state's work for it in dissolving the revolutionary body. In March 1920, the Freikorps made an attempt to install its own puppet candidate, Wolfgang Kapp, as Reich Chancellor in Berlin, supported by a show of military force in the streets. While the constitutional government fled in terror to Stuttgart, the Kapp putsch was terminated after four days by a lethally effective general strike that short-circuited all methods of official communication. That these spectacularly subversive ventures got as far as they did testifies to the lack of resistance, itself exacerbated by lack of foresight, offered by the central authority.

3. A state authority is not truly an authority when there are other countervailing hostile entities abroad in its territory. The Freikorps had become a law unto itself, acting as an

unofficial extra-judicial body outside the executive control of the state. When a workers' uprising with a coherent portfolio of political demands broke out in 1920 in the Ruhr industrial region, the SPD government relied not just on the regular army, but on elements of the Freikorps as well, to suppress it, a task they had already begun without awaiting the nicety of official sanction. This action above all others would result in an irreconcilable split within the corpus of the left, enfeebling it in the face of the concerted anti-constitutionalism of the far right.

4. A chronically unstable state is characterized by an atmosphere of unbridled violence. The normal parameters of the law are thrown into continual suspension by the actions of organized and opportunistic agents in the national conflict. Clashes between striking and non-striking workers, attacks on workers' demonstrations by the Freikorps, heavy-handed crackdowns by law enforcement units on outbreaks of unrest, and regular assassinations of leading figures became part of the daily miasma of Weimar life. The breaking of bones ceased to be a purely criminal act, or one confined to the battlefield, and became instead the methodology of political confrontation in the civil polity.

5. Adrift within its own milieu, an embattled state often looks to unlikely external allies, as did the German state when it concluded the Treaty of Rapallo with the Soviet Union in 1922. Under its terms, the wartime enemy of five years earlier was to be supplied with military technology in an arrangement that would enable Germany itself to breach key clauses of the Versailles Treaty, which set strict numerical limits to the extent and composition of its armed forces. For

his pains, the German foreign minister who signed the treaty, Walther Rathenau, was assassinated by nationalist army officers two months later.

6. Political precariousness is always attended by economic instability, a situation aggravated in Germany by the reparation terms of Versailles and by its lack of trading partners in the isolation of defeat. Against this background, the Treasury resorted to the self-deluding strategy of printing unlimited quantities of new money to pay the reparations and keep the economy going, a policy that led to the calamitous hyperinflation that peaked in 1923. By November of that year, banknotes in the denomination of fifty billion marks were being issued, money that was, proverbially and literally, not worth the paper on which it was printed. Two of them would buy a loaf of bread, if you managed to get to the head of the queue before the price had increased again. This state of affairs undeniably contributed to widespread hardship and deprivation, but remains the most salutary episode modern capitalism has to offer of the contradictions inherent in the money system. If it is pushed to its limits, and indeed beyond them as it was in Germany, money itself is rendered functionally meaningless, and the economic system that it underwrites turns entirely chimerical. The redenomination of the currency in November 1923 led to the resumption of war reparations, the strengthening of the economy and the advent of a relatively pacific period in the middle to late 1920s.

For all these reasons, and supremely for the reason that it turned out to be powerless to prevent the transition from a system that preserved at least the lineaments of a representative democracy to one of brutal repression and dictatorship, and an even more spectacularly destructive war than the first one, the Weimar Republic is classed with the great political catastrophes of human history. And yet this is not by any means the full picture of how it was experienced by those who lived through it. Nor were its positive legacies entirely extinguished by the twelve years of Nazi hegemony that succeeded it, but instead lay in cold storage in society's cellar, awaiting a return to the daylight of political liberalization after 1945. To say so is not to essay a facile search for the silver lining in every crisis, on the flawed Nietzschean assumption that what does not kill people makes them stronger. Instead, what emerges on the credit side of human development in periods of chaos is precisely what enables a productive critical attitude to the forces that have brought about the chaos in the first place. Far more so than in periods of apparent stable consensus, the self-dissolution of a chaotic polity positively mandates the formation of alternative conceptions of it, conceptions that in turn, as they gather force within public opinion, serve further to undermine the disintegrative system. Something of this perception was voiced by Mao Zedong in the turbulent early onset of China's Cultural Revolution, in his remark, 'There is great disorder under the heavens – the situation is excellent.' While the decade that followed would prove to be one of the most notorious in the history of the People's Republic, Mao's contention that the centre of the 1949 state apparatus might be vulnerable to popular onslaught was an acknowledgement that, if there was to be any chance of a return to dynamic political initiatives in such circumstances, they could only come about through the surrender of the state to radical instability. In one sense, the systems of Western parliamentary democracies are founded on a not dissimilar notion, which is that, at a certain fixed point every several years, the entire executive apparatus dismantles itself. The space of political power is made vacant, other than for unforeseen contingent emergencies, and the electorate is called upon to initiate the next historical phase. The new start thereby launched may well be nothing other than a continuation of the old regime under the same personnel, but nonetheless a moment's pause, during which something that passes for a debate leads to a final decision, is allowed to take place before the everyday administration of political authority resumes.

In a state of ostensible consensus, whether imposed or commanding ready consent, critical consciousness and its expression is a marginal endeavour, unwelcome other than at the peripheries of public discourse for its questioning of the ideological narratives a society tells itself. There may still be many forums for debate, including parliamentary inquiries, combative media interviews, the televised interactions of politicians and the public, and the tide of dissension in online social networks, but these are the forums precisely that have been prescribed. Where the articulation of dissent refuses the very terms of discursive engagement, eschewing the expected clichés, eliding the finite range of choices on offer, it is met either with ridicule or with blank incomprehension. By contrast, in a state that is rocking on its foundations, critical thought becomes a more overt and prominent aspect of the public conversation and, in many cases, of the public conduct of sociopolitical affairs. Indeed, the very same forms of opposition now take on more salient subversive force, just because the centre is no longer strong enough either to resist them or to absorb them.

In the case of the Weimar Republic, the phenomenology of dissension appeared in manifold forms. Progressive political initiatives abounded: the formation of workers' and soldiers' councils, on the model of the soviets that preceded the October Revolution; the abolition of the last of the imperial monarchy; advances in workers' terms of employment, from compulsory rest periods during the working day up to health insurance committees elected by the workforces themselves; the reinstatement of demobilized workers; rent controls and protection for tenants; the abolition of Prussian legislative assemblies elected on the basis of social class; the extension of the franchise to universal suffrage at the age of twenty in all national and local elections; and much else besides. Even in the explosive month-long existence of the Bavarian Soviet Republic, run from Munich under the leadership of the Leninist revolutionary Eugen Leviné, in April and May 1919, and which was constituted in bitter opposition to the Weimar settlement, the government had chance to enact policies such as putting factories under workers' control and ownership, and redistribution of the property of the wealthiest sectors of society to the homeless, before it was blown from history in an uproar of street-fighting.

The Weimar period was furthermore distinguished by tumultuous cultural ferment. In the visual arts, it produced the movement known as Neue Sachlichkeit (New Objectivity), a current also given the name of 'magic realism' by the critic Franz Roh in 1925. Painters such as Otto Dix, George Grosz, Conrad Felixmüller, Max Beckmann and Jeanne Mammen moved away from the obscure interiorities of the expressionist mode and towards an overtly allusive documentary style that shone an unforgiving spotlight on the hypocrisies of an establishment generation that had led Europe into the Great War. In a style that hovered somewhere between graphic art and the satirical cartoon, Grosz depicted generals, bankers and industrialists engaged in the sordid transactions of an ethically moribund society. Artists looked to the circus and the cabaret for their subjects, or depicted the monumental architecture of the factories towering over the churches and tiny dwellings of the workers in the modern cityscape. Suicides and sex murders fill the canvases of Dix and Rudolf Schlichter. They reflect the prevalence of a social type identified by Peter Sloterdijk as the 'impostor', the personification of a social process in which nothing can be taken at face value and nothing happens as intended, 'the existentially most important and most understandable symbol for the chronic crisis of complexity of modern consciousness'.[3]

The literary traces of dissension and duplicity were many and varied. Alfred Döblin's great montage novel *Berlin Alexanderplatz* (1928) employs the discontinuous modernist techniques of Joyce to draw a documentary picture of a fragmented and fissiparous urban world. Erich Maria Remarque's important war narrative *All Quiet on the Western Front* (1929) attempted finally to put the experience of the ordinary German soldier in the great imperialist conflict centre-stage, at a decade's cautious remove from the defeat. Even as canonical a figure as Thomas Mann sought to weave the textures of a radically faulty reality into allegorical form in the great fabular expanses of *The Magic Mountain* (1924), in which the remnants of the intellectual and social elite, cloistered in an Alpine sanatorium for the good of their health, read the last rites in Socratic dialogues to an etiolated culture drifting towards its doom. In the documentary register, Mann's often-overlooked novella *Disorder and Early Sorrow* (1925) makes oblique reference to the Weimar hyperinflation as a life-context that its characters have all but learned to endure. As Todd Kontje puts it in a point with wider resonance, '*Disorder and Early Sorrow* depicts a social order teetering on the brink of chaos, but one that has also unleashed new creative energies'.[4]

In architecture, the Bauhaus sought a break with decorative and bombastic principles, the pilasters, cartouches and statuary of the ornamental style that had dominated the built environment of the nineteenth century, and aspired to an ethic of pure functionality, albeit one that incorporated popular craft elements in place of heroic classical references. The American-influenced jazz of the cabaret scene, spurred by the extravagant popularity of Josephine Baker, brought a new sense of demotic excitement to the tradition of popular song, itself reflected in the scores of the *agitprop* stage-works that composers such as Kurt Weill and Hanns Eisler produced in collaboration with the dramatists Georg Kaiser and Bertolt Brecht. Meanwhile, the German cinema produced Europe's most revolutionary experiments in the possibilities of film, in an arc that stretched from Robert Wiene's *The Cabinet of Dr Caligari* (1920) and Friedrich Wilhelm Murnau's *Nosferatu* (1922) to Fritz Lang's *Metropolis* (1927) and Georg Wilhelm Pabst's *Joyless Street* (1925), *Diary of a Lost Girl* and *Pandora's Box* (both 1929).

The concurrent strands of political effervescence and a vigorously productive oppositional culture combined to provoke advances in social consciousness. Life as an ordinary member of society undergoes a qualitative transformation in such circumstances, departing from the mere fulfilment of traditional economic and familial roles, and lighting out instead into more uncertain zones, in which social identities become fluid, more responsive to a greater range of experiences. The besetting context of risk into which objective conditions have pitched everybody, where it does not entirely immobilize its victims, can encourage them into a corresponding willingness to court hazardous chance and contingency. People discover more about themselves in a society that has become too weak to impose itself fully on them. The fear of exposure through ruined reputation comes to seem less appalling than returning to a life of conformity, when conformity has so signally failed to pay off. Failure of the traditional political and economic structures makes the shadow of personal failure less forbidding. If society as a whole has not the faintest idea how to hold itself together, what obligation is there on its members to do so? This was pre-eminently the mood among many sectors of Weimar society, a phenomenon by no means confined to a leisured or decadent elite. The sexual licentiousness of the cabarets, with their disruptive gender codes and the propagation of divergent forms of desire to which they gave expression, was only the most visible manifestation of non-conformity turned into a cultural style. Added to a carnivalesque rejection of the straitlaced morality of the Wilhelmine era, which had after all proved itself sufficiently morally unhinged to countenance mass bloodletting the length and breadth of Europe, the accelerating worthlessness of the national currency abolished the most concrete admonition against impulsivity that the capitalist economy can muster – the fear of being unprovided for tomorrow. In the nightclubs of Berlin, people spent the zero-festooned banknotes precisely as though there were no tomorrow, which, for the banknotes themselves at least, there wasn't. If you didn't blue it tonight, it would buy considerably less by next morning. 'During the hot inflation years of 1921–23,' Sloterdijk writes, 'literature and the "history of morals" registered a first flickering of crass neohedonistic currents … a new middle-class illusionism celebrated a dress rehearsal while the zeroes on the banknotes galloped on. The show began.'[5] Fluid erotic relations with no guarantees, in which an episode of sex with somebody initiated no more of a future with them than cash deposits at the bank had, reflected the loosening of the political and economic moorings of existence.

Weimar social life may have been represented ever since as a paradigm case of partying on the edge of the volcano, but it nonetheless allowed for partying. By the time the NSDAP assumed the reins of government and set about laying waste to the constitution in a violently imposed heteronomy of monolithic order, the world of the 1920s had, for good and ill, disappeared forever. The current of sexual libertinism did not entirely disappear, but it was driven back to the subterranean regions in which it had dwelt before Weimar, while the cultural life of the Third Reich was subjected to an arid conventionalism defined as much negatively – through the infamous *Entartete Kunst* (*Degenerate Art*) exhibition that opened in Munich in

1937, before touring the country – as in the exemplary neoclassical architecture and statuary that furnished the Nazi state. The economy underwent a near-miraculous recovery, through a combination of public works projects and default on the terms of Versailles, and before long everybody had his or her role to play within a society of total mobilization.

What is important in the estimation of any historical epoch is first and foremost how it represented itself to itself, and predominant among its own impressions of the genesis and instability of the Weimar Republic was the fact that it had emerged from the catastrophe of defeat in war. It had to remake itself amid conditions of exigency and the undoubted impact of the humiliation visited on it by the victors, who in the Paris peace conference were generous in assuring each other that none of them had wanted a continental war, or even dreamed it might happen. The German nation was reborn on the economic terms dictated to it, but politically it was allowed to piece itself together again as well as it could. If the psychological mindset of many of the surviving combatants was a nostalgia for the certainties of the front as against the sectarian bickering of peacetime political sects, as Sloterdijk argues, the wider cultural image the war had bequeathed, which has never entirely dissipated throughout Europe to this day, was of the individual reduced to a regimented subject of vast impersonal forces. These repercussions were felt throughout the nation, for all that, as so often in periods of national convulsion, the explicit culture that the defeated state engendered was largely restricted to the bigger urban centres – Berlin, Hamburg, Frankfurt. The cities, as elsewhere, were the arenas of a reckless new drive in consumption, of a nascent internationalist architecture and other manifestations of the artistic avant-garde, as well as being the chief beneficiaries of the advancing frontiers of a new welfare state, but inasmuch as reports of such developments percolated to the provincial peripheries, these cultural trends only opened a gulf of alienation between city and country. An internally divided nation is the natural setting for the most precarious of political dispositions, which in Weimar's case was exacerbated by the restless, hectoring influence that an army, refusing to confine itself to its constitutional barracks, continued to exert on national events. The place of power was constantly contested between civil and military elements, which inevitably led whole sections of the populace to take one or the other side. A state of emergency was declared by the army no fewer than three dozen times in the troubled early years between 1919 and 1923, with calls for a strong leader uttered repeatedly by the top brass in the frantic autumn of 1923. This period saw ten different cabinets, though in that sense, Weimar was no more helpless a victim of governmental discontinuity than was post-war France, and in any case, as the deck was shuffled each time, the successive administrations were largely composed of much the same personnel. On one account, at least, the eventual appointment of Hitler as Chancellor in January 1933 was less a vote of confidence in him than an acknowledgement that all other alternatives had been exhausted and that his turn had come.

Against the background of a national polity that was unable to decide what its own best composition and course ought to be, the economic calamity of the hyperinflation exercised the strongest psychic influence on people's sense of the value of their own lives. The received historical wisdom has long been that it was the war reparations imposed in 1919 that accounted more or less solely for the inflation but, as Harold James points out,[6] there were many other factors in play – among them the weight of unfinanced debt incurred in funding the conduct of the war, the payment of benefits to surviving veterans after 1918, the programme of substantial social expenditure aimed at reforming or at the very least pacifying, post-war society, not to mention the persistent overvaluation of the Deutschmark. As the prices of basic goods rose to levels that would once have sounded sufficient to furnish a plutocrat's country estate, profound social anxiety set in, to be replaced in some quarters with a certain cynical insouciance. It bears emphasizing, as James does, that these were also the circumstances that stabilized employment levels, created conditions in which revived demand mitigated the worst aspects of the depression and arguably generated the liberation of the imaginative faculties that prompted a cultural efflorescence to rival that of France and put British culture's prosaic resort to heroic battle stories and light satire in the shade. Elias Canetti suggested that the meaningless figures on the banknotes helped prepare the Nazi climate in which life would become meaningless for both the favoured and the unfavoured alike, sacrificing themselves or participating in a state murder programme organized with Taylorist efficiency, but the evidence is more that it was money itself that was nullified, thereby freeing people, albeit in desperate times, to live lives outside the socio-economic nexus. The victorious Allies may not have been entirely misguided in treating warnings about the incendiary potential of the reparations policy to foment revolutionary unrest as a case of crying wolf, and in any case when the end of reparations was successfully negotiated at the Lausanne conference of July 1932, their cancellation did nothing to prevent the Nazi electoral victories of the following year.

The picture of the Weimar Republic as a culture of defeat, the image of the whipped cur that eventually bares its snarling teeth at its tormentors, remains hard to dislodge in the prevailing historiography. In a more nuanced assessment, Anthony McElligott throws this picture into relief by providing much of the sociocultural detail that it either overlooks or misinterprets. The celebrated German historian Detlev Peukert's monumental 1987 study of Weimar[7] identifies in it 'the crisis of classical modernity', seeing it as the gladiatorial arena in which the politics of reason, enlightened self-interest and the Hobbesian consensus came to die, but such narratives are overdetermined by the period of the Nazi nightmare that followed.

> The idea of a doomed republic is difficult to shake off, even among a new generation of younger scholars. There is hardly a title without some reference to the impending disaster awaiting the republic and which places the republican experience firmly in the antechamber of the Third Reich ... And the picture is problematic, not least for the obvious reason that as historians we are trained not to read history backwards ... But to approach the history of Weimar Germany from this perspective in order to ask: 'How was Hitler possible?' and: 'Was the Nazi "seizure of power" avoidable?' skews our historical vision ... and it militates against a nuanced understanding of the complex interplay of forces that shaped and reshaped the republic from its beginning. The fact is, in 1918 the republic's future was open and its history yet to be determined; Hitler was neither its predestined nor its obvious conclusion.[8]

McElligott's point may well be readily taken, until, that is, one attends again to certain prominent voices writing from amid the very milieu itself, with no knowledge that the fluidity and incontinence of the times would end with Hitler's forces coming to rapidly undisputed power. Siegfried Kracauer, commenting contemporaneously on the techniques and ideological bearings of the German cinema of the 1920s,[9] weighs the competing claims of politically tendentious art and romantic escapism, addressing directly the charge that the latter style occludes true social insight. Perception of the nature of society can be had even from the most apparently superficial and gaudy of cinematic spectacles, he suggests.

But this is the case only if distraction is not an end in itself. Indeed, the very fact that the shows aiming at distraction are composed of the same mixture of externalities as the world of the urban masses; the fact that these shows lack any authentic and materially motivated coherence, except possibly the glue of sentimentality, which covers up this lack but only in order to make it all the more visible; the fact that these shows convey precisely and openly to thousands of eyes and ears the disorder of society – this is precisely what would enable them to evoke and maintain the tension that must precede the inevitable and radical change. In the streets of Berlin, one is often struck by the momentary insight that someday all this will suddenly burst apart. The entertainment to which the general public throngs ought to produce the same effect.[10]

A later iteration of mass-cultural critique from the heart of the Frankfurt tradition, Adorno and Horkheimer's chapter on the culture industry in the *Dialectic of Enlightenment*, would refuse any truck with the idea that the Hollywood film industry might produce anything other than obfuscation, a dreamy acquiescence in its own spectacular delusion by the mass audience, an effect that became more suffocating with the technological breakthrough that added a soundtrack to the originally silent images. Kracauer's argument, though, is not that the audiences are undeceivable, but that the figuration of images of glamour and stylistic perfection on the screen speak all too eloquently of the lack of these in the actuality in which their spectators have to live. A radical art might prepare radical social transformation through the paradox of escapist visions, what Adorno will persistently call the utopian impulse in art, by the improbable means of taunting the audiences with its unavailability. Whether that will turn out to be effective or not in the very different transatlantic context, in which such impulses would be entrusted to Warner

Brothers, RKO and MGM, is perhaps beside Kracauer's point, but what arrests us here is the closing point from the cited passage, in which he speaks from a visceral consciousness that everything on the streets of Berlin looks ready to blow. Something, perhaps cinematic art, could light the fuse at any moment.

If anything began to prepare individuals and social collectives for the shock of simultaneity at the last-but-one fin de siècle, it was the attempt to reflect precisely that sense of dynamic action, of everything happening at once, in the arts. The era in which elements of a genuinely popular culture, before the mass entertainment industry appropriated that category to its own more or less nefarious purposes, were inveigled into the productions of high art was the era in which previously unknown social alignments and political upheavals advanced to prominence in Europe and the wider world. Iconoclastic theatrical productions, the plethora of formally mutational styles in the visual arts, and above all the techniques of classical musical composition, in seeking to represent the intensive pace of life in the sprawling urban centres, the mechanization and impersonalization that helped make it possible, in the epoch of the assertive nation-states, to flirt openly with the idea of a new cleansing war in Europe, such as had not been seen since Bonaparte was consigned to St Helena nearly a century earlier, all seemed to train the neurasthenic consciousness – and who among Austen's or Balzac's characters had ever heard of that diagnosis? – in the ways of formlessness and discord as much as representing a pre-existing condition. Fredric Jameson captures this point with regard to the symphonic music of Mahler. Amid the competing layers of orchestration, one hears

> a call to order, occasionally, in which one type of sound – no matter whether loud or soft, monumental or chamber-like in its

intimacy – rebukes the increasing disorder of the other parts of the orchestra and summons it to combined and disciplined action: or failing that, suddenly releases the pandemonium of sounds of all kinds and descriptions building up and pressing towards the excitement of chaos.[11]

Something like the latter effect happens recurrently throughout the opening movement of the gigantic Second Symphony in C minor, known as the 'Resurrection'. Restless rhythmic figures keep stirring and turning, as preoccupied as the metrical intensities of the late Beethoven quartets but lacking their urgent drive, disinclined to let the instrumental currents around them coalesce into anything like an obvious theme, an atmosphere of chthonic brooding that unfolds over nearly twenty-five minutes. Teleologically, this fragmentation will be resolved four movements later in the great choral resolution of the Finale, an affirmation of faith in spite of everything, which provides both the spiritual and the philosophical closure to a work that has plumbed the deeps of doubt and of unaffiliated incapacity for hope. True, its provision of a stately Ländler in the second movement, where a moment's remembered sunlight is reflected by the transition to a major key, A♭, seems to hint at a world of uncomplicated country joys, but the mood is fleeting enough, and the music soon returns to a sombre third movement that pulls in Jewish folk themes on the way to what Mahler himself referred to in correspondence as a 'death shriek', of which there are conventionally held to be at least two, and probably three, in the Second Symphony.

The first comes at the climax of that third movement, when a flowing melody in the strings is suddenly interrupted by the unconscionable apparent brightness of a brass fanfare, a moment of unnerving confident assertiveness that sets the strings whirling into a rapid billowing pattern beneath it, its agitation growing until it culminates in the fortississimo blast of a chord laden with inescapable doom. Its furious irruption has the effect of a door abruptly being blown open to admit a raging gale, the blizzard of destiny, in which everything that is not nailed down is scattered, a mercilessly sustained roar that only with difficulty manages to climb down through hobbling intervals to the grimly triumphant hammering of timpani. It is the sound of the last of subjective integrity being torn away, an instant of pure panic, of coerced surrender and helpless grief. Directly recalling it, the fifth and final movement opens with exactly the same fatalistic statement, brass fanfares filling in the texture of a screaming minor chord, descending figures in the harps and turbulent undulations in the strings. Here, if we are attentive throughout to the devotional text of the choral parts, it seems to set the note of dread that will be banished by the paradoxically gentle nature of obstinate faith, the choir entering, when it finally does, not in apocalyptic mood, but in breath-holding pianissimo, an effect particularly striking in performance, when the massed ranks of the choir behind the gigantic orchestral forces Mahler inherited from Wagner open not in full voice but in auditory tiptoe, picking their way through the debris of shattered hopes that have littered their path. The third shriek comes later in the final movement, when, during the silence of the choir, the music comes to a last anguished, bitterly comfortless gasp of pure horrified fright, as though even amid the assurances that simply believing, putting one's tattered trust in the Almighty ('*O glaube!*'), might just be enough, the soul yields to one more gust of momentous, consuming hysteria. It might not be. All three of these moments are achieved with sustained minor chords that are cut ragged at the edges and at the root with dissonances, the octave Cs in the bass in the first of them in argumentative conflict with the B♭, D♭, F and upper B♭ in the chord above them. They are moments of the kind of musical cathexis that even the untutored ear scarcely needs to be told how to hear, which dispel the insidious nature of all other listening in a world given over to sheer functionality or to the aesthetically tendentious, in which, as Adorno puts it in one of his literary essays, 'ears that have preserved their sensitivity cannot help hearing that someone is trying to talk them into something'.[12] Nobody is being talked into anything in these Mahlerian shrieks. Their cries of despair, of spiritual chaos, are dire articulations of the emptiness in every soul when it is confronted with the ineluctable.

What is particularly important for the present analysis is the way these sudden crises are presented musically as though, for a few bars at least, the composer had released his grip on the compositional tiller and allowed the orchestra to shoot out crazily across the stream of the music, the only unity in the dissonance residing in the phenomenon of all instruments pulling tonally in different directions at the same time. In other words, the instrumental layers are united inasmuch as they all sustain the same horror-stricken chord at once, but precisely because they do not conform to any classically recognized tonal scheme in doing so, the effect is one of purer chaos than would unfold from everybody branching out – rhythmically, dynamically, melodically – away from each other. Clinging together for the duration of a single monstrous, wounded and wounding cry, they have the same effect as an outbreak of panic in an overcrowded lift that has lurched to a halt between floors in a very high building, the pandemonium accentuated through different responses occurring simultaneously in the same confined space.

Scoring this sensational affect in the mid-1890s, Mahler anticipates a good half-century of dramatic shock-tactics in all the arts, a technique that will serve the various modernist schools of the post-Versailles period as they seek to find aesthetic analogues for the barbarically sustained shock-effect of the war, and that will last most durably into the affectless minimalism and postmodern irony of the next post-war period in the context of the film industry, where sudden nasty surprises are the regular sustenance of commercial film plots. In one obvious sense, the irruptions of chaos in film narratives are as desirous of provisional and ultimate resolution as are the dissonant outbreaks in even the most formally daring tonal music, but while they are in full spate, and pandemonium – in the shopworn usage – reigns, there is a sense of everything having been thrown into the mix. The outstanding masterclass in this rhythm of desperate mayhem and subjugated respite comes in Hitchcock's enduring eco-thriller *The Birds* (1963), inflated from a windswept Cornish mystery in Daphne du Maurier to a vision of the end-times among arriviste socialites and repressed locals in the peaceable coastal California of the nuclear age. The film gradually but remorselessly grinds the fledgling flawed romance between its two principals under the millstone of a gathering natural catastrophe that will neither be disregarded nor explained away. By the end, despite the fragile embattled liaisons that have arisen among characters who gladly profess not to understand each other earlier on, the birds are all that matter. Each successive attack is more audacious, so that the one swooping seagull that takes a bite out of Tippi Hedren's forehead at the close of the long unhurried narrative preamble multiplies into massed ranks of heterogeneous avian species banding together to launch what look like concerted attacks on humanity, both in previously tranquil Bodega Bay and, it seems from the gasps of news caught on the car radio later on, beyond. More than ever seduced by the potentialities of everyday sadism that film could mobilize, Hitchcock externalizes it here, its human avatars in his earlier career – the obsessional loners as represented by the simpering, simmering Bruno Antony (Robert Walker) in *Strangers on a Train* (1951) or Anthony Perkins' gauntly vulnerable but ruthless Norman Bates in *Psycho* (1960), whose own avian preoccupations and mannerisms anticipate the real thing in the film that will follow –

now superseded by a menacing force that can be freed from the last
vestiges of human moral scruple and of human accountability alike.
The assaults of the birds need no rationale at all. They are liberated
narratologically to torment schoolchildren, petrify the elderly and
tear the eyes out of those defencelessly trying to defend each other.
They illuminate for a while what humans might do when faced with
the same kind of incomprehensible threat that the previous decade
had imagined in the form of Martian invasions, themselves birthed in
late Victorian England by HG Wells, who is more interested in what
human beings might do when they have no means of understanding
their motiveless foe than when psychology, and a lot of scrupulous
Jamesian conversation, patiently unlocks its motives for them. After
the characters in *The Birds* have been variously broken down or killed,
though, nothing happens to bring restitution, and one of the most
archly tantalizing open endings in cinema history leaves its audience
with a deliberate empty chill. In the meantime, the upheavals and
implosions of modern experience, the everything-at-once we have
been considering in this chapter, are figured with the full box of
contemporaneous cinematic tricks in those moments when a house
is suddenly filled with a torrent of birds that come pouring from the
chimney flue, or a children's outdoor birthday party is set upon by
vengeful shrieking gulls. There is famously no music soundtrack in
the film, only an electronic soup of bird-calls and relentless wingbeats,
in the midst of which crockery faintly shatters and festive balloons
are popped, while the thin screams of children are no match for the
raucous cackling of their attackers.

Despite the authentically unhinged nature of these interventions of
the chaotic principle, in Mahler and Hitchcock and in the subversive
potentials of the popular Berlin cinema that Kracauer could readily
envisage, there is still a sense that these are episodic interruptions
in a narrative process that otherwise tends towards a resolution of

such instabilities, where it does not, that is, image a final condition of satisfied stasis, the 'happily ever after', the 'quiet earth' or the 'unharming sharks', the 'yes I said yes I will Yes', to which the great bulk of narrative works still implicitly tend, whatever their ideological or formal commitments. What about a chaos of everything happening at once that functions as a culmination, or even the desired end, of a narrative sequence? The paradigmatic instance of such an outcome in Victorian literature is the festive occasion at the close of *Through the Looking-Glass* (1871), when Alice, newly crowned a queen, presides over a rackety banquet of which she has been given no prior notice and which, despite it being ostensibly given in her honour as a coronation feast, appears to be proceeding first in accord with the dictates of her fellow queens, especially the imperious Red Queen, and then in accord with no discernible social or diplomatic protocols at all. If we have been attentive to the schematic structure of the tale, which has its origins in a game of chess, Alice starting as a white pawn moving forward the permitted two squares across a landscape mimetically resembling an expansive chessboard, and ending with her being exchanged for a queen at the opposite end of the field of play, this promotion would seem to mark the last move of the game. Her elevation to the notional monarchy, encapsulated in the golden crown that oneirically appears on her head as she crosses into the eighth rank on her winning trajectory, is immediately ratified by a kind of demented viva voce examination by the two existing regal authorities, the Red and White Queens. No game of chess may have three queens on the board, which is where the ontological problems begin. When Queen Alice enters the banqueting-hall, an instant pin-drop silence greets her, as though the entire company is discomfited by her mere appearance. Indeed, what can she be but a transgression of the rules, unless, that is, one of the other two queens is prepared to make way for her? At first, she is given rough-and-ready lessons in etiquette by the Red Queen, who reproves her for wanting to slice and serve up the food items – a leg of mutton, a plum pudding – to which she has been formally, socially introduced. A verse riddle to which the solution will go begging is then recited for her to puzzle over, but in the meantime, the Red Queen screams out a toast to Alice, and as the guests respond, the true nature of the occasion becomes apparent:

> Some of them put their glasses upon their heads like [candle-] extinguishers, and drank all that trickled down their faces – others upset the decanters, and drank the wine as it ran off the edges of the table – and three of them (who looked like kangaroos) scrambled into the dish of roast mutton, and began eagerly lapping up the gravy, 'just like pigs in a trough!' thought Alice.

A children's fabulist of the 1870s is hardly free to say so, but what is abundantly evident is that everybody is roaring-drunk and getting drunker. The Red and White Queens now insist that Alice return a gracious speech of thanks for the toast, to aid her with which they support her physically on either side at the head of the table, so that she actually does 'rise to return thanks'. At this point, the White Queen, a delicate old creature with an incipiently senile demeanour, has a presentiment of the gathering apocalypse. '"Take care of yourself," screamed the White Queen, seizing Alice's hair with both her hands. "Something's going to happen!"' And many somethings do happen.

> The candles all grew up to the ceiling, looking something like a bed of rushes with fireworks at the top. As to the bottles, they each took a pair of plates, which they hastily fitted on as wings, and so, with forks for legs, went fluttering about in all directions: 'and very like birds they look,' Alice thought to herself, as well as she could in the dreadful confusion that was beginning.

The White Queen's blandly grinning face is last seen disappearing over the edge of the tureen as she takes refuge in the soup. Several of the guests are now lying down in the serving-dishes, while the soup ladle comes striding furiously up the table towards Alice, 'beckoning to her impatiently to get out of its way'. Everything has taken on an animated life of its own, and in being alienated from its everyday purposes, succumbs, much as people will in such circumstances, to hoggish self-indulgence or to mere anarchy for its own sake. The transformation of the banquet from the sloppier end of a Greek symposium, only one with women as the hosts, its inebriated parodies of speeches and the licensed vandalism of the *komos*, into a scene from Bosch, with its grotesque Ovidian metamorphoses and hellish retributions, is now complete. All that remains is to assume the most decisive controlling role of all, as Alice duly does. "'I can't stand this any longer!" she cried as she jumped up and seized the tablecloth with both hands: one good pull, and plates, dishes, guests, and candles came crashing down together in a heap on the floor.' Her final act is to shake the diminutively scurrying figure of the Red Queen, the overbearing paralogical tyrant now shrunk to the size of a doll and surrendering her adulthood to the child heroine herself, into the kitten Alice will turn out to be holding as she wakes up.[13]

The chaos of the banquet is Alice's chance finally to seize control of a world through which she has travelled as a patient and attentive voyager, but also in a state of thraldom. A society in which everything is a mirror image of the one she knows, in which not just left and right, fast and slow, moist and dry, are reversed, but the physical logics of cause and effect by which things work are subverted too, has finally revealed that there is a greater opposition than walking away from a destination in order to reach it, and that is that there are no laws at all. The great deception mounted for her by all the characters, from the moment she clambers through the glass above the fireplace, is that if only she thinks in inversions, she will attune herself to life on the other side. It is the Red and White Queens who hold the key, as they emphasize through their twin strategies towards Alice of rote learning and distracted anecdotalizing. The world, like the words in Humpty Dumpty's linguistic regime, means just what they say it will mean, so that the final banquet, which has no analogue in the chess game, is a state of pure unregulated chaos. By the time she takes her place at the head of the table that has become a microcosm of the whole of Looking-Glass society, it has become more than just a drunken revel. An element of Bakhtinian carnival survives in the banquet – the principle of inversion itself has now surrendered to thoroughgoing disorder – but there is something more malevolent at play too, a destructive urge in which both the table accoutrements and the guests themselves have liberated themselves from their allotted functions and roles and turned on themselves. Martin Meisel makes the percipient point that the exciting ideological notion of chaos as a liberation from petrified order was effectively over by the end of the nineteenth century, its potentials withered amid scenarios of sociopolitical affray such as the Crimean War and the hostilities unleashed when institutional religion, as it was increasingly given to do, escapes its moorings. This is how we might see the collapse of Alice's second sojourn in an alternate dreamworld. There is fear and excitement combined in the endings of both of her adventures, in the hubbub of the closing trial scene in Wonderland and in the psychotic banquet of the Looking-Glass creatures, the fear and excitement generated by a situation spiralling out of control that, in so doing, allows her to assert an authoritative influence over it. If chaos has ceased to be liberating, it has surely not lost its power to be productive – and productive precisely of the human agency that will transform it. A placid-natured Oxford mathematician and divine with a possibly troubling photographic interest in pre-pubescent girls hardly fits the role of prospective revolutionary theorist, and yet the resonant lesson of both the Alice stories is that when a historical situation that escapes the bounds of normative social decorum and numbing regulative tranquillity arises, it urgently awaits the agent, be it an individual or a class, that can give it the requisite Nietzschean push and, by scattering the pieces on the board, create a new world in accordance with its own rules. And of course create itself in the process.

What is alluring about everything happening at once, where a situation at least seems sufficiently dynamic as to be experientially rewarding, delivering multiple hits of whatever it is that ought to comprise life, is just that it permits little or no time for reflection on each development before the next supervenes. In most organizational structures, and indeed in the conduct of the kind of quotidian life we have to live regardless of whether it is surrounded by dynamic, multi-faceted patterns of occurrence as well, the absence of such breathing-spaces – more properly, thinking-spaces – is more or less of a disaster. Unless some order is imposed somehow, life degenerates to a sedimentary layer under the tidal waves of the contingent, which need not be momentous at all, needless to say, but is far more likely to be obstinately stifling in its banality, but where the currents of excitement and the best kind of unpredictability – the liberating kind, not the tightrope contexts of angst and insecurity – hold sway. Whatever happens next may well turn out to throw another richly coloured filter over a scene that is already iridescent, rendering order entirely beside the point. Perhaps in these seasons, events generate their own order, one that defies the sclerotic predication in which all but the freest spirits have been trained up through what passes for a lifetime, but the lens of order, of the methodical sorting of experiences by degree of magnitude and, most crucially, one by one, seems obsolescent.

The literary theorist Stanley Fish, in a work on the classical history and diverse potentials of the sentence, returns us to the point with which we opened this chapter. For him, as for so many others in the tradition of literate humanism, the hierarchically structured nature of experience, and the way we perceive it, derive from correct grammar, a normative impulse in which one can unabashedly make the large claim that a grammatically cohesive sentence 'ranks, orders, and sequences things, events and persons in a way that strongly suggests a world where control is the imperative and everything is in its proper place'.[14] For Fish, comments Jan Mieszkowki, 'the sentence is fundamentally a defence against the random, the irrational, and the chaotic'.[15] If the high-modernist era in European letters in the early twentieth century attempted precisely to undo that link, whether explicitly at Nietzsche's behest or under the impress of the broadening chasm between urban experience and the narrative arts, so that language might draw nearer to human life by its radical self-dismantling, it has clearly, at least as far as the whole scholastic tradition represented by Fish is concerned, failed in the attempt. One of the ways it sought to break out of the hierarchies of predication was by repetition. 'Repeating then is in every one, in every one their being and their feeling and their way of realizing everything and every one comes out of them in repeating. More and more then every one comes to be clear to some one.'[16] So says the narrator of Gertrude Stein's *The Making of Americans* (1925), one of the century's most dogged experiments at stopping the mouth of traditional narratology so that unmediated experience might be heard. If its effect is more that of a parody of narratology than a metamorphosis of it, there would be more felicitous results in Stein's shorter texts than in this beached leviathan which she would ambiguously declare a failure later on. In *Finnegans Wake* (1939), Joyce would process the literary culture, historiography and demotic customs of an ageing and tottering Europe through a linguistic mincer to produce a polysemic stew of allusions, jokes, riddles and academicisms that would, he fondly hoped, keep the professors busy for generations to come. In the post-war period, it found itself stranded on a prison island of public and professional incomprehension, consigned, like Stein's opus, to the category of 'unreadable' until its predecessor, *Ulysses* (1922), was similarly caged, its length and discursive obscurities proving too much in the era of the creative writing programme. In another couple of generations, *Ulysses* will in turn find itself shuffling along the unreadable perch to make room for its diegetically slippery prelude, *Portrait of the Artist as a Young Man* (1916).

Joyce's works, most notably the *Wake*, posit that experience is cyclical, not linear, a primordial circular chain rather than a line-dance. What literary history has not managed to achieve, despite a century and more of formal dissolution and reconstitution, is the effect of everything happening at once. The aleatory principle of chance has played its part, as in BS Johnson's anti-novel *The Unfortunates* (1969), which consisted of a set of loose-leaf texts of varying lengths delivered in a box like pizza, intended to be consumed in whatever order the pieces came out, but not the idea of many things coinciding. In this regard, Johnson's experiment bears the same relation to unmediated experience as mathematical chaos theory does to actual chaos. The simultaneity principle of chaos is exactly what helps it evade capture by discursive artforms. If we are to find it represented aesthetically, it will be in the textures of music at the moment – both during and after Gustav Mahler's attenuated life – that it frees itself from the structural discipline of tonality.

3

Discordance

When everything is in the wrong place, and everything is happening at once, it seems axiomatic that a state of discord reigns, and that the internal elements of a system or scene are at variance with one another. On this reading, a harmonious chaos would be a wilful oxymoron. The principle of order connotes not just every entity being in its assigned place, and every event happening in due succession, but precisely by virtue of such dispositions, that everything thereby fits together in natural and intuitive ways. Anything that appears to militate against this schema creates a state of dissonance that is always implicitly asking to be resolved.

The readiest paradigm of dissonance and its resolution arises in the very field to which it lexically refers, that of music. In the grand narrative of Western music, one of its most seismic revolutions occurred when the gold standard of tonality, on which all composition had been based since the old modal musics of the pre-Renaissance graduated to the whole-tone scale and the key signature, began to fragment under the expressive – eventually expressionist – dynamics of the late Romantic composers. There are blasts of more or less programmatic dissonance in the music dramas of Wagner and in Mahler's symphonies, but they gain semantic force exactly through their ill-fitting abrasiveness in the generally harmonic contexts that surround them. By the early years of the twentieth century, in the

compositional practice and musicological theory of the modernist
lodestar Arnold Schönberg, dissonance began to emerge from the
shadows of tonality and become a constituent part of the battery of
compositional technique. The musicology is virtually as important
as the writing of music in Schönberg's case. Without the corpus of
painstakingly argued theory, dissonance in atonal music might
have been nothing more than the stylistic quiddity of a particularly
nonconformist dissident and his small band of acolytes.

What became known as the Second Vienna School – the first
being the hitherto unquestioned classical forebears of Haydn,
Mozart and Schubert – was founded not on an aggressive ideological
oppositionism, in the manner of Zürich Dada or Italian Futurism,
but on a scientifically argued theory of sonority. If it aimed at
what Schönberg's 1926 essay 'Opinion or Insight?' called, with a
polemical enough vocabulary in the revolutionary era, to be sure,
the emancipation of the dissonance, it was a liberation to be pursued
not for the purpose of confounding the detested bourgeoisie, guilty
by this epoch of everything from the inanities of the state theatres
to the bloodwash of the world war, but in the interest of freeing the
untapped potential already latent in tonal music. For dissonances
were not the barbed antitheses of tonal chords, but only their
remote and unrecognized kin. As Schönberg summarizes it here,
'Consonance and dissonance differ not as opposites do, but only
in point of *degree*; that consonances are the sounds closer to the
fundamental [note], dissonances those farther away; that their
comprehensibility is graduated accordingly, since the nearer ones are
easier to comprehend than those farther off.'[1] In this respect, there are
no dissonances, *stricto sensu*, only consonances you haven't yet met –
or haven't yet heard. Eventually, with repeated exposure to the new
music, the listener would begin to comprehend what had previously
been foreign, or what had sounded as though it were sorely in need

of resolution into the tonic key, with the proverbial force in which, as Schönberg states, all roads led to Rome.

The theory was expounded in detail in the otherwise stolidly traditional context of the composer's earlier key work *Theory of Harmony* (1911):

> In the overtone series which is one of the most remarkable properties of the tone, there appear after some stronger-sounding overtones a number of weaker-sounding ones. Without a doubt the former are more familiar to the ear, while the latter, hardly perceptible, are rather strange. In other words: the overtones closer to the fundamental seem to contribute more or more perceptibly to the total phenomenon of the tone – tone accepted as euphonious, suitable for art – while the more distant seem to contribute less or less perceptibly. But it is quite certain that they all do contribute more or less, that of the acoustical emanations of the tone nothing is lost.[2]

Schönberg's argument, that the ear hears, and the sensibility responds to, these more distant tones, whether the listener be objectively conscious of them or not, resonates all too clearly to subsequent generations with the psychoanalytic categories also being formulated and theorized by Freud and his school in the same contemporaneous Viennese milieu. Just because one is not immediately aware of an impression does not discount either its existence or its psychic efficacy, and what is deliberately repressed is fated, somehow or other, to return in another guise. Historical precedent, evinced against this argument from virtually every quarter of a traditional musicology that suddenly felt itself under siege, and which held tonality to be somehow acoustically natural, could scarcely be the arbiter of the matter, since if we could but train our Eurocentric sights a little beyond the august, imposing walls of the Musikverein, we would recall that the tonic scale is itself an entirely unsuspected idiom in the traditional musics of numerous other cultures. Such is proved by

> the incomplete or unusual scales of many other peoples, who have, nevertheless, as much right as we to explain them by appeal to nature. Perhaps their tones are often even more natural than ours (that is, more exact, more correct, better); for the tempered [Western] system, which is only an expedient for overcoming the difficulties of the material, has indeed only a limited similarity to nature. That is perhaps an advantage, but hardly a mark of superiority.[3]

The productions of this emergent theory emerged tentatively enough, to be sure. What is often held to be one of the breakthrough works of Schönberg's passage to free atonality, the Second String Quartet, op 10 (1908), is notionally in the key of F sharp minor. Its third and fourth movements are scored for a soprano voice as well as the chamber ensemble, and it is the finale, 'Entrückung' ('Rapture'), to a text of the Symbolist poet Stefan George, that is usually held to mark the departure from conventional musical discourse, not least because it is bereft of a key signature. Its famous opening line, 'Ich fühle Luft von anderem Planeten' ('I feel the air of another planet'), casts the singer's spirit adrift from the present sublunary world, the voice wandering without restraint or melodic moorings into a hitherto unknown medium of weightless liberty. And yet, almost as though a final prank is to be played on its appalled first audiences, the music ends with a suddenly obvious, even facile, resolution into F sharp major. If this is not to be taken in the coy spirit of a return to reconciliation with the present world after the excursion out of it, it can be seen as laying bare the evident snare in seeing the tonal and atonal modes as entirely distinct. This is the construction put on it by the music historian Richard Taruskin: 'The movement, in its implied progression from tonal indefiniteness to regained definition, demonstrates the location of "tonality" and "atonality" on a contextual continuum, and the impossibility of drawing a categorical line between them.'[4] This dialectical view of the matter, while watertight enough with regard to the Second String Quartet, becomes harder to maintain when one turns to the Six Little Pieces for Piano, op 19 (1911). Here all tonal reference points are shunned like the plague in an idiom in which, as Taruskin himself puts it, 'the whole conventional vocabulary of music has been suppressed in favour of a private language.'[5] If what passes for a melodic line in the first piece appears entirely random in its progression, that is the one thing it cannot be, since even a random line might light, quite by chance, on a tonal relation, a familiar cadence, here and there, on which the ear would, in its ironbound classical way, immediately seize. There are shapes to the music, if we insist on finding them – little semiquaver flurries, pointed striding patterns of single notes, a deceleration to a fermata at the twelfth bar that seems to unite the previously disparate left and right hands for a moment – but nothing that would appear to unite its constituent parts into a unified whole other than the minuscule dimensions of the piece itself. More than any dogmatic insistence on an antithetical stance, however, Schönberg's conception of dissonance as having been released from its shackles, emancipated from the slavery in which it had been bound for centuries, is a call for the relative terms of consonance and dissonance to be abandoned, a point Taruskin succinctly catches: 'As far as dissonance itself is concerned, it is not so much liberated as conceptually erased.'[6]

The conventional error has been to see in these early atonal works the expression of negative feeling in the late Romantic sense, the Second String Quartet in particular thought to register Schönberg's desolation over his wife Mathilde Zemlinky's extramarital relationship with the painter Richard Gerstl. This is to mistake the relation between the composer and the work for the same exercise of subjectivity by which traditional music had been informed. In this respect does tradition submit to a second annihilation. As Adorno puts it, 'Tradition is the presence of the forgotten, and Schönberg's vigilance is so great that it itself exercises a technique of forgetting.'[7] Even an early work of his pupil Anton Webern, the Five Movements for String Quartet, op 5, still evinces a desire to use motifs in the material for expressive purposes, whereas Schönberg, in the 1911 Piano Pieces, which still employ motivic patterns, 'lets them go unimpeded and, eyes shut, allows himself to be guided where tone after tone takes him'.[8] If there is a veritable image of disorder in atonality, in the manifestation of music that appears not to be governed by regulative convention, including even the convention of subjective expression, it would arguably sound more like the Schönberg of the early atonal years than the kind of bombastic effect that more obviously suggests a musical representation of chaos.

At around the same time, on the other side of the Atlantic, the American composer Charles Ives was working on an orchestral suite, *Three Places in New England*, that took a very different approach to the evocation of disorder in music. Although it incorporated melodies written a decade earlier, with a further revision of the whole undertaken in 1929 for its New York premiere in 1931, the bulk of the compositional work on the three-movement piece occupied Ives between 1911 and 1914. Far from making himself into an antibody in the canonical tonal system, Ives saw himself as working squarely within the popular traditions of American music, even if, as would be the case throughout the ascendancy of North American culture in the twentieth century, those traditions were often at demotic odds with the academic practices prevalent in the European conservatories. European orchestral music, particularly in the Teutonic and Slavic heartlands, had itself long incorporated folk elements into the repertoire of classical expression. We have already noted the presence of the Ländler in Mahler's Second Symphony, but American music did not simply incorporate popular tunes as grist to a classicizing millstone. It rather foregrounded them as the very matter of American musical culture itself. If anything, the reverse of European priorities is the case in Ives. The numerous borrowings of popular catches, parlour ditties, regimental marches and plantation songs into the gliding, shifting, densely sonorous textures of his orchestra are not intended facetiously, but are the very lingua franca of American musical vitality. The orchestral timbres recall evocatively enough the Stravinsky of the period, and even, in their chromatic instabilities, the cosmopolitan Delius, whose own brief sojourn in Florida in the 1880s – to manage an orange orchard, of all the counter-intuitive occupations for the offspring of German-Dutch-English wool merchants – had left with him an instructive predilection for African American melody. In the midst of Ives's orchestra is a stubbornly discorporated piano that, liberated from the domestic parlour in which it might once have knocked out 'The Battle Cry of Freedom' while the family gathered round, offers largely atonal chordal commentary in the Schönbergian manner, as well as the percussive 'piano-drumming' effect (thick hammered chord-clusters in the left hand) that anticipates Stravinsky, amid the tangling and snagging melodic miasmas that surround it.

The central movement, 'Putnam's Camp, Redding, Connecticut', memorializes General Israel Putnam, one of the field tacticians of the Battle of Bunker Hill in 1775, which resulted in the most calamitously Pyrrhic victory British forces were to register in the Revolutionary War, against colonial forces that were only shambolically organized at best. The camp, established three years later in the embattled aftermath of Independence, would afterwards become the customary site of Fourth of July celebrations, and it is on one such occasion that Ives imagines, as detailed in the programme note he wrote for this movement, a small boy's mingled vision of the independence fighters, a sorrowful allegorical figure of Liberty who implicitly decries the placid amnesia into which their cause has fallen in modern experience, and the joyous rowdiness of his confreres at their games and dances. The shade of Putnam appears to banish the pensive moment and restore that triumphalist defiance that properly belongs to the day. Opening in jauntiest quickstep, the music soon finds itself tripping over its own bootlaces as competing snatches cut in – a fragment of 'Yankee Doodle Dandy' sounding both impudent and fatuous as it puts in its dime's worth, promptly lurching out of key – and colliding cross-rhythms argue the toss. A subsidence to a moment of general calm casts a wool-gathering pall over the scene, rather than prompting conciliatory reflection, after which the music gradually picks itself up and makes a heroic effort at reassembly, with offbeat snare-drum tattoos and tootling flute recalling it to a girding of its martial loins. When a stormy brass section has momentarily exhausted itself, a sweet moment of legato strings allows a moment of Ives's own 'Country Band March' to be heard, but then everything blurts in again, determined to be heard, producing the famous effect of two or more marching bands, their itineraries crossed, meeting in the same festooned and choked street, with nobody inclined to give way, until the movement comes to an abrupt stop with a sudden propulsive lift to a final unresolved discord. In the pause before the final movement, 'The Housatonic at Stockbridge', we might hear the continuing firecrackers and distant whoops of an Independence Day worth the uproar.

There may be a musically barbaric, inebriated quality to the polytonality of 'Putnam's Camp', but the music is ultimately on the side of celebration. There is a ludic, comic overtone to it, recalled in the most recent era by Peter Maxwell Davies's riotous orchestral tone poem, *An Orkney Wedding, with Sunrise* (1985), in which the nuptial festivity that has gone on all night, culminating in a bagpipe cadenza to greet the rising sun, is reflected in bibulous departures from key, stumbling dance rhythms and fractured traditional airs in the Ivesian fashion. Nothing could be further removed from this mood than the musical melee in Stravinsky's primitivist dance score *Le Sacre du Printemps* (*The Rite of Spring*), premiered in Paris in 1913 to an audience in famous full-throated repudiation of it. In later life, Ives would rather deprecate the ingrained suggestion that he had borrowed some of his percussive orchestral technique from Stravinsky, specifically the *Sacre*, pointing out that he was at work on his *Three Places* before Paris had heard so much as the opening coils of Stravinsky's bassoon tune, itself a borrowing from Lithuanian folk melody ('Oh sister!'). Adorno for one notoriously found no room for Stravinsky in his capacious repertory of modernist emancipation, largely because of what he contemptuously dismissed as the restorationist tendencies of the composer's later neoclassical works, which perhaps suit a more obviously postmodernist analysis unavailable to the hawkish Adorno of the *Philosophy of New Music* (1949). The latter work forced Stravinsky's entire oeuvre to cower in the elongated shadow cast by the Schönberg to whom the first half of the book is consecrated, even in the context of Adorno's final abjuration of the twelve-tone system as bringing a sterile mathematicity to the open fields that the free atonal works had ploughed. His ambivalence on the question of the *Rite of Spring* lies in his recoil at the rejoicing in savagery that it seems to connote. It describes the ritual sacrifice of a young maiden, but with cruel excitement rather than any evidence of compassionate reflection. The means by which the horrifying event is recorded are fetishized until they take priority over subjective expression itself, which they fraudulently disavow, resulting in a work that invites its listeners to disregard the suffering it depicts as sadistically as ballet tutors paradigmatically discount the agonies of their pupils:

The severity of *The Rite of Spring*, which makes it insensible to all
subjective impulse as does ritual to pain in initiations and sacrifice,
is at the same time the power of command that trains the body –
denied, under threat, the expression of pain – to do the impossible,
just as it trains the body to ballet, the most important traditional
element in Stravinsky. This severity, the ritual exorcism of the soul,
compounds the illusion that the result is not anything subjectively
produced, reflecting the human being, but rather something
existent in itself.[9]

The sacrificial dance closes the work, but its counterpart at the
concluding sections of the first part, from the 'Ritual of the Rival
Tribes' to the 'Dance of the Earth', in which the people first form up
into two hostile groupings shaking their weapons at one another and
then celebrate an animistic unity with the earth in the presence of their
elders and sages, is if anything even more sonically violent. Despite the
broken-backed rhythmic hammerings that lace the whole passage, the
music rushes along mindlessly, unstoppable in its determination, with
broad discordant brass themes bellowing across the jabbering strings,
until the entry of a chieftain brings the hubbub to a sudden halt. He
sanctifies the ground on which the people will dance, and the chosen
girl will be forced to embrace her fate. The music obediently pauses
until everybody pitches in, reverently observing the preposterous
performance with the same detachment that relativist anthropology
would bring to its fieldwork. Mass culture's version of inoculating
itself against empathy would eventually be delivered by the genre of
comedy horror, in which every obscenely inventive killing is greeted
with laughter and cheering by its audiences.

If the programmatic elements of the work have been deducted
with its passage into the modernist orchestral repertoire, or at least
reduced to the incidental colour of a programme note, what remains

compelling about the *Rite of Spring* – and remained so in the era of imperial belligerence that was about to conjure a hell on earth out of Europe – is its heedless celebration of cacophony. Who had not, perhaps during the initial tuning of the orchestral sections prior to the entry of the conductor, momentarily imagined what a frightful commotion a large convocation of classical musicians could make, were they so disposed? The properly subversive element of Stravinsky's work is not just the pandemonium of polytonality of which large sections of it are constituted, but the horrible polyrhythmic impetus that drives them on. One of its triumphalist moments is reached in Part 2, in the single bar in 11/4 time, when a relentless battering of eleven chords in fourths abruptly announces the Glorification rite of the doomed girl. In the piano transcription of the work, the player's thumbs interlock in crashing them out. As Peter Hill puts it in his monograph on the *Rite*, 'One can imagine Stravinsky discovering this sound, gleefully pounding these chords on the muted upright piano in his tiny studio at Clarens'.[10]

The question of whether polytonal works could ever sound anything other than furious, despite the ruminative quietude of many of Schönberg's early works, seemed a legitimate one at this historical juncture. Darius Milhaud's *Five Studies for Piano and Orchestra* of 1920–1 are more obviously in the Ivesian mode, extending characteristically to a passage in which four fugal themes gallop along simultaneously in three divergent keys. The opening piece is a bustling, tripping excursion into the unstable and argumentative mood towards which cross-tonalities so readily tend. Not to be outdone, the fourth stages a swirling battle of stately brass, roiling strings and clanging piano, all at obstreperous odds with each other, in fuming fortissimo. The piano's chiming discords, surfacing out of the morass, stage their own internal dissension amid the agitation of the orchestral writing. In the final piece, the tempo is again brisk, ominously so, with sudden drops preparing a muted build-up of forces that culminate in apoplectic fury, concluding on the abrupt, unresolved staccato chord that was the favoured ending of many atonal and polytonal composers of the era. The second piece in the group is the only gently reflective one, with chromatic harmonies in the piano that closely evoke the recently deceased Debussy, and meandering flute melodies adding to a pastoral mood at variance with the companion pieces in the set. In the context, it sounds frankly soppy.

With the development of the dodecaphonic, or twelve-tone, system, in which every note of the chromatic scale is heard once before any of its elements is repeated, and the theme appears forwards and backwards, in inversion and in retrograde inversion, introduced a scientific regulative principle into the dissonances of early-twentieth-century modernism, transforming atonality from a language into a system. For Adorno, whose argument did so much to provoke Schönberg's disgust in a book that was otherwise a complex articulation of the composer's genius, this is what capsized the libertarian momentum of atonal music. It turned composers into arithmeticians, subjecting them to exactly the kinds of calculative discipline that people originally drawn to music, to aesthetics rather than to the abstract sciences, thought they were escaping. There are masterworks of the twelve-tone system, to be sure. They would have to include Schönberg's own Violin and Piano Concertos; the String Trio, op 45; the war-memorial cantata, *A Survivor from Warsaw*; the unfinished opera *Moses und Aron*; Alban Berg's Lyric Suite for string quartet; his Violin Concerto; Webern's String Trio; his tiny Symphony; the Variations for Piano, op 27; and the late String Quartet. 'He [Webern] expected nothing less of it,' Adorno writes of that last work, 'than that it would bridge the gulf in the history of Western music between objectivity and the subject, a gulf that seemed to him to be embodied in the historical forms of the fugue and the sonata.' The problem was whether it was indeed such a breakthrough, or simply a recurrence of the older formal language to which it addresses itself. Despite its leaping intervals, plentiful resort to pizzicato textures, deconstructed harmonic relations between the parts and forensically detailed construction, Adorno for one can only hear a decline from the composer's earlier, freer style: 'Hardly anything happens anymore; the composer's intentions scarcely make any impression, and instead he sits in front of his notes and their basic relationships with his hands folded as if in prayer.'[11] The further the twelve-tone system elaborated its own possibilities, the more it proceeded towards its own appointment with a post-war funeral rite that would clear the air for the aleatory, improvisational work that pupils of the serialist school would espouse in its place.

The principal problem with the notion that atonality represented a break with the centuries-long harmonic tradition is that it overlooks the contradictory tendencies within tonality itself, which would come to its own historic moment of self-realization when its own inadequacy as a musical language was recognized. This would be cathected in the theoretical writing of the Second Vienna School, but it was encapsulated in the work of many a major figure, throughout different aesthetic disciplines, where they survived into the development of a mature – indeed late – style for which the earlier schema would no longer suffice. Adorno again catches this point with suggestive concision in the *Aesthetic Theory* (1970):

> From the perspective of the philosophy of history, it is hardly an improper generalization of what is all too divergent if one derives the antiharmonic gestures of Michelangelo, of the late Rembrandt, and of Beethoven's last works not from the subjective suffering of their development as artists but from the dynamic of the concept of harmony itself and ultimately from its insufficiency. Dissonance is the truth about harmony.[12]

The abandonment of harmony is not the strategic choice of an artist looking to express the decompositions and anxieties of late life, but emerges anyway from a lifetime's exploration of its possibilities and limitations. In music, thematic motifs began to dissipate in the late quartets of Beethoven, surrendered to the propulsive effect of obsessive rhythm, with each part assuming moments of autonomy from the general structure within what remains of the contrapuntal format. Invoking Carl Dahlhaus's narrative of the dichotomous evolution of nineteenth-century music, Fredric Jameson opposes the melodic tradition of the arias of the era's great opera composers, beginning with Rossini, to 'a symphonic organization of absolute music whose logic leads toward a fragmentation and an atomization of the old thematic "subject" and then on into atonality and the end of the Western tradition'.[13] And yet conventional music appreciation, expressed through its accustomed narrative, doughtily resists the idea that harmony, like every other evidently watertight and integral system, was at a certain point, or points, pregnant with the seeds of its destruction. It prefers the didactic image of the tree-felling gang, led by the reliably dour Schönberg, coming to chop down the arboretum of Western harmony and its towering productions. How else, after all, explain the fact that, to put it coarsely, audiences subjected to over a century of atonal and polytonal music still prefer tunes, themes, cognizable structures, melodies that proceed in contiguous or proximate intervals so that one can whistle them on the way out of the concert hall, or as they occur to one while out on a sunny spring walk? If abstract painting caught the post-war public mood, in many cases for its propinquity to sheer design or its occasional optical tricks, and novels written in interior monologue would progress to being the default mode of popular narrative art, to the extent that expository passages, descriptive writing and reflective authorial intervention in the late Victorian manner would become personae non grata, music that shuns key signatures is still widely denigrated as sounding like incompetent amateurs indulging themselves or, notoriously, the aggravated plinking of a cat picking its erratic way over the piano keys.

The discordance of chaos in political affairs has its obvious point of concentration in outbreaks of war. Nothing that happens in the arena of human endeavour, and its failure, denotes quite the disintegration of order into its opposite as the resort to armed hostility, especially where it has no particular end in sight other than the continuous, imperative enactment of hatred. Wartime conditions notoriously fail to be limited to what opposing armies do to each other, and instead lay waste to the surrounding country, its human habitations, its cultivated land, its structures of morality and mutual respect. History has done nothing to soften this tendency. The conduct of nearly every war since the Boer Wars has been an exploratory exercise, among other imperatives, in discovering how far destructive depravity is prepared to go in the prosecution of a cause, just or otherwise. Wholesale targeting of civilian populations was largely an invention of the twentieth century, as were concentration camps, extermination camps, the judicial abandonment – and reintroduction – of torture, and while impressment and forcible conscription were hardly novel, they were resorted to on previously unprecedented scales in the world wars whose conduct occupied over a tenth of the century. Notwithstanding the stark statistics that have accompanied every resort to hostilities since the profligate cost in life of the Great War began to be computed at the end of 1918, the crimes against humanity, the horrendous cost of reconstruction, the phalanx of fugitive and displaced persons that the conflicts both generate and leave behind, the notion that war was somehow a cleansing, purifying process, indeed an ennobling one, in which, as at Shakespeare's Agincourt, men who were dozing in bed when the heroics were ensuing will subsequently curse their luck for not being part of the action, endured well into the era of Auschwitz and Hiroshima. The steadfast belief that one side must eventually prevail, and that it will probably be ours, together with the protocols of self-censorship in which the news media readily acquiesce, proves a powerfully effective analgesic for those who will not be sent to the battlefield, or have the misfortune to live anywhere near it. If war is indeed chaotic hell, it can perhaps be endured, vicariously at least, until a surrender or a ceasefire comes into view.

For all its gargantuan appetite for life and livelihoods, war remains obstinately entertaining at all levels of cultural access. It provides the action-settings for video-games from earliest childhood on, and it has been one of the most enduring thematic currents in cinema history. This is so even where something like the intention to sound a sombre warning is present, or where culture feels the imperative to remind its audiences of the human cost. A strong tradition of unsparing graphic art runs from the documentary depictions of executions, punishment beatings and mass pillage in the Thirty Years' War by Jacques Callot in *Les Misères et Mal-heurs de la Guerre* (1633), through the bestialities of the Spanish resistance to Napoleonic France after 1808 in the series of etchings by Francisco Goya entitled *Los Desastres de la Guerra* (1810–20), to the multifarious impressions of the squalor of the Western Front in the paintings, etchings and drawings of the First World War artists, most notably on the German side. Among the last are the works of Max Beckmann, who served in a medical unit in East Prussia before being shipped to Belgium, in due course being discharged from tending the wounded of Flanders in a state of total nervous collapse in 1915. In a set of drypoint works on paper, he scratches out attempts to capture the nightmare. *The Grenade* (1916) shows the panic of troops in a trench into which an explosive has been hurled, the traumatized faces and contorted bodies caught amid slashed black lines of sonic force. *Resurrection* (1918) is a Bosch for the tragic times, its relics of humans reduced to the stylized, jerking poses of marionettes on strings, some naked, others half-clad in whatever they have salvaged. An elderly man clutches a dead baby while a cowled figure hurries by. Squatting, striding, cowering figures fill a flat picture plane in which all perspective, fittingly, is lost. If there is to be a general resuscitation of the dead in the Christian sense, this is what it could well look like by 1918, a point that draws its potency from Beckmann's own journal, in which he records, in the aftermath of the fighting, passing 'cities of the dead, both the newly massacred and long-since buried, hurled into the air time and again like a mockery of the Resurrection'.[14] In a passage at the lower right, Beckmann himself with his wife and son stand at the gaping window of a house that has been torn open by a bomb-blast, observing the scene like a party of the gentility visiting Bedlam, the nightmare having reduced those it has not annihilated to a state of benumbed, passive witness. The whole scene is lit simultaneously by a gigantic moribund sun and a black moon for the final apocalyptic note.

A common factor in the pictorial technique of many of the Great War artists is a kind of dark matter that fills the space between the figures, in partial acknowledgement that where they physically are has ceased to matter as they are reduced to the bare ontology of mutilation and pain, and also because to the ripped nerves and shattered senses of combatants, the blackness that had taken possession of them was also somehow exuding from them too, infecting everything around them. Otto Dix's drypoint etchings of bombings, battlefield burials and dying soldiers are set in a thick black ether, his *Cemetery between the Lines* (1917) a mass of jagged crosses amid barbed wire emplacements, even the sun shooting out lacerating spikes rather than gentle rays. László Moholy-Nagy draws a *Dying Soldier* on the Isonzo Front in 1916, his bulbous, doomed face all but buried already amid dense black skeins like unspun wool. Further west in the same year, Fernand Léger sketches a confabulation of helmeted soldiers in their emplacement at Verdun, their tunics and the wooden posts around them covered in a jagged scribble that, in the London cultural milieu, at least for the five minutes that it seemed like a good idea, would have earned it a pass into the Vorticist school. Beckmann had begun with what, in hindsight, look to be almost gentle documentary sketches of wounded troops in their beds in the field hospital in the opening months of the war, but it would not be long before the unbridled mayhem drove into all the artists the same tone of infuriated subjectivity with which Goya captions his atrocities. The tone of objectivity and impersonality that would sweep through the European arts in the 1920s has its origins, at least partially, in the rage of indignation that the 1914–18 war bred in more or less everybody who experienced it, and survived it long enough not to bury the memory of it in layers of neurasthenic repression.

Notwithstanding the great tradition of historical painting, for which scenes of battle represented the most demanding call on an artist's technical resources – Altdorfer's crowded panorama of 1529, narrating Alexander's victory over the Persians at Issus in the fourth century BC; the slashing sabres and trampled bodies of Girodet's French colonial troops mercilessly reducing the rebellion at Cairo, done twelve years after the fact in 1810; William Sadler's contemporaneous cast-of-thousands staging of the Battle of Waterloo; the monochrome inferno of Picasso's *Guernica* (1937), the flashbulb illumination of a single incident of the Spanish Civil War – what the visual arts have been paramount in representing is the epilogue of war, its after-effects, the trail of waste, the continuation of suffering. In the twentieth century, the representation of war itself would become the classic preserve of a medium that dealt only in moving pictures, and with DW Griffith's two-reeler *The Fugitive* (1910), a tale of two soldiers in the American Civil War, to a screenplay by the Tipperary playwright John MacDonagh, who had transposed it from the context of the Irish nationalist struggle against the British, cinema found one of the métiers it has dutifully served ever since. The first film to win the Best Picture accolade at the inaugural Academy Awards in 1929 was William Wellman's *Wings* (1927), starring Clara Bow and Richard Arlen, set amid history's first air battles on the Western Front and drawn from the director's own experience. It was shot on location at an air force base in Texas with as much attention to technical precision as the circumstances and budget would allow, and is still admired for the convincing realism of its sequences of aerial combat. Nearly a century later, the awards for Best Cinematography, Visual Effects and Sound Mixing would be presented to Sam Mendes's *1917* (2019), set during the same deathless conflict as its predecessor, this one filmed in long sequences with an unresting mobile camera to give the immersive feeling of a single unedited take.

One of the ideological problems with which film has confronted itself, and barely ever solved, is how to portray war while at the same time decrying it. Fighting is the paradigm manifestation of motion-picture action, the more so when it involves aerial bombardment, spectacular destruction, bodies being thrown into the air, hideous wounds and injuries. The combination of noise, devastation and total disregard for the niceties of civil conduct, driven by a sense that one side deserves to win, engage an audience's receptivity like nothing else. Deploring the effect of it in the aftermath does nothing to cheat the spectator of his retrospective enjoyment of the ferocity. The films that try to pull off this ethical balancing-act are innumerable, but exemplary of the ambivalence is Francis Ford Coppola's *Apocalypse Now* (1979), a transposition of Joseph Conrad's novella of colonial Africa *Heart of Darkness*, to the context of America's embroilment in Vietnam. A scene in which the scouting party led by Captain Willard (Martin Sheen) stops to search a Vietnamese family's sampan, only to end up slaughtering them all when one of the Americans misinterprets the movement of a girl to protect a puppy, encourages the viewer to reflect on the chilling relativism of killing in wartime. The young soldier who has pre-emptively opened fire on the family is in one sense guilty of a war crime, but in another, as Willard's narrative voice-over observes, is only following protocol. Willard himself acts with clinical efficiency in administering a coup de grâce to the only woman who has not quite been killed, shooting her dead while the boat's pilot is still talking about getting her to a medical station, throwing an unsparing new light on his own degree of ethical compromise. The episode intends to leave the viewer stunned with revulsion, but is staged with the maximum resort to prolonged automatic rifle fire, the screaming bloodlust of the young soldier doing the firing, and the bodies of non-white indigenous people, referred to in the boilerplate military racism of the war as 'gooks', being consumed like incinerated refuse. Earlier in the film, the beach rendezvous with an unhinged American officer, Colonel Kilgore (Robert Duvall), offers another lesson in rebalanced priorities. What Kilgore dearly wants to do is enjoy a spot of surfing off the newly captured beach, a leisure activity that can easily be fitted in between ordering napalm attacks on the enemy. The bomber pilots conduct their mission to the accompaniment of the celebrated theme from the opening of Act III of Wagner's *Die Walküre*, which is not an addition to the film soundtrack itself, but is worked into the action as the insane stipulation of Kilgore for inspiring the airmen on their killing sprees. Here too is a cinematic technique steeped in ethical ambiguity. From one angle, Kilgore's cold-blooded cynicism is naturally to be deplored, while from another, the film can settle into a thrilling action sequence full of minutely relished suffering and death, with Wagner dragooned into taking part in a way that allows Coppola the alibi of blaming one of his characters.

The productive indeterminacy of cinema's attitude to war, which for many films throughout its history consists precisely in exploiting the potential for gratification of a specific audio-visual desire in its audiences – which is to say, mostly in its male audiences – while abluting its conscience with more overt disapproval of its deathly outcomes in the personal lives of its heroes and those who love them, has the merit at least of echoing a level of undecidedness among people's reactions to real-life war. Few people can see the wisdom of the now perpetual presence of Western forces in the Gulf states and Afghanistan, where they are locally seen as helping to perpetuate the very dangers, of the exportation of organized terrorism primarily, they are there to forestall. It only takes the next murderous rampage in a Western city, however, a grimly determined volunteer swerving a hired van on to a crowded pavement perhaps, to rally support for another bombing raid in the Hindu Kush. In the long preamble to the outbreak of European hostilities in July 1914, war was much talked and written about, politically and philosophically, as the answer to what was perceived as the inexorably tilting balance of power on the continent. With the exception of the Crimea, there had not been a war in Europe, as distinct from localized revolts and uprisings, since Waterloo. The Greek War of Independence against the Ottoman Empire occupied over a decade of the 1820s and 1830s, to be sure, and in due course drew in Tsarist Russia, the France of the Bourbon Restoration and the British Empire as unlikely allies in the radically militant cause of Greek self-determination. In these narratives, war remained a heroic and noble proceeding, an act of social and political cleansing that resulted, by divine blessing, strategic brilliance and the mercurial attribute of luck, in history being reset. In this optic, a successful war, from the victors' viewpoint, is the paramount example of ends justifying the means by which they are brought about. The relative peacefulness of the European nineteenth century produced, among other cultural manifestations, a series of cognate outbursts of anti-conventional sensuality in Aestheticism, Symbolism, *l'art pour l'art*, the Pre-Raphaelite Brotherhood, the Decadents and – as the century turned – the decorative gratuity of Jugendstil and Art Nouveau with their curvaceous furls, torsions and tendrils. All of this was evidence, in the eyes of the conservative retrenchment, of a lotus-eating society crying out for the curative intervention of the martial spirit. The retrenchment would eventually get what it wanted, bringing back the advancing dark and the withering of hope after the long summer languish.

As though to propitiate the pugilistic impulse in human beings, war has been subjected since ancient times to rules of engagement, protocols of conduct with regard to the treatment of prisoners and civilian populations, and the batteries of weaponry with which it may be waged. The whole constitution of fighting forces, especially where trained through peacetime in standing armies that are theoretically ready to meet any eventuality, has historically been founded on the tautest regimes of physical and hierarchical discipline in the soldier's relation to himself, his own fitness and conduct, to his uniform and his equipment, to his comrades and commanding officers, to the land and people and principles, indeed the whole sociopolitical dispensation, he has been recruited to defend. At its heart, the practice of war depends on his ability and willingness to obey orders without ruminating too much, or at all, on the consequences of them. In the most recent era, in the armed forces of many nations, these duties and expectations have been equally extended to women soldiers, an innovation that would surely have bemused Sun Tzu. This discipline is the notional microcosm of war as it will be fought, to which end, as Martin Meisel describes it:

Untold intellectual effort has been expended on the task of eliciting the 'laws' of war, both in a scientific sense and in a legal and social sense – the latter, a body of thought, argument, and legislation intended to set limits upon under what circumstances and provocations (*jus ad bellum*) and by what means (*jus in bello*) aggregations of humanity may legitimately slaughter each other.[15]

A question remains as to whether these formalized accords assist humanity in taking small steps away from the abyss, or whether, by applying rationally calculated juridical principles to them, they perpetuate the existence of the abyss. The invention of the submarine and its deployment in wartime was once thought so offensive to the conduct of fair play that it would surely be outlawed for such purposes by international agreement. If the forgoing of toxic gas against frontline troops in the Second World War, after its regular deployment in the trenches of the First, was counted an advance for civilization, its use as an instrument of mass killing in the Nazi camps marked another giant leap downwards. Arms control treaties that took many years of wary, distrustful overture and negotiation turn out to endure just as long as it takes one of their signatories to tear them up. At the heart of war itself is precisely the sense that anything goes, the motivation of eventual victory licensing every abandonment of the codes of honour, every firebombing and sinking, every maltreatment of the captives. The retrospect of history offers not the reassurance that we are not as depraved any longer, only that depravity has the deepest-rooted precedent in human behaviour.

The Spartans, for example, often threw bound prisoners live into a pit not far from town, the feared Kaiadas, where the disabled and wounded slowly starved or bled to death.

The Athenians [storming the garrison at Mount Istone in 425 BC] ... claimed they would grant leniency to the

captured garrison, on the provision that not a single one of
the prisoners dared to escape. But after tricking a few to risk
flight, they executed the rest on grounds that the accords
had been broken. Apparently the remaining captives were
roped together in twos and whipped by special executioners
equipped with cat-o'-nine-tails as they were forced to run a
gauntlet between two long lines of [spear-] jabbing hoplites.
After sixty or so were torn apart, the rest refused to come out
of their barracks. They either perished under a hail of arrows
and roof tiles or killed themselves by jabbing captured arrows
into their throats or hanging themselves with nooses made
from their own clothes.[16]

These events, occurring during the Peloponnesian Wars, in the very
heartland of the war for independence that would be waged there over
two thousand years later, are at least as evil as anything perpetrated
by the Nazis in the 1940s, or under the regional commanders of the
Daesh in the present day.

Walter Benjamin's recollection, in a 1936 essay on the decline of the
storytelling tradition, of the generation that returned from the trenches
was of men returning mute, the latest stage in human development
being the theft of experience itself from consciousness. Hardly
anybody wanted to talk about what they had seen. The recounting
of stories, the passing on of life's lessons from the elder generations
to the younger, the ready proverb and homily that, however glibly,
captured a moment of worldly wisdom: all had been sandblasted away
by the ruthless application of technology to the business of slaughter
as never before, and by the concomitant destruction of social mores
that followed the armistice.

For never has experience been contradicted more thoroughly
than strategic experience by tactical warfare, economic experience

by inflation, bodily experience by mechanical warfare, moral experience by those in power. A generation that had gone to school on horse-drawn streetcars now stood under the open sky in a countryside in which nothing remained unchanged but the clouds, and beneath these clouds, in a force-field of destructive torrents and explosions, was the tiny, fragile human body.[17]

The chaos of warfare and its aftermath had bequeathed a traumatized stasis to those who had returned from it and, while the rest of society did its desperate best to move on – culturally, behaviourally, morally, philosophically – from the enormous waste of the war, no such recourse seemed psychically available to the surviving combatant. This cauterizing of living experience would only be ratified by the even larger arena in which the next world war would be fought. Not merely the loss of life and the destruction itself, but the way each development of the war is reported in the broadcast media, conspired to produce what Adorno, writing in the autumn of 1944, towards what was by then the war's inevitable end, calls a society of 'subjectless subjects', people who still retain the ghost-impression of what it was like to be a living, thinking, feeling person, but whose own capacity for experience has been excised from them. The temporality of the war has been made to resemble the plot structures of the films that will be shown in the same venues as the newsreels. 'Life has changed into a timeless succession of shocks, interspaced with empty, paralysed intervals. But nothing, perhaps, is more ominous for the future than the fact that, quite literally, these things will soon be past thinking on, for each trauma of the returning combatants, each shock not inwardly absorbed, is a ferment of future destruction.' This is Freud's return of the repressed enlarged to the societal level, and will also unfold in an atmosphere in which, as Benjamin predicted, culture itself will have withered into desuetude,

not least for its feeble impotence in standing against the descent
to barbarity. The mediatization of the war, in Adorno's analysis,
'is another expression of the withering of experience, the vacuum
between human beings and their fate, in which their real fate lies. It
is as if the reified, hardened plaster-cast of events takes the place of
events themselves'.[18]

A hardened plaster-cast is what had become of European aesthetic
life itself by the later reaches of the 1920s. Initially heralded by what
became known in France as the *rappel à l'ordre* (return to order) and
in Germany as the Neue Sachlichkeit (New Objectivity), painters and
poets, composers and – especially – architects, departed from the
free-form subjectivism and emotional outbursts of the early Futurist,
Fauve and Dada moments, and sought refuge in a restorationist formal
impulse, albeit in the service of the most fastidiously topical concerns,
duly applied to figurative painting, photomontage, documentary
work, classical tonality, and the spare, hard-edged outlines in building
design at the Bauhaus and by other exponents of the International
Style. The theatre director Oskar Schlemmer voiced the mood when
he wrote in his diary in April 1926: 'If today's arts love the machine,
technology and organization, if they aspire to precision and reject
anything vague and dreamy, this implies an instinctive repudiation of
chaos and a longing to find the form appropriate to our times'.[19] What
that meant in everyday practice was the unadorned white bedroom
of Erwin Piscator's house, designed in 1927–8 by Walter Gropius and
Marcel Breuer, in which such spartan necessities of furniture as there
are are pushed uniformly back against the walls, to which are also
fitted items of gymnastic equipment, leaving an expanse of bare floor
lit by a bare globe light fitting, not so much the epigrammatic 'machine
for living in' of the functionalist school as a spotless cool-box in which
an organic specimen might, if not dwell, then at least be stored. It was
as though the disintegrative trends of pre-war aesthetics, the grisly

howls of pain in the Expressionist theatre, fractured poetry, atonal music and the anything-but-repressed hysteria of Marinetti's first Futurist manifesto, had been massively overwhelmed and reduced by the gargantuan storm of the European war, so that artists and designers could only respond by insisting belatedly on principles of rational construction once more. Constructivism itself emerged, in both the Weimar Republic and Soviet Russia, as the first significant current to ignite after Dada's fizzling, and it would be accompanied by geometrical abstraction in painting, neoclassicism and the countervailing elegance of the twelve-tone system in music, objective reportage in film and photography, and that comfortless white block of Piscator's, and many others like it, in architecture. The human element was elided where it was not actively despised, and it was in the light of these currents that Benjamin suggested that, with the abandonment of buildings that looked like buildings, and of representations of true experience in the visual arts and in literature, people were assiduously, even cheerfully, preparing to survive the loss of culture, if that was the pass to which things would come. It was. If the first war put paid to the turbid swells and threatening skies of subjective expression in the arts, the second outdid the impulse to rationally planned order and efficient execution by rationally planning and efficiently executing the entire populations of towns and villages, with a whole race in its ultimate sights.

War is the outcome of inadequately managed chaos in political affairs, at least as much as it is the calculated response to provocation or, in previous centuries, the thoroughly scouring hygiene of a society – a masculine society, pre-eminently – grown flaccid with ease. It substitutes a vast, exponentially destructive and squalid chaos for the disorder to which it claims to be the antidote, and yet there is hardly an age in global history that has managed to do without it. Despite the proliferation of rules and protocols in the eras of the League of Nations and the United Nations, its outbreak nearly always comes as a kind of relief, the abandonment of a hopelessly punctilious or glib diplomacy, and the supervention of a time in which more or less anything now goes. The start of the aerial bombing of Saddam Hussein's Iraq in 1991, after the Western coalition's ultimatum to him to withdraw from Kuwait had expired, was accompanied by an atmosphere of barely concealed relish among television audiences at home in the United States and the United Kingdom, who could at last be treated to coverage of the nocturnal obliteration of selected urban targets, and each morning's aftermath of smoking ruins, for as long as it took to drive Iraqi forces out of the territory they had illegally occupied. Our side is punishing an act of aggression by bringing chaos and destruction to the perpetrators, since, in the primal logic, it is now widely perceived and accepted that there is no other way. That there was no alternative to the Second World War, or probably to the foreign-sponsored civil war that engulfed Russia in the immediate post-October period, or even to the English Civil War by which the constitutional future of a nation was fought out on fields and moorland between the abstract principles of monarchical supremacy and popular elective self-determination, did not make the resort to killing any more tolerable at their respective times, or any more regrettably necessary in historical memory. Each act of dignified commemoration, for all its common decency and intent to honour, makes straight the way for the next unavoidable outbreak.

For all that there may be social-anthropological benefits to living, even if only for defined intervals and even supposing such an enterprise is at all allowable or possible, outside the usual structures and hierarchies of the global capital economy, the question persists as to whether there could ever be a disordered simultaneity in a social collective, as distinct from the eremitical ideal of utter solitude, that does not involve certain conflict. And if there is, how long could we live with it, given the antecedent millennia of acculturation in which we are embedded, that progress in the alienation of human beings from their world and everything in it, including each other, identified in the central argument of the *Dialectic of Enlightenment*? A theory of the primordiality of conflict has it that the first hostilities arose from perceived inequality, particularly where one group, at the extremes of survival, sees that another group is in possession of a surplus that it is loath to share. If this were something near to the actuality, it would be hard indeed to adjudicate which party had the ethical advantage – the one trying to sustain itself, or the one trying to protect its resources. Even in that scenario, the question that presses itself is why two groups of the same species from different localities should see themselves as different, opposed entities. In the Judaic origin myth, the perception of inexplicable undue favour by the deity is what leads one brother to kill the other. There is no other way, it seems to him, to enjoy his own share of providence, and the psychological dynamics of this are a fair representation of what drove the first hominin groups to begin deliberately killing each other. At one level, with ominous implications for every age to come, it solves the problem. What else is the deprived group supposed to do? Accept its own starvation? It can hardly do that when it is endowed with exactly the same instinct for self-preservation as the contingently favoured group. The answer of today's anarcho-syndicalist movement is that the first group should be encouraged to share what it has, but that depends on an absent external social authority, or indeed whatever hegemonic ruling force the groups believe in, to arbitrate the matter, which is precisely what turns out to be unavailable. If this is the true scenario, then social antagonism genuinely is a matter of economics, as Marx and Engels argued, with the happy implicit proviso that economic inequality relentlessly generates the political forms that will eventually overthrow it. But what if, Adorno posits in *Negative Dialectics*, the emergence of antagonism was something much more obviously contingent, the product of 'archaic arbitrary acts of seizing power. With that, of course, the construction of the [Hegelian] world spirit would fall apart. The historic universal, the logic of things that is compacted in the necessity of the overall trend, would rest on something accidental, on something extraneous to it; it need not have been'. In the case of the historically determinist theory of Marx and Engels, the hope for an imminent overthrow of existing relations of production led them to tie the project of political economy very specifically to its most recent manifestation in the capitalist economy. They at least would have no truck with the anarchism of their time, which they saw as only wanting to alter the political disposition of social collectives while leaving intact the economic motive of self-preservation. Only a wholesale revolution on both fronts would stand the chance of not being overthrown in turn by the forces of retrenchment. As such, the solecism of primal communism was conjured, as an Edenic state from which economic realities had ruthlessly separated the human spirit, but the ghastly truth was that the principle of domination survived into the planned economies of the socialist countries, precisely because of their appeal to a human tendency that was allegedly stronger and that had prevailed in the earliest communities. If there is such a thing as historical inevitability, in either the Hegelian or the Marxist sense, there can be no freedom to escape, and not simply because of its own remorseless logic. The necessity itself is a piece of ideology, of what Marxist thinking otherwise knows as 'socially necessary semblance', but no less semblance for that. 'Theory cannot shift the huge weight of historic necessity', Adorno argues, 'unless the necessity has been recognized as realized appearance and historic determination is known as a metaphysical accident.'[20] Whatever catastrophe now threatens global societies, whether economic, ecological, nuclear or natural, shares its homology with the meaningless calamity that initiated the whole process of antagonism, confrontation and war.

The chance element, which supplies physical chaos theory with its principle of unstable dynamics, was theorized by the Epicurean school as a founding structure of the physical universe from the third century BC on. Where Democritus had held that the atoms of which everything is composed move in straight lines in all possible directions, in accord with invariant laws of necessity, Epicurus gave to this theory a literal twist, in the sense that he argued that atomic motion was uniformly downwards, and at uniform velocity, but what was not uniform about it was that each atom was capable of deviating slightly from its path. This *clinamen*, or swerve, produces collisions of atoms that accidentally result in new organic structures, the same principle argued two centuries after Epicurus by his greatest epigone, Lucretius, in the *De Rerum Natura*. For the latter thinker, the apparently random nature of atomic *clinamen* is what underwrites the notion of free will, which, so far from having been accorded to humankind by the benevolent gods, is instead, like everything else, a spontaneous occurrence. There is no purpose in this; it just is. On this view, the physical world and its processes emerge not from an abysmal empty chaos, but from a chaos of accidentally clashing and interacting tiny particles, invisible and unpredictable, but whose behaviour determines the entire context of human life and its habitat. One extrapolation from this is that the postulate of a harmonious, rationally ordered universe cannot possibly be true, but that the confrontations and abrasions of atoms capable of divergent motion are what make everything happen. Similarly, the collisions of human beings endowed with free will are what constitute the immense evolution of contingency we call history.

An important aspect of the shapeless pre-ontological heap in Ovid is that it is *non bene iunctarum discordia* (an 'uncoordinated and discordant' mass). Every element within it lacks attunement with every other. If this had not been the primal state of humanity in the ancient myths, it would become so by means of the divine punishment of, firstly, the natural curiosity of humans in the Garden, and then subsequently the hubris of human communities. What enables the construction of the Tower at what would become known as Babel – by biblical etymology at least, so named from the Hebrew verb *bālal*, to jumble, confuse, confound – is that the human race is still united by one universal tongue. Their creative ambition goads the deity, who had reserved such rights to himself, into a particularly spiteful bit of vengeance: 'Go to, let us go down, and there confound their language, that they may not understand one another's speech' (Genesis 11:7). Nothing daunted, in time to come, they will learn one another's speech, but for the time being, the mutual incomprehension visited on them is enough to force them to abandon work on the Tower, which in later iterations of the myth, the Lord then prudentially destroys.

Enfolded into the textures of this myth and its later exegesis is the notion that the cost of creativity in human aspiration is dissension, with the concomitant risk that dissension then produces states of radical disorder in which nobody knows where they stand, or what to expect, or whether the earth will provide. The dialectical motor force that Hegel saw in history, and which in its materialist livery furnished the Marxist philosophy of historical development, carries with it by definition the assumption that the world is a site of constant conflict, at its worst the 'slaughterbench' of Hegel's own rhetorical conception, at its least worst the crucible of competing versions of reality that, in striking sparks off one another, produce new configurations of ideas, new social dispensations, horizons of hope and, indispensably perhaps, the impression – however ideological or illusory – of progress. At least one working definition of war is that it is the outcome of one side or the other in a national or political standoff refusing to accept that the sun is setting on its own version of reality. This does not, however, preclude the possibility that its defeat is a matter of mere logistical contingency and, where so, it may tactically retreat before regrouping and mounting another stand. The English Civil Wars initially began to dwindle in the early 1650s as Royalist forces were defeated in all quarters of the British Isles, militarily outmanoeuvred and infiltrated by intelligence officers of the Parliamentary ascendancy. A substantial wing of the Royalist cause now accepted its fate, a change of temperament reflected in the softening of its cultural priorities. 'Royalist literature,' writes Blair Worden, 'which in the late 1640s had offered solace to the victims of Puritan supremacy but had also incited resistance to it, now rarely ventured beyond its consolatory purpose. Izaak Walton's *The Compleat Angler*, one of its high achievements in the 1650s, pays homage to rural retreat.'[21] Within the decade, as the government of the Commonwealth unravelled amid continued military rule and political agitation in the provinces and the evident toxicity of Puritan stricture among the population at large, Royalism saw its chance of resuscitation. The dialectical tide had rushed in and promptly receded.

If defeat brings with it a mixture of resignation and the residual buried hope that all might be different one day, victory, no matter how appalling the cost, carries the obligation to celebrate. The immediate aftermath of Waterloo in Britain was a country teeming with demobbed veterans reduced to mendicancy in the streets, their numbers swelling an already substantial cohort of the luckless, all competing with a massive brigade of women in reduced circumstances selling their bodies in order to get by. Slum children foraged for what they could amid the passing strollers and carriages of the more salubrious districts. Abandoned babies lay in gutter and ditch, sometimes still clinging to life. Before long, cheap gin would notoriously come to figure as a staple part of the daily diet, the purity or otherwise of its distillation brutally commensurate with its target clienteles at all levels of society. All of this was generated or aggravated by the years of war and the national expense it entailed. In the *Quarterly Review*, however, the ideology of national victory and the indomitable motherland poured forth thick as risen cream: 'Never was any other nation the object of such universal and boundless honour, admiration and benediction ... Wealth seemed to spring from expenditure, armies and fleets from the waste of battle, and courage and hope from disaster. She entered the conflict poor and feeble, she came out of it rich and invincible'.[22] The retrospective conception of war and its mayhem as the fair wind that has blown the civil polity as a whole some good, notwithstanding the loss of life and waste of resources, is an irrefragable aspect of the taking stock that follows it. Even the respect accorded to the dead in the solemn memorializations of cenotaph and annual national thanksgiving is blended, indigestibly for those who feel that all commemorating connotes a tacit complaisance with the militarist mentality, with an admixture of one of ideology's most refined cordials, the disguised blessing.

A critical engagement with the existing world and with certain forces within it will by no means disappear in even the most far-reaching wagers on social perfectibility, for precisely the reason that perfectibility has always to begin from the present state of affairs. Marx and Engels in *The German Ideology* (1845) conjure a vision of the typical day's activities in a liberated state as involving opportunity to 'hunt in the morning, fish in the afternoon, rear cattle in the evening, criticize after dinner, just as I have a mind, without ever becoming hunter, fisherman, herdsman or critic'.[23] The fact that nobody will be defined, as under capitalism, by what they do for a living does not preclude a state in which the intellectual endeavour of criticism will continue to flourish. The critical essay is as needful as the material provisioning of life. In 1956–7, the much-disputed Hundred Flowers Campaign was launched in the still fledgling People's Republic of China, its slogan, personally endorsed by Mao, drawn from classical poetry: 'Let a hundred flowers bloom, let a hundred schools of thought contend.' Originating from Zhou Enlai's concern that constructive theoretical input from the people as a whole was being stifled by the operations of the party-state, the policy should have worked to dynamize the socialist state, much as a refreshing breeze was blowing through the Soviet Union of the period, following Khrushchev's denunciation of Stalin. 'We stand for freedom of independent thinking, of debate, of creative work; freedom to criticize and freedom to express, maintain and reserve one's opinions on questions of art, literature or scientific research,' claimed one of the party's chief theoreticians and veteran of the Long March, Lu Dingyi.[24] A year after its implementation, in the midst of a tidal swell of rancorous disgruntlement from workers and peasants as much as government employees and academics, the policy was thrown into a handbrake turn and those who had been incautious enough to voice their resentments hunted down and imprisoned as Rightist enemies of the state. The first impulse, however, that internal contention was nothing to fear, could have produced the world's first truly participatory communist state, instead of being retroactively reinterpreted by historians as a Machiavellian booby-trap. A conflict of ideas would be one of the prerequisites for a reconciled society, exactly because it would be the external evidence that people had not been dragooned into supporting what merely already existed. There is an ocean of ethical difference between that realization and the cynical wisdom that says that war is an inevitability, with which we just have to learn to cohabit, the international arms trade's self-perpetuating bill of rights.

The elevation of war to the paradigm manifestation of chaos is what has also determined the interpretation of disorder and confusion as essentially evil, the theological ramifications of which remain to be unpicked.

4

Malevolence

It was while residing at Ephesus on the western coast of today's Turkey in the mid-50s AD that Paul of Tarsus received gathering evidence that the church he had founded in the Peloponnesian city of Corinth was in a state of disarray. Internecine squabbles and dissension plagued it, there were frequent outbreaks of competitive babbling in tongues, and little or no sense of proper structure, particularly in the matter of the correct form of worship appropriate to the new ecclesia. In a notorious verse of his first letter to Corinth, which may well be a later interpolation by another hand, he excoriates the practice of allowing women to speak in church, not the custom of any of the rival faiths of the region and therefore not likely to impress anybody with the dignity of the newest community. Immediately prior to that, however, he gives a definitive declaration of divine irenity. 'For God is not a God of disorder but of peace' (1 Cor 14:33). The Greek word translated by 'disorder', 'confusion' in the Authorised Version, is *akatastasías*, the genitive form of *akatastatos*, literally 'instability', but customarily indicating a state of unruly disorder. In the view of the apostle, disorder is not merely an inconvenience, an inefficient obstacle to sound proceeding, but the very theocratic principle that should underscore all devotion. As the final verse of the same chapter instructs, 'everything should be done in a fitting and orderly way'

(1 Cor 14:40), where 'orderly' (*táxin*) announces the very principle that supports the disposition of knowledge and understanding, of regular arrangement and fixed succession, as in a taxonomy. Confusion, turbulence, chaotic disorganization are alien to God's nature. Chaos is, in a word, evil.

To understand the true nature of malevolence, however, there is no point in lingering among the fractious adepts at Corinth when we could go to the master strategist, the organ-grinder indeed, himself, as he is presented to us in Milton's cosmology. At Satan's first appearance in the great mythopoeic epic *Paradise Lost* (1667, 1674), we find him lolling, half-stunned, on the fiery billows next to his companion-in-arms Beelzebub, having suffered his first decisive defeat in being cast out of Heaven, literally pitched over the 'Chrystal Battlements', by the Creator, like a drunk being ejected from an exclusive reception. A hideous silence prevails, the silence of the vanquished, in which, however, the first stirrings of his next defiance might foment, but while Satan is all for regrouping and mounting the counter-attack, Beelzebub, while reassuring his Prince that their work will continue to be nothing but evil, frankly doubts that they have the resources to outmanoeuvre God. Satan's first rallying call is a classic exhortation to make a virtue of infernal necessity:

> Farewel happy Fields
> Where Joy for ever dwells: Hail horrours, hail
> Infernal world, and thou profoundest Hell
> Receive thy new Possessor: One who brings
> A mind not to be chang'd by Place or Time. (I: 249–53)

Spreading their sodden and singed wings, the pair of them flit over to the dry shore, aware, nonetheless, that the only reason they can do this much is that they have been humiliatingly permitted to do so by the heavenly victor. Gathering his strength once more, Satan summons his wounded myrmidons, and forth they come, a motley company of shape-shifting, ambisexual demons, defeated kings and shopsoiled deities, many of whom are still the objects of cultic worship among the more deluded fraction of humankind. Their leader then stirs them to their mettle with something like a profane version of Queen Elizabeth's address to the troops at Tilbury, except that this call to triumph is uttered from the bilious recumbency of defeat, and Satan must three times choke down tears before he can begin his speech. Once he has gathered himself, what emerges is pure defiance. Like the manager of a beaten team, he begins by reminding his forces of their fearsome reputation, shored up as it is by their incalculable number, attributes that entitle them to put the contingency of the present vanquishment to one side. After all,

> what power of mind
> Foreseeing or presaging, from the Depth
> Of knowledge past or present, could have fear'd,
> How such united force of Gods, how such
> As stood like these, could ever know repulse? (I: 626–30)

And the reawakening of that awareness of their own multitudinous power is what ought to inspire them with the belief that they will once more rise up, 'bounce back' as the manager might put it. They now know what they are up against, and how their own resources compare to it, knowledge that, artfully borne in mind, could be put to strategic use. Intelligent logistical thinking, that 'art of war' of which we were reminded in the previous chapter, must henceforth replace the clash of force: 'our better part remains / To work in close design, by fraud or guile / What force effected not' (I: 645–7). That way, if the Almighty continues to concentrate his firepower in simply overwhelming the satanic legions by brute strength alone, a dim enough tactic anyway for the allegedly omniscient, he will only have won half the battle.

Evil now has its own habitation, with its own cultural space, its own physical lineaments and its own geographical extent, and that, as any ethnic group seeking to run its own affairs within its notional borders knows, is an asset. 'Space may produce new Worlds,' Satan suggests, envisioning a sub-celestial *Lebensraum* in which his regathering people may find themselves again. All acknowledgement of defeat, if the surrender to it is not to be unconditional, must include the glimmer of renewed possibility, however nebulously sketched, and it is there, in that putative unexplored space, that he inspires his desolate following with the vision of a recovered sense of self: 'Thither, if but to prie, shall be perhaps / Our first eruption, thither or elsewhere' (I: 655–6). The detail, for now, as so often in such extremities, hardly matters.

For the time being, their first task must be the establishment of a capital city for the new netherworld. The architectural vision is nothing less than a shining city on a hill:

> There stood a Hill not far whose griesly top
> Belch'd fire and rowling smoak; the rest entire
> Shon with a glossie scurff, undoubted sign
> That in his womb was hid metallic Ore,
> The work of Sulphur. Thither wing'd with speed
> A numerous Brigad hasten'd. (I: 670–5)

Led by Mammon, the pecuniary Spirit whose chief interest when resident in Heaven had been the gold-paved walkways at which his gaze was permanently downcast, the builders dig deep into the hillside land and uncover their own seams of gold. The reader need not be surprised that there is gold in the hills of Hell, as there is in Heaven: 'Let none admire / That riches grow in Hell; that soyle may best / Deserve the pretious bane' (I: 690–2). Indeed, it is Mammon himself, and those who worship him, who have perverted any innocent enjoyment of the beauty of gold and turned it vile. Whatever achievements of art high-minded endeavour can produce can be matched by those with nefarious intent. Dictators have fairytale palaces built for themselves. The devil, according to rueful evangelism, has all the best tunes. Satan's temple duly arises as effortlessly as if the infernal earth had blown it out, and it looks remarkably similar to the most opulent productions of antique architecture:

> Anon out of the earth a Fabrick huge
> Rose like an Exhalation, with the sound
> Of Dulcet Symphonies and voices sweet,
> Built like a Temple, where PILASTERS round
> Were set, and Doric pillars overlaid
> With Golden Architrave; nor did there want
> Cornice or Freeze, with bossy Sculptures grav'n,
> The Roof was fretted Gold. (I: 710–17)

No sooner is the work finished, on time and under budget, than a cacophonic fanfare sounds, calling the ranks of loyal troops to the first meeting of the supreme presidium, in a city that now has a name:

> Mean while the winged Haralds by command
> Of Sovran power, with awful Ceremony
> And Trumpets sound throughout the Host proclaim
> A solemn Councel forthwith to be held
> At PANDAEMONIUM, the high Capital
> Of Satan and his Peers: (I: 752–7)

There are innumerable swarms of them, so densely crowded that they clog the entrances, hovering in buzzing clouds like spring bees over the palatial halls, every available golden throne occupied by seraphic nobility and demigods, others of vast but less material composition obligingly transmuting themselves to fit the space – 'incorporeal

Spirits to smallest forms / Reduc'd thir shapes immense' (I: 789–90).
There is a plenary address, and then the 'great consult' gets under way.

Despite the licking flames and the perpetually smouldering
atmosphere, the salient attribute of the temple of Hell is that it looks
substantially similar to Heaven, or at least the more luxurious precincts
of Earth. Where one might have expected an architecture of petrified
sulphur, its cisterns flowing with boiling ichor, there is a golden palace
with classical detailing, Doric columns and fretted ceilings, cornices
and pilasters, the referential, derivative style of a kind of infernal
postmodernism. This carries an important theological charge. If
Good, ultimately, can be called forth out of Evil, it matters that there
is some topological relation between them, the very relation by which
the whole hellish cohort can trace its origins back to Heaven. God's
desire to see malevolence return to the fold of Good is what offers the
Satanic hordes a certain measure of freedom in their realm, which
could as easily, after all, have been a place of eternal bondage. Satan's
own commitment to demonic liberty, however, is such that he intends
to use that freedom, among other things, to turn benign purposes to
bad. Whichever way the traffic flows, it only does so because there
is a contiguity between benevolence and ill will, each deriving its
ontological status in contradistinction to the other.

There follows, in the second Book, the conference in which each
of the staff-officers of Evil has his say – the volcanically tempered
Moloch, the more pacific Belial, whose irenic disposition has made him
the greatest loss to Heaven, Mammon, prototype of an early modern
capitalist, urging his compatriots on to a great enterprise that will see
Hell overtaking Heaven in splendour, and finally the master-strategist
Beelzebub, the Lavrenti Beria of state Satanism. Word is that God is
intending to create a brand-new race of beings, whom he will favour
even over the angels. What better way to earn a revenge against Heaven
than for evil to inveigle itself into the primal scene of the new progeny,

and spoil it from the outset? In a flurry of grandiloquent posturing, Satan resolves on a solo espionage mission to Heaven, for which he must first negotiate an exit-permit from Hell. The gates are formed of a ninefold thickness – three each of brass, iron and rock-solid adamantine – guarded by a pair of hideous doorkeepers. These are the incestuously related couple of Death and Sin, the former shapeless but unassailable, the latter a hybrid sorceress, half-woman, half-serpent, girdled with snarling curs, with whom Satan, who appears to have forgotten that she once sprang from his own head, must engage in a dialectical negotiation. Eventually persuaded, she unlocks the gate and lets him out.

There is, inevitably and constitutively, a No Man's Land between the infernal and celestial realms, but it is anything but the fathomless absence of the Mosaic legend. There is a boundless expanse of water, to be sure, but also an uproarious tumult overseen by a Hesiodic pantheon of distinctly familiar mythic figures:

> a dark
> Illimitable Ocean without bound,
> Without dimension, where length, breadth, and highth,
> And time and place are lost; where eldest Night
> And CHAOS, Ancestors of Nature, hold
> Eternal ANARCHIE, amidst the noise
> Of endless warrs and by confusion stand. (II: 891–7)

The realm of Chaos is, fittingly, without order or dimension of any kind, so that its boundaries and its location cannot be computed. Its ambience is incessant conflict, uncontainable by temporality, unimpeded by regulative force, subject only to those anti-monarchs, 'Chaos and old Night', already prefigured in Book I, who preside over the scene in a parody of arbitral supervision, only to ensure that it never ends. 'CHAOS Umpire sits, / And by decision more imbroiles the fray / By which he Reigns: next him high Arbiter / CHANCE governs all' (II: 907–10). And here we might parenthetically note, against the proponents of mathematical chaos theory, that Chaos and Chance in the Miltonic optic are properly two separate entities. Through this raucous mire, Satan must now improvise a passage, and finds that his usual airborne mode of locomotion will not suffice for long, and that he must employ all the laborious indignities of less illustrious creatures than himself to make his way.

> So eagerly the fiend
> Ore bog or steep, through strait, rough, dense, or rare,
> With head, hands, wings, or feet pursues his way,
> And swims or sinks, or wades, or creeps, or flyes: (II: 947–50)

Since there are no physical laws, no one strategy can be expected to serve. Somehow, in the intensifying hubbub, he must find someone to ask directions to the farthest border, where the region of light begins, but comes instead upon the whole convocation of the region's Lords of Misrule –

> the Throne
> Of CHAOS, and his dark Pavilion spread
> Wide on the wasteful Deep; with him
> Enthron'd sat Sable-vested Night, eldest of things,
> The consort of his Reign; and by them stood
> ORCUS and ADES, and the dreaded name
> Of DEMOGORGON; Rumor next and Chance,
> And Tumult and Confusion all imbroild,
> And Discord with a thousand various mouths. (II: 959–67)

Satan explains that he is on his way to investigate the new world that has lately been willed into being, along with a new prodigy to inhabit it, and inasmuch as he intends to introduce the principle of maleficence into the spotless realm, wrecking its entire purpose, will thereby open up a whole new province of disorder and strife for Chaos to colonize. Chaos, who has no particular interest in relations between Heaven and Hell, or their presiding chieftains and their armies, but does relish any chance for mayhem – 'Havock and spoil and ruin are my gain' (II: 1009) – reassures Satan that he has not far to go now.

The hard part over with, it only remains to construct an immense bridge over the abyss of Chaos, by which Satan's minions will enjoy an easy passage to the mortal world on their missions of temptation and torment, and an equally easy one back again with each captured soul. Chaos and his dominion, then, are not in themselves the abode of evil. Satan's realm, as we have seen, is a paragon of order compared to the metereologically turbulent, conflict-ridden, howling din of the abysmal zone. Instead, classical elegance is the stylistic habitus and the deliberations proceed in punctilious courtesy, everybody hearing out each speaker with attentive respect, and somebody, presumably, taking the minutes. That these proceedings are a subtly parodic version of the harmony that prevails in the former heavenly home is, in one sense, beside the point. The hellish clans prefer to behave with pompous decorum rather than in bestial disarray, but the contiguous intermediate realm in which permanent uproar predominates is what will facilitate the transpontine traffic between Hell and the newly populated Earth. Chaos, while it is not somewhere one would willingly choose to dwell, is not in itself evil, but it is the precondition of a descent into evil. If there had been something like the watery void of Genesis stretching between Hell and the distant horizon of light, it would have been inconceivable that anybody would cross it, but the existence of a Chaos redefined from chasm to mayhem, is what builds the high-speed link between them. In this respect, it does Milton's epic something of a disservice that 'Pandaemonium', his own coinage, should have become another of the synonyms of chaos, instead of designating a stately convocation of demons. And the Milton whose view of the malevolent potentials of parliaments and religious assemblies, their baleful tendency to cloak iniquity in procedural nicety and constitutional fustian, was already publicly known, ensures that the satirical tone of the kingdoms of Hell and Chaos, their disastrous adjacency, rings resonantly through the opening two books of *Paradise Lost*.

Notwithstanding that, there has been an enduring academic debate as to the precise – or perhaps imprecise – moral valence Milton gives to his characterization of Chaos. Is it a place of evil, the begetting and abetting of evil, or is it rendered in softer, more neutral lighting, an ambience in which it could even, as with the original void, be the essential setting from which the creation will be sculpted? An influential essay of 1985 by Regina Schwartz, 'Milton's Hostile Chaos: " ... And the Sea Was No More"', robustly argued for the first option, enumerating the various strategies by which later commentators in the liberal tradition had sought to detoxify chaos.[1] Martin Meisel too, while acknowledging the competing strands of this debate, opts for the clinching force of Schwartz's case:

> There is a better argument for its evil disposition and for its moral identification with the uncreating, retrograde principle that is left free to contest the perfection of the evolving universe, an argument based less on Milton's cosmology and theology than on the affective coloring in his representations of the chaotic. In its unstructured boundlessness, its indiscriminate mixing, its confusion and indeterminacy, chaos in Milton is felt as profoundly unclean, allied to the monstrousness of Sin and Death as well as to the transgressive, degenerate Satan from whom they emanate.[2]

Such ambivalence as there is in the text itself surely reflects the liminal state of conceptions of chaos at this, the last era in English understanding that it retains both its meanings – of elemental emptiness and of teeming, formless confusion. Indeed, Milton is cited in the OED as the last author in English still to deploy the original Greek sense of chaos as void. This results, not accidentally, in a shape-shifting conceptualization of the properties of chaos. In Aaron Santesso's words:

> One might do better to recognise Chaos in *Paradise Lost* as neither primarily good nor evil but both. If Creation is generally good, then Chaos has moments of goodness. If destruction is evil, then Chaos has moments of evil. If it is good to obey God, then Chaos is good when it obeys God during creation … If it is evil to aid Satan and attempt to thwart God, then Chaos is evil when its Anarch directs Satan towards Eden.[3]

The astute point here is that it is both, not neither: the one thing Chaos cannot be, in contrast to what some commentators have suggested, is neutral, since its director does not stand above the cosmic fray, but opts to assist Satan on his way to corrupt humankind. The salient topographical feature of the realm of Chaos is its vast extent, across which a weary, thwarted and ultimately lost Satan must make his way, and it is this which ensures that it retains its original attribute of a gaping abyss as well as its seething ferment of tempest and racket. If, as Santesso points out, chaos as emptiness is a spatial element, and chaos as disorder a more obviously physical one, there is also a suggestion, at this transitional moment in English letters, of the former hermeneutic being more readily suited to poetic diction and the latter to prose. Perhaps this, at the prolusion to the English Enlightenment, was what finally divided them.

In the century after Milton, Alexander Pope conjures no such ambiguity from Chaos. Explicitly echoing the Miltonic formula of 'Chaos and old Night', he opens the fourth book of *The Dunciad* (1742) by fearfully invoking an uncertain shaft of light to half-illuminate those elemental forces: 'Yet, yet a moment, one dim ray of light / Indulge, dread Chaos, and eternal Night!' (IV: 1–2). At the setting of the direful scene, they prepare to do their worst: 'The moon-struck prophet felt the madding hour: / Then rose the seed of Chaos, and of Night, / To blot out order, and extinguish light' (IV: 12–14). All the humanizing arts – Science, Logic, Rhetoric, Wit – are put to languish by the new goddess, Dulness, a force of benighting stupidity who is the daughter of those Hesiodic parents, Chaos and Night. She is tastelessly beseeched in the florid address, 'O Cara!' ('Dear lady'), familiar from Italian opera, a particular Popean bête noire, to unleash that same opera's cacophonous strains to confound the procession of the traditional Muses:

> O Cara! Cara! silence all that train:
> Joy to great Chaos! let Division reign:
> Chromatic tortures soon shall drive them hence,
> Break all their nerves, and fritter all their sense:
> One trill shall harmonize joy, grief, and rage,
> Wake the dull Church, and lull the ranting Stage;
> To the same notes thy sons shall hum or snore,
> And all thy yawning daughters cry, *encore*. (IV: 53–60)

There follows a pageant of dunces, a celebration of every form of social and moral asininity imaginable, from those Oxbridge dons who banished the work of Locke to the cane-happy master of Westminster School, whose special penchant is whipping the native intelligence out of boys in a regime more punitive than pedagogical. At the close, a reign of idiocy has descended on the fallen world, Truth, Morality and the spark of human intelligence having been driven from the scene or extinguished utterly:

> Lo! thy dread Empire, Chaos! is restor'd;
> Light dies before thy uncreating word:

Thy hand, great Anarch! lets the curtain fall;
And universal Darkness buries All. (IV: 653–6)

The 'uncreating word' is to be contrasted with the divine fiat that inaugurated the world, and also to the Logos, the Word made flesh, that dwelt among us. All the word of Chaos can do is bring down the curtain on it all. The contiguity of Chaos and Hell in *Paradise Lost* is superseded here by a personified ruler who casts the gloom of ignorance, the evil disorder of obtuseness, over the creation.

As both Milton's and Pope's visions propose, Chaos more than Hell is pre-eminently the country of mayhem. Even if Hell's proceedings in Milton are a fraudulent imitation of order, they pay tribute to the genuine and perfect order that reigns in Heaven. Any aspirant to the divine kingdom must be aware that the principle of order connotes not just a commodious way of living, but a sacred duty. The formalism that Paul enjoins the church at Corinth to observe continues to inform not just the practice of worship but the deliberative procedures of the established churches today. There is, to be sure, a degree of latitude in those evangelical communities that insist that the formal liturgy has proved alienating to people in the post-war Western world, and is what accounts for the widespread decline in attendances, but very often the degree to which services are unstructured, making do without the Georgian and Victorian hymnal of traditional worship and promoting personal outbursts of beatitude, reflects precisely the degree of exegetical sternness with which the revealed word of the Bible is treated. The brutal cause-and-effect by which the interventionist God of American fundamentalism punishes moral backsliding with hurricanes suggests that nobody is about to abandon the idea of structure in the enactments of belief. Where a commitment to formality in observance remains, the Vatican and the Church of England's General Synod still recurrently preoccupy themselves with issuing proclamations touching the conduct and structure of the liturgy, as well as the conduct and structure of personal life. The crisis prompted in the worldwide Anglican communion over the elevation of women to the episcopate, and the obligation felt by both Roman and Anglican confessions to maintain a stance not just on gay marriage and civil partnership but on the constitutive physical conduct of homosexuality itself, speak of an impulse to formal institutionalism that is, to a significant extent, at loggerheads with the anti-institutional propensity of the original Christian teaching. Whoever the true author of the letter to the Phrygian faith community at Colossae was, he is at considerable variance with the Paul who adjures the Corinthians to formalize their devotions. Instead, the sacrifice of Christ is just what releases the community of believers from the legalism inherited with the notion of original sin, and which henceforth has been 'nailed to the cross' along with the corporeal body of the Redeemer:

> Since you died with Christ to the elemental spiritual forces of this world, why, as though you still belonged to the world, do you submit to its rules: 'Do not handle! Do not taste! Do not touch!' These rules, which have to do with things that are all destined to perish with use, are based on merely human commands and teachings.
>
> (Col 2:20–22)

It is true that the writer goes on in the next chapter to entreat the faithful to live in accordance with those rigidly hierarchical social precepts that should see wives acquiescing in their husbands' authority, children in that of their parents, servants in that of their employers, with the concomitant requirement in each case that those to whom deference is shown should be appropriately gentle in the exercise of command, but these obeisances should be performed not for the benefit of their respective superiors, but because they help ensure that tranquillity and mutual respect in human affairs that is pleasing to the Lord. The heavenly kingdom, on this latter view, is just that – a wise constitutional monarchy in which peace is guaranteed.

The sin of Satan, for which he is evicted from the presence of the Almighty, is rebelliousness, a refusal to accept the existing structures of authority. If chaos is evil, or if it provides the transit from a state of grace to unrepentant maleficence, it is because it signifies a refusal of the regulative principle, and where this has been instituted by God, the church or society, in the form of a heteronomous body of law that must be observed inasmuch as it is not actively defied, the result is the communal disorder and moral anarchy that leads to pernicious consequences. In an easy slippage, moral strictures require the individual not just to observe the law but to 'obey' it, as though its formulations always had an imperative propositional value, as though they always instructed and mandated people to undertake certain actions. The law both prohibits and commands: it forbids theft and arson, but it also requires its clients to pay their taxes and complete the census form. If everybody disregarded it, the result would be chaos. These obligations are fortified by the ancient moral tradition in which obedience is a virtue. The submissions that the writer of Colossians solicits among the communities of the faithful specifically require obedience, of the weaker to the stronger, the younger to the elder, which are in turn replicated throughout those institutions of society, including armies, academies and churches themselves, that would be unable to function without it. In the canons of piety, in the monastic rule and in the strictures for living that are urged on secular society too, the virtue of obedience lies in its abnegation of the self. In making oneself over to authority, personal or institutional, the subject denies his own subjecthood, or brackets it as subsidiary to external command. Self-denial is not only a Lenten observance, but is the proper attitude of the Christian at all times, since conflict arises from the clash of opposing self-assertions. The ontological problem with general humility as a system is that it needs some authority below God before which to humble itself, or there will be no opportunity for it. Somebody, however reluctantly, has to occupy the position of authority to which others must submit. The invention of the autonomous self in the subjectivity of Romanticism began to make humility chafe at its bonds. Servitude is the antithesis of that untrammelled freedom of spirit that the natural world has conferred on everything in it, with the troubled exception, since the origins of consciousness, of humankind. In the shackles of a mercantilist society, with every social purpose tending towards the worship of money and indigent labourers uprooting themselves from their organic communities and heading towards the cities in search of a living, individuals and the sensory capacities with which they are born need to be carefully nurtured, nursed back to a state of open-hearted wonder, a transformation that can only be achieved by solicitous attention to the damaged self. Obedience, subjection to the insolence of the propertied and plutocratic classes, is just what there is too much of. Far from being a virtue, it has become a system of socio-economic fetters that have bound human beings so tightly that Marx and Engels can assure them that, in rebelling against the present dispensation, they would have nothing else to lose.

If obedience were always a matter of occluding the self in the interest of promoting social harmony, and if everybody observed it, it would be an evident virtue, but what makes it obscene is the countervailing impulse by which those to whom people submit enjoy their submission. The theological teaching in the matter concentrates entirely on the suppliant and has nothing to say about those whose superiority makes his suppliance possible. For as long as there have been structures of power, there have been people who wish to commandeer the uppermost positions in them, their psychological reward for doing so being the sense of gratification that comes from giving the orders that enable those who yield to them to feel virtuous. The disastrous alternative to obeying others, according to established church teaching, as outlined by American theologian Donald DeMarco, is obeying oneself, and 'there is no more certain route to personal disaster than obeying only oneself. We are not so wise or self-sufficient that we can afford to shut our minds to all others and find our way through life solely by listening to and obeying ourselves … Obeying only oneself is a formula for … alienation as well as anarchy'. Obeying a self alienated by the division of labour, or the lack of self-respect that poverty visits on individuals in a money economy, can doubtless unleash the hostile forces that society ought to fear, and certainly ought to have foreseen, but perhaps the problem lies in the very concept of obeisance. Obedience is by its nature alienating, because it assumes an extraneous force, and where that force appears to emerge from within the subject, he has certainly already been alienated from himself. Alienation is not the consequence, but a precondition, of the destructive self. 'Obedience … is closely allied to service', continues the theologian.

> Hence the expressions 'your will is my command' and 'it is a pleasure to serve you.' The person who loves is happy to serve, eager to obey the needs and desires (legitimate ones, of course) of the beloved. Obedience allows a person to transcend the narrow confines of egotism and respond to the good of those he loves with alacrity, enthusiasm, and cheerfulness.[4]

And yet the obedient who craves to serve cannot do so without a steady stream of commands to obey, and if the beloved truly returned his love, they would scarcely keep giving in to the impulse to issue them. The constitution of all love relations as relations of power, from ancient patriarchy to today's consensual sadomasochism, hammers into every participant that even here, in the very realm of feelings that ought properly to exist outside social obligation, heteronomy reproduces itself. 'Love,' Adorno observes, 'you will find only where you may show yourself weak without provoking strength.'[5] For many, he might have added, it remains an undiscovered country.

Those who wish to bring chaos to systems of order are constructed as evil because they have not learned, or more likely have consciously repudiated, the virtue of obedience. That there are peripheral figures in even the most closely regulated societies, civil polities whose regulative structure has been ordained of God, haunted the imagination of the Elizabethan and Jacobean theatre. The malcontents of the classical and modern urban communities portrayed in the drama of the period are not necessarily motivated by personal gain, but more often by status envy, sexual jealousy, contempt for the law and the Lord Almighty who instituted it, and a consuming spite for their fellow creatures. They alone see that happiness is a chimera, sincerity a cynical front and the supposed bonds of loyalty nothing but disguised self-interest, and only subversion of the social and moral order might bring the deluded to look honestly upon themselves. In Shakespeare's oeuvre, the prototype of all such malevolence is Aaron the Moor, secret lover of the Gothic empress Tamora, in the lurid early revenge confection, *The Tragedy of Titus Andronicus* (c. 1590), implicitly set in the final deterioration of the Roman Empire. Aaron kidnaps the mixed-race baby he has fathered on Tamora, having killed the infant's nurse to prevent her from revealing the scandal. Cornered in the fourth act by Titus' eldest son Lucius, he confesses to his accessory role in the rape and mutilation of Titus' daughter Lavinia, a crime that brought him ecstatic hilarity, for which enormity he is to be hanged as soon as the baby boy has been similarly dispatched. At his moment of execution, Lucius asks Aaron whether he feels any remorse, to which the reply is only that he has not had chance to commit countless other

such deeds, although there is some valedictory relish to be had from
recalling those he has committed:

> Even now I curse the day – and yet, I think,
> Few come within the compass of my curse, –
> Wherein I did not some notorious ill,
> As kill a man, or else devise his death,
> Ravish a maid, or plot the way to do it,
> Accuse some innocent and forswear myself,
> Set deadly enmity between two friends,
> Make poor men's cattle break their necks;
> Set fire on barns and hay-stacks in the night,
> And bid the owners quench them with their tears.
> Oft have I digg'd up dead men from their graves,
> And set them upright at their dear friends' doors,
> Even when their sorrows almost were forgot;
> And on their skins, as on the bark of trees,
> Have with my knife carved in Roman letters,
> 'Let not your sorrow die, though I am dead.'
> Tut, I have done a thousand dreadful things
> As willingly as one would kill a fly,
> And nothing grieves me heartily indeed
> But that I cannot do ten thousand more. (V: i)

The enumerated catalogue of his crimes, and the obscene enjoyment
with which he recounts them, which derives much of its intensity
from the anticipated reaction to it, are what mark out the irredeemable
perversion of his character. Then too, what makes the malefactor
truly chilling is that he knows that what he has done is hideous. He
is not morally benumbed by his outcast status, but energized by the
imaginative cruelties he has been able to perpetrate against the society
that cast him out in the first place. Those thousand deeds are 'dreadful'

in the older sense – full of menace and terror to the civilized – but also in the looser, later colloquial sense of shocking, appalling, dire. In this respect, he is unsettlingly capable of standing aloof from his own malevolence and judging it in the same light as do his accusers. Only the true sadist refuses to exonerate himself, but readily acknowledges the ghastliness of his activities, which would not be so enjoyable if they were not ghastly. For this searing self-disclosure, Lucius decrees that hanging is too good for him, and he is hauled down from the makeshift gallows.

In the culminating scene, which derives from the Roman dramatist Seneca's grotesque tragedy *Thyestes*, Tamora's sons Chiron and Demetrius, rapists of Lavinia whose throats Titus has personally cut in the previous scene, are fed to her unwittingly, their decapitated heads having been baked in a pie. Obscene consumption had always been one of the enduring cultural tropes of Roman imperial decadence, expounded in bilious comic detail by Petronius in the first-century prose narrative, *Satyricon*, and Shakespeare exploits its disgust value to the full. It only remains for Titus, having revealed the horrible truth to Tamora, to kill her, and be killed in his turn by her lover, the emperor Saturninus, before the prisoner Aaron is brought once more before Lucius. His sentence of execution is that he is to be buried chest-deep in the ground and left to starve to death. Anybody showing pity to him will themselves incur the death penalty. Unlike his spiritual godson, the nefarious lieutenant Iago, Othello's tormentor, who remains obstinately silent at the discovery of his plot against the general and his wife, Aaron spits out a final venomous tirade:

> O, why should wrath be mute, and fury dumb?
> I am no baby, I, that with base prayers
> I should repent the evils I have done:

Ten thousand worse than ever yet I did
Would I perform, if I might have my will;
If one good deed in all my life I did,
I do repent it from my very soul. (V: iii)

He almost has the play's last word, but for Lucius' few lines of wrapping up. Tamora is to be denied a proper burial, her body to be thrown out instead for wild animals and raptors to consume, and the sentence on Aaron closely superintended. His perfunctory final couplet – 'Then, afterwards, to order well the state, / That like events may ne'er it ruinate' – is the least convincing *rappel à l'ordre* in all Shakespearean tragedy, a merely gestural instruction that cannot stand a chance of fulfilment in the morally chaotic swamp in which we have been submerged.

The Elizabethan villain is a direct descendant of the blood-hungry tyrants and schemers of Roman tragedy, a lineage in which Seneca's universe of predation and vengeance figured prominently. There are overt currents of supernaturalism – ghosts and conjurors, witches and other occult forces – in his works, which ensured them an unimpeded passage from the world of courtly recitation for which they were written to the fully enacted events of the Tudor stage. Sackville and Norton's *Gorboduc* (1561), generally considered the first English tragedy, privately performed before Queen Elizabeth in January 1562, is saturated with Seneca through and through, a tale of revenge killings within a mythical royal family of ancient Britons, stemming from the gratuitous murder of one brother by another. In a reversal of the primal tale of Cain and Abel, it is the younger brother, Porrex, who murders his elder sibling, Ferrex, generating a series of events that engulfs a whole community. The sibling rivalry arises from the baseless suspicions of two brothers whose several titles to their father Gorboduc's realm have been decided by apportionment.

If everything had been left to the elder, the younger might have had
the motive of envy, but would have had no choice but to accept the
ancient principle of primogeniture. It is the attempt to divide the
largesse that causes the contestation, as Gorboduc is indeed warned
from precedent, which he will no more heed than will Lear when
parcelling his kingdom out among his daughters. As the retaliatory
killings multiply, they draw in factions and legions of supporters
on either side, until everybody in the realm feels impelled to take
one side or the other. The bitter wars between the royal houses of
York and Lancaster, which consumed the English polity for thirty
years in the fifteenth century, until the male lines of both families
were entirely wiped out, were doubtless uppermost in the minds of
Tudor dramatists. There is a sense, though, in the entire tradition
of the tragic conception of life, already identifiable in the domestic
embroilments of the house of Atreus in the *Oresteia* of Aeschylus,
that dire events – hatred, bloodshed, vengeance, the unhinging of
rational and just social relations – are not solely the responsibilities
of each individual who helps perpetuate them, but happen as a result
of extraneous, irresistible fate, a force in human affairs that may
derive, at various junctures in history, from the whims of inscrutable
deities, or from some other equally intangible current – perhaps the
movements of the astral bodies, the stain of original sin, the active
influence of Satan, the indomitable fact of predestination, the reifying
effect of capitalist exchange relations, the spellbinding distractions of
consumerist enchantment. The theatrical villains may provoke what
diabolical mischief they can, but they are themselves only the most
obvious conduits through which disembodied mischief leaks into the
human world. They could not themselves cause chaos if the world
were not already in some sense homologous with the condition of
chaos in the first place. What the characters plotting against society
in these plays want to create more evidently than disorder is fear, and

while fear can certainly create the disorder of panic, it more often results in a static condition that imposes its own order.

The transcultural symbol of malevolent chaos par excellence is the snake or serpent, sometimes expanded to the dimensions of a dragon or reptilian sea-monster, but more often to be found lurking in the undergrowth of the ordered habitat, slithering up on its victims unseen, polishing them off by constriction or with secretions of convulsive venom. The serpent in Eden is not so stealthy, but must draw Eve's attention to it so as to beguile her, like Disney's (though not Kipling's) version of the Indian python Kaa in *The Jungle Book* (1967). It is unimaginably ancient, as old and seductive as sin itself, leading her astray through the tempter's standard strategy of assuring her that the worst fate she can imagine, instant death, is very unlikely to befall her. In the roughly contemporaneous book of Job, the serpent has resorted to a maritime habitat and taken on monstrous dimensions in the form of Leviathan. A 'twisting monster' in the Hebrew etymology, Leviathan is widely considered by present-day biblical interpreters to equate to the Nile crocodile, once fished out of the waters by hook, an enterprise scorned in the opening words of God's final fulmination to the tortured Job: 'Can you pull in Leviathan with a fishhook or tie down its tongue with a rope?' (Job 41:1). Whatever its precise zoological inspiration, it is not only sinuously evasive, but has become an overweening power, impossible to subdue, negotiate with or control, albeit one that flatters to deceive humankind by appealing to its own instinct for dominion. It has become the objective correlative, in other words, of evil itself, as the thundering God points out in an excoriating sequence of rhetorical queries: 'Will it keep begging you for mercy? Will it speak to you with gentle words? Will it make an agreement with you for you to take it as your slave for life?' (41:3–4). The point is that if humans shy away from laying hands on the sea-serpent, how much less likely are they to have the wherewithal to stand up to the sea-serpent's maker? If it cannot be commandeered, nor can it be attacked, its armour being impermeable, its monstrosity more than a match for anything they might throw at it: 'A club seems to it but a piece of straw; it laughs at the rattling of the lance' (41:29). By the end of this extraordinary poetic disquisition, one of the greatest lyrical passages in the Tanakh, the wretched Job can only indicate that he has taken the point.

Leviathan is a probable derivation from the Canaanite sea-creature Lotan in the Ugaritic legend-cycle of the storm-god Ba'al. In the extinct Semitic language in which the myths were told, Lotan means 'coiled', indicating that its original incarnation was indeed something in the nature of a serpent rather than a crocodile. In the legend, Ba'al triumphs over the serpent, subduing its destructive influence, which may well have symbolized the devastating effects of sea-borne storms and flooding on subsistence crops. A glancing interpolation of the Ugaritic mythos appears in the Prophet Isaiah, in invocation of the terrible Day of Judgment: 'In that day, the Lord will punish with his sword – his fierce, great and powerful sword – Leviathan the gliding serpent, Leviathan the coiling serpent; he will slay the monster of the sea' (Isaiah 27:1). There is no single and obvious lineage for this scenario, though, which forms one of a cluster of transcultural and transhistorical myths grouped in comparative ethnology under the concept of *Chaoskampf*, the struggle against – and inevitable victory over – the malign forces of chaos. In antique Babylonian cosmology, the serpent is a manifestation of the sea-goddess Tiamat, eventually slain by the storm-god Marduk. In the Vedic texts, the king of Hindu deities Indra annihilates the serpent Vritra ('the constrictor'), incarnation of drought, with a thunderbolt. Its Norse counterpart, Jörmungandr ('monstrous serpent'), is a northerly paradigm of the ancient Egyptian *ouroboros*, an image of a serpent swallowing its own tail, creating in the process a seamless enclosing entity, wrapping the world up in malignity, but doomed eventually in the Nordic myth to be slain by the storm-god Thor. The serpent of the Greek origin-myths is Typhon, cast down into the underworld by the thunderbolts of Zeus, who thereby gains mastery of the pantheon of divinities. At least two millennia before any of them, the Egyptian sun-god Ra had engaged in successive battles with Apep or Apophis, the serpent-god who represents chaos and darkness, whose stirrings and thrashings within the underworld bring periodic thunderstorms and earthquakes to the world above.

In an imaginative work of evolutionary science, Lynne Isbell points out that, for millennia, snakes were the only natural predators of anthropoid apes and hominins. She speculates that a giant leap in the development of communication skills took place when human ancestors learned to alert each other to the presence of a deadly snake by pointing to it, thereby initiating another type of gestural language that said something of potential benefit to its recipient, rather than simply announcing something about the self. While attempting to interest a colony of monkeys at the California Primate Research Center with a dummy snake in one of her experiments, Isbell was fortunate enough to observe their reactions to the unexpected appearance of the real thing:

> In an enclosure holding about 80 monkeys, at least 30 gathered around in a mob to watch the snake, some on the ground, others clinging to the fence. As the snake progressed into the enclosure, the mob parted like the Red Sea for Moses, giving it a wide berth to pass through unhindered. Snakes elicit fearful fascination in captive-born-and-raised rhesus macaques who likely have never been harmed by one.[6]

By contrast, they still appear able to cohabit peacefully after all these millennia with predatory humans, unless the latter's intentions are overtly hostile. Isbell attributes this to the fact that humans have not been inimical to the safety of other primates for as long in the evolutionary record as snakes have, which would also explain the findings of the 1999 survey she cites that showed ophidiophobia to be the most commonly occurring irrational fear, outstripping fear of flying by more than two to one, the two nonetheless combining to subtend the self-explanatory premise of the cultishly enjoyed action-thriller *Snakes on a Plane* (2006).

At the heart of the reptilian conception of evil is the notion that evil itself has an ontology, that its very indomitability stems from its perfectly self-enclosing organic form, the serpent eating its tail, making itself, like an eternity ring, into a shape that is literally endless, self-renewing. But what if evil, like chaos, is inherently formless? If the Creation brought shape to what was shapeless, its beneficence derives from its state of rounded Being, of having become at the behest of the Creator. St Augustine, musing on the relative status of good deeds and evil in the *City of God*, reaches his way towards a conclusion that evil cannot be a created entity, for which the Creator could be held responsible and which would cast a dubious light on his intentions, but is simply the absence of good. 'Evil has no positive nature,' he declares, 'but the loss of good has received the name "evil"' (XI: 9). It makes no sense to conceive this as a fissure or faultline in good, since the good could, by definition, harbour no such flaw, but is more to be looked for in the act of refusing the good. 'For when the will abandons what is above itself, and turns to what is lower, it becomes evil – not because that is evil to which it turns, but because the turning itself is wicked' (XII: 6). Still, what one would be turning towards is precisely nothing, the void from which acts of malevolence issue. If evil is more an activity than a substance, it is in itself necessarily formless, a manifestation of incompleteness, an illimitable and random morphology that allies it to the principle of chaos. As Augustine was aware, this theodicy works perfectly well as an explanation for why human beings commit evil deeds, but less well when it comes to the perennial bugbear of all Christian theology, the existence of natural evils, the earthquakes and droughts and cancer. On this point, he is unable to offer anything more satisfying than the postulate of original sin, that initiatory deviation from the prescribed regulations, for which humanity is to be punished ad nauseam until the present world is overripe for abolition. A redemptive post-Calvary theology ought to have subjected the concept of original sin to its dialectical sublation, and at the very least reinterpreted the natural disasters as paradigms of perennial suffering, rather than let them stand in the shadow of original sin as the malfunctioning earth's own evidence that God scarcely minds now whether human beings sink to its own level or not.

The free will that humanity has been granted, and which, in the eyes of orthodox theology, it has never ceased misinterpreting, is what introduces the wayward element into the world. Strictly conceived, despite the imperatives of the Kantian moral law by which it should innately do what is expected of it in any given crisis, human freedom is what stains the otherwise orderly natural world with an admixture of the unpredictable. Even where people, like the malefactors of the Elizabethan theatre, are forsworn to destructive acts, there is still an evanescent possibility that they might not, if only through missing the chance rather than through unbidden attacks of conscience. The chance element, which mathematical chaos theory knows as the stochastic principle, is what throws the laws of ethics as much as of Newtonian physics out of kilter. Its very resistance to regulative iteration preserves the alienating note in a reality that was once nothing but an entire context of alterity, and explains why Kant has to found the postulates of the *Critique of Practical Reason* on the subjective self rather than on anything in external reality that might securely anchor them. The fact that history keeps undoing constituted morality is not so much the cause of ethical fragility as the evidence of it. As society has bound its clients within ever tighter nets of regulated consciousness, even while jubilating over its ideological progression towards individual freedom, it has trapped the liberated subject within an inescapable double bind. In Adorno's words, 'In the socialized society, no individual is capable of the morality that is a social demand but would be a reality only in a free society.'[7] It is precisely that freedom, though, that is to be feared for its very formlessness, according to a conventional bourgeois homiletic that is happy to celebrate the liberating moments in history – 'Bliss was it …' – before turning quickly to disparagement of the chaos in which they are held ultimately to result.

Where the present world itself is imaged as dominated by a chaotic strife from which only their extinction, or translation to the metaphysical realm beyond, will deliver its victims, chaos becomes the absolute evil to which men and women have been consigned. That same benighted existence that the Gnostics saw in the creation, still deprecated by Schopenhauer as the homeland of misery, was also means by which the darkest scepticism of the middle years of the last century – that of Antonin Artaud, Georges Bataille, Emil Cioran, Thomas Bernhard, the absurdist currents in existentialism – fulfilled Spengler's dictum that civilizations in decline resort to nihilistic habits of mind. The fractious ambivalence at the heart of nihilism, though, is that the *nihil* at which it snorts its contempt is also the only state that would resolve the present agony, which classical theology knew as the longing for restitution in a state of peace. Between the yearning for a better place and the Sophoclean intimation that it would have been better not to have been born to begin with, there is only a wafer-thin membrane, and it is with that in mind that Adorno points out the homology in Beckett's plays between redemption and a return to nothingness: 'The last absurdity is that the peacefulness of the void and the peacefulness of reconciliation cannot be distinguished from one another.'[8] In this vision, death is strictly a state of indifference, of undifferentiatedness, in which the distinction between heaven and hell evaporates. If the former reflects 'the messianic state in which everything would be in its right place', the latter is the state of absolute heteronomy, 'the hell in which time is completely confined within space, in which absolutely nothing changes any more'.[9] A reconciled state would require the abolition of temporality, not its confinement, and would be incompatible with megalithic invariance, but the world has become such a catastrophe that only the total annihilation towards which it seems, to the desperate satisfaction of Hamm and Clov in *Endgame* (1957), to be heading, is left as an image of deliverance. Hamm's dialectical correction of Clov's observation that there are so many terrible things – the external evidence seen through the telescope at the window each day is that there are in fact progressively fewer – is the belated form of hope. Beckett's world is the final habitat of a race for whom there remains little but the undecidability of whether the creation, the precipitation of differences from homogeneous emptiness, put paid to chaos once and for all or recklessly initiated it.

The perception of disorder as evil is ultimately and obviously totalitarian, in that it assumes that there is, or ought to be, in the world as it is a putative state of harmonious regulation, to which all give their consent, perhaps freely, in some unimaginable state of pure purposeful uniformity, or – more likely – as a matter of imposition. If a mature polity is to be conceived on the principle of consent, however, it must accept that outbreaks of dissent and disorder are not just inevitable, but capable of being fully metabolized within the social process. The conservative inflammation of such incidents is always predicated on the fallacy that any disorder at all betokens the complete breakdown of order, and must therefore be suppressed ruthlessly and urgently. There is no such thing as a society endowed with untroubled civil stability and certitude, even where most subjects accept the disposition of political and ethical authority within it. The system may generate its own friction through the enactment of unjust and unworkable legislation, or it may accommodate popular antipathy towards an existent state of affairs and thereby ameliorate widespread dissatisfaction, but either way, the idea of ordered acquiescence is inadequate or irrelevant, and the disorder that has disturbed it is not maligned. There is nothing to recommend the notion that all civil order should be stable and uncontested, because no such order is a paragon of justice. Moreover, this is not even a particularly radical argument, but one that could emerge from the tradition of liberal political ethics:

> Although an order would come *closest* to being absolutely stable where all subjects yielded unconditional obedience, we can also see that such a form of obedience would be completely irrational and could not fairly be demanded: for rulers, being like other men, commit their share of errors and excesses too, and these often require to be disobeyed and opposed.[10]

In this respect, the elevation of order to a perfect social good is as misconceived as the recommendation that all societies should live in peace. Peace may be axiomatically preferable to war, but not at any price. And so with order, the demand for it, which it is assumed is what everybody wants, is nearly always made in support of a particular kind of order, which is to say, one in which people know their place, accept inequities of opportunity and access to services, and do not question the means by which those in power attain their positions, among many other such assumptions. If order is always better than disorder, human beings are sooner or later expected to turn a blind eye to whatever strategies are deployed to ensure its maintenance, and its restoration after outbreaks of unrest. The tide of historical evidence is that people do not always prefer order to disorder, and the insistence on it is nearly always undiluted ideology. As the political theorist Preston King expressed it:

> Since order cannot be achieved *per se*, it is pointless to demand it as such. Since order cannot be established in any total sense it is important to recognise that the demand for it is always implicitly a demand for some specific kind of social arrangement, for some limited species of order.[11]

As so often, Auschwitz, a meticulously planned and minutely ordered death factory, stands as the grim paradigm of where unexamined ideology leads.

King's word, for all that its meditation on authoritarianism grew from the chastened soil of the generation that had taken the testimony of Nuremberg to heart, is hardly the dew-fresh reflection of post-war liberality alone. It precisely echoes thoughts that had been in currency since the European Enlightenment tradition, which had proved so frail in the face of the systematic barbarity of totally administered malevolence. Enlarging on his earlier *Treatise of Human Nature* in the intellectual crucible of Edinburgh in the 1740s, David Hume too wrote that society ought have nothing to fear from critical disturbance of its certitudes:

> The character[istic]s which engage our approbation are chiefly such as contribute to the peace and security of human society; as the characters which excite blame are chiefly such as tend to public detriment and disturbance: Whence it may reasonably be

presumed, that the moral sentiments arise, either mediately or immediately, from a reflection of these opposite interests. What though [if] philosophical meditations establish a different opinion or conjecture; that everything is right with regard to the WHOLE, and that the qualities, which disturb society, are, in the main, as beneficial, and are as suitable to the primary intention of nature as those which more directly promote its happiness and welfare?[12]

If it subsides into placid acquiescence, the civil polity will quickly connive at every piece of injustice, every misapplied moral stricture and aggravated law that tends to corrupt it. It positively relies for its well-being as much on percipient dissidence as it does on sound administration, and what destabilizes it ought to be seen as equally apposite to 'the primary intention of nature' as what reinforces its constitutional solidity. Whether the intentions of nature have anything more to do with human social purposes at this late stage may be as moot a point as whether nature has teleological intentions at all, but Hume's liberal political vision, in implicitly harking back to deliberative traditions such as those that underlay the democratized Greek polis after Cleisthenes, also projects forward a proto-Hegelian dialectical schema in which the intermittent disturbance of harmony guarantees harmony.

If order can be quite as much the force for malignity as which chaos is normally figured, a countervailing intuition should illuminate the ways in which disorder can be positively benign. Any such investigation ought to begin by counterbalancing the equation under which order emerges from the resolution of chaos with the insight that a return to disorder can seem to be sweet relief after subjection to a regime of regularity. The yearning for spontaneity, unpredictability, the unforeseeable, calcified into a cultural ideology between the decadence of the Victorian fin-de-siècle and the transvaluation of all values that the decade of the 1920s ushered in as its counterblast to war and privation. If there were to be an escape from the regimented life, and indeed of regimented death, it seemed to lie in the refusal of heteronomous social strictures, the defiance of manners and decorum, a contempt for the ideal of just proportion with regard to appetites of every kind – for food and drink, liberated sex, and a pharmacopoeia of exotic intoxicants. These last, in particular, offered exaggerated sensual experiences that proved waywardly irregular in their effects, all the way to the squalid comedowns and long-term ruination of health that invested them with the coveted element of risk. Cocaine, especially, which sustained under-occupied party animals, the spare scions of heritable fortunes, the personnel of the nascent film industry, and anybody with a substantial capacity for pick-me-up soda-pops (Coca-Cola was not by a long chalk the only proprietary tonic drink to contain the alkaloid of coca in its early days), by prompting a rush-release of dopamine, had a potentiating impact on its users and the social occasions in which they took it. Its spangling effect on consciousness, underpinned by the jittering muscular response and gasping respiration that went with it, hard to reconstruct from the etiolated street coke of the present day, created a sense of expectation, of extravagant possibility, that it was implicitly daring its user to fulfil. If a little alcohol relaxed its consumers, a little cocaine exercised an incomparably more dramatic imperative. There was, and to some extent still is, a deeper moral valence to the use of intoxicants, whether legitimate or proscribed, which consists in the fact that the heterogeneous psychotropic effects they command are nothing to do with anybody else. Intoxication, while it generates many secondary social effects among groups of users, is not in itself dependent on interaction with others. This is not to reiterate the dull homiletic observation that all drug-taking is a solipsistic self-indulgence, only to note the relative autonomy of altered states in comparison to most other mental and emotional sensitivity. The moods intoxicants create are nobody else's responsibility, and nor are they wholly the responsibility of the user, despite the recurrent impulse people have to find culpability in even the most unpromising contexts: 'You have only yourself to blame'.

The evil that is perceived to lurk in the liberation from regularity is predicated on its apparent licence of any and all moral enormities, the very sentiment encapsulated in the apocryphal adage generally attributed to Chesterton, that when people cease to believe in God, they don't believe in nothing, but believe in anything. Believing in anything at all has indeed taken on pestilential dimensions in the era of New Age spiritualism and the kinds of arcana the internet has made more plentifully available than when they were confined to tiny publishers and small meetings in hired halls. The defiance of social strictures often took precisely those forms – the British sculptor Eric Gill raping his daughters, his sisters and his dog – that reminded the horrified cultural onlooker why the strictures came into being in the first place, while the refusal of decorum propagated as much boorish egoism as it did unpresumptuous liberty. The turn of the twentieth century brought with it the sensualist desideratum of 'living life to the full', which connoted as a minimal requirement not doing, or at least not invariably doing, what was expected of one. For women especially, bound to the home as part of the marital and parental compact, living life to the full might involve scarcely anything more daring than taking up a legitimate opportunity rather than dutifully turning it down, but for men who saw themselves as free spirits, at every level of aspirational dignity from Nietzschean *Ubermensch* to slippery chancer, a certain measure of experimental delinquency was key to the stance. When that surrender to disorder in turn resulted in the greatest unhappiness, rippling out from the doer to the dismayed ranks of his loved ones, its malignity lay exposed. Not for nothing was the straight path also narrow. In fact, it was nothing but narrow, the gate it led to, in the Authorized Version of the Sermon on the Mount, being also 'strait' (Matt 7:14).

Where a disordered liberty follows the release from routine, its reputation might already have been ruined by its alleged synonymy with destitution of life's chances, the freedom to do without. In the era of globalization, of the free movement of capital across the borders of nation-states that are porous when it comes to financial resources but entirely impermeable to impoverished people, there is all too little structure in the lives of the least favoured. Unable to rely on the guarantee of work from one year to the next, or from one week to the next, in a labour market of relentless outsourcing and zero-hours contracts, with social services and welfare provision increasingly precarious even in the advanced economies, the freedom from obligation resembles the freedom of the open road for the vagrant. A parody of freedom thereby gives all liberty a bad name, since it becomes something to be avoided at all costs. Between the kind of employment that occupies the lion's share of a worker's waking hours, both within the workplace and outside it, which leaves little or no time to enjoy what remuneration it offers, and the unrolling empty time of unemployment without the material resources to fill it, there is only the thinnest of borders. Earning the right to freedom means giving up freedom until one is neither fit for it, nor has the slightest idea what to do with it. Now that state pension systems are pressed to the limits of their munificence, the imperative to go on working for longer before one can draw on them will help ensure that more people than ever are physically unfit to make the most of their dwindling retirement when it does belatedly arrive.

What became known as the negative definition of freedom – which relied on an abstract conception of depredations and deficiencies that it was constituted as the freedom from – has likewise marked the experience of those moments in which the subject is liberated weightlessly from the structure of obligation. Adorno remarks in his essay on free time that it cannot be properly free when it is still defined by the unfree time from which it is the respite. It 'refers to a specific difference, that of unfree time, time occupied by labour and ... time that is determined heteronomously'. Thereby is many a bank holiday ruined by people comforting themselves with the luxury of not having to spend today at the office to which they will have to return tomorrow. 'Unfreedom is expanding within free time,' Adorno writes, 'and most of the unfree people are as unconscious of the process as they are of their own unfreedom.'[13] This is why the notion we have proposed of a creative disorder as being the liberation from the straitjacket of an oppressive order will not suffice as anything more than the most modest preliminary to the disorder of true liberty. As long as it is nothing more than the cessation of external imposition, it remains tied to such imposition, indeed is functionally inconceivable without it. In this sense, what we are calling liberty is precisely as bivalent a concept as chaos itself – as both vacancy and plenitude – has been. Freedom is at once the blank page, the meandering path, the empty horizon, and a condition of existence that is brimful of divergent elements, as much a state of potential as it is an ontological actuality. If it is to be realized, it must also keep returning to a state of potentiality in which new things can happen. It makes possible a self-revolutionizing that is more than the desperate extemporization that globalized precariousness demands of its vassals, in which every month or two of relative stability is to be pitifully embraced, but is instead a continuous project of self-realization, of uncovering aspects of the self that did not exist until one started prospecting for them, in congress or in solitude. If anything but smoothly automated regularity, the click of the metronome that measures life out in precisely calibrated segments, is to be dreaded as evil, people are being cheated of the first requirement of a full life, a life that would be too full indeed to squeeze its every last event into an allotted place.

5

Hilarity

As long as it isn't happening to us, chaos as a spectator sport, and as the undergirding of an ancient comic tradition from Aristophanes to sitcoms, is supremely funny. The seed of comedy may be the incongruous, the failure of the external world to conform to the expectations an individual may have of it, or indeed to its own measurable laws and principles, but it takes on tenor of true hilarity when such failures ramify into the total breakdown of order. Comic plots in which the events become increasingly entangled in misunderstandings, accidental collisions and polymorphously destructive consequences, are reliable provocations to paroxysmic laughter, the more so in that they confound the dignified intentions of a character we have been given licence to despise. The punctured self-esteem of the righteous, the pratfalls of the bombastic, are the worn but still valuable coinage of comic drama, which would not be comic if such characters were not either shamefacedly reformed under duress, or else vanquished altogether by circumstance, on behalf of those whom they would seek to tyrannize – the suffering poor, humble believers, abused servants, thwarted lovers.

At the least dignified level of comic entertainments, in the Rabelaisian inversions of carnival and the slapstick of the circus, chaos needs no narrative frame. Rather like sexual activity in pornography, it is sufficient unto itself. All that is required is that somebody trips and falls headlong into a tray of whitewash, or that some mechanical item blows up in their face or falls to bits at a touch, and an audience is exhilarated – the more so if, unlike its hapless victim, they can see the catastrophe coming. So ingrained is this response that it very often carries over into everyday life, so that people's first reaction to something falling out of a cupboard and hitting somebody on the head, or seeing them topple over on an unnoticed patch of ice, is the apparent heartlessness of laughter. A belated expression of concern then takes on the extra dimension of contrition, perhaps accompanied by the gratuitous admonition to others that 'it isn't funny'. It isn't, of course, and yet it resonates with such a strong echo of fictional comic calamity, that it is. All drama depends on inversion of the existent, but if tragedy inverts the world through one individual's acting against the precepts of divinity, comedy seems to show that the world is all too ready to stand on its head all by itself, and thereby act against humanity. The lighter side of malevolence is cast in comedy's magical investment of the inanimate with intentionality. It is as though the roller-skate knows that somebody who will not see it is sure to come downstairs. Even in extremity, especially in extremity, things resist human volition with something like their own rebellious animus and, when misfortunes concatenate, seem to prove the paranoid hypothesis that the object world is in conspiracy to frustrate human purposes. When his fiancée's suitcase bursts open during their dead-of-night elopement in *Our Wife* (1931), Oliver Hardy is thrown into a panic as the alarm-clock in it starts ringing. In futile desperation, he tries muffling it by putting it under his top-hat, and when that fails, hurls it into the dark, where it naturally finds a glasshouse window to smash through. If *Othello* had been a comic tale, the handkerchief wouldn't have needed to be stolen, but would have just turned up in the wrong place anyway.

An essential aspect of much chaotic comedy is that the person to whom the calamities are happening should try to act as though they are not, in the vain hope that if they appear not to notice the torn-off trousers or the top-to-toe splattering of mud, then nobody else will. The insistence on dignity where it is most in ruins is an indispensable comic element of its loss. If the victim perceives his own degradation, the humour can feel too sadistic, as at the closing nemesis of Ben Jonson's *Epicoene, or the Silent Woman* (1609), when the noise-hating misanthrope Morose is reduced to his own humiliated silence by the nephew, Sir Dauphine Eugenie, who has plotted his downfall for disinheriting him. Morose has been tricked into wedding a comely and delightfully reticent young girl, who is no sooner married to him than she turns into a clamorous scold. The ruse is that she is a boy in disguise, so that when the inheritance has been extorted out of him again, the miserable old Uncle can be released from a marriage that never was in the first place. Sir Dauphine plays the moment of triumph with an obscene Sadean relish that seems designed to turn the innocent merriment to cruelty. 'I'll not trouble you, till you trouble me with your funeral, which I care not how soon it come' (V:i). The play is liberally invested with the Jacobean vision of the world as a purgatory in which almost everybody is corrupted, the whole plot having been motivated after all by nothing but pecuniary gain. In this profound ambivalence, the theatre of what might be called revenge comedy exhibited a finely tuned understanding of the mechanics of retribution and comeuppance that would begin to drain away from the moral complexion of the English theatre after the Restoration. What twentieth-century film slapstick was left with was the simple monochrome of pretension punctured and virtue salvaged. Nobody need feel guilty for laughing at the destruction of the blustering colonel, the sanctimonious vicar, the dehydrated moralist, the legions whose own backgrounds of deprivation and oppression have turned them into criminal thugs and bullies.

The lineaments of comedy derive, in any case, from the ritualistic practice of disordered revelry, which had their origin in the orgiastic celebration of the rites of Dionysus. These demanded nothing less than intoxicated abandon, with no half-measures, the consequences of a censorious approach to which are depicted with hideous graphic cruelty in Euripides' late play *The Bacchae*. There is laughter in the worship of the god who brings the gift of wine and transfigured consciousness, but there is also a licensed uproar that snaps the bindings of everyday decorum. Commenting on the chaotic dimension of the ritual, Ingvild Gilhus explains that 'the laughter of Dionysus points to a dimension beyond normal human thought and experience. It is a laughter that is disruptive and unpredictable'. The laughter of the gods, where it is represented in both rituals and natural occurrences, far from being a reassurance that their purposes are benign, is destabilizing in its ambiguity. Like much human laughter for that matter, it is poised uncertainly between the warmth of innocent glee and cold derision. Gilhus writes that 'common to all its expressions is the laughter's unexpected and ominous nature. This divine laughter made humans tremble with fear, both repelling them and fascinating them at the same time'. The result was that the laughter of drunkenness during the Dionysia, the obscene phallic songs that the revellers sang, which Aristotle identifies in the *Poetics* as the origin of comic drama, took on a particularly hysterical quality, a recklessness that prompted certain civic authorities from time to time to try to curtail the more riotous manifestations of it, the terrible error that Euripides' King Pentheus makes. Laughter, rowdy amusement, unbridled hilarity, was at once a vulgar human response in imitation of the inscrutable habits of the gods, but also a portal into subterranean levels of being that for the most part lay concealed. 'Strange and inexplicable, it opened up a channel into the chaotic dimensions of being,' says Gilhus.[1]

Inebriated laughter was also the principal impetus of the *komos* into which the classical Greek drinking party, the symposium, disintegrated. In the theatre, it became *komoidia*, the Aristophanic or Old Comedy that was an integral part of the Dionysian festival in the sixth century BC, and whose terminology identifies it as a 'revel-song'. The revel itself probably originated in the previous century, a gentrified social descendant of the riotous feasts of triumphant homecoming warriors, a ritual of maximalized male bonding and of cathartic release. Many ancient cultures retained such practices in more or less sanctioned form, occasions in which energetic conviviality was encouraged to proceed towards what the classicist Oswyn Murray calls 'a ritual of licensed chaos'.[2] The celebration is only complete when it has overflowed its bounds. To this degree, the Greek symposium that flourished during the ascendancy of the aristocratic Athenian polity opened with a solemn prescription of measure – how much was to be drunk, in what proportions of wine and water, the length of the speeches, and so forth. As the evening progressed, and the guests became openly inebriated, as lascivious with the brutally objectified naked serving-boys as they were with their own erotic favourites, the rules were gradually abandoned until they collapsed altogether. Pleasure is hardly more intense than when it is sensible of itself as transgressive, whether the strictures it is violating are external or self-imposed. Even so, its licentiousness did not stop there. Inasmuch as it was an aristocratic practice carried on within a private household, it was so far invisible to the society at large, and so the concluding affray created by its spilling out on to the streets in the dead of night or, better still, in the first light of dawn was the public face of its challenge to plebeian decorum. As

Murray expresses it, 'The *komos*, the drunken revel through the streets which terminated the *symposion*, was an essential element in the sympotic lifestyle, and a necessary corollary as a public display of aristocratic self-definition.'[3] Its activities typically included physical rough-housing with passers-by, the vandalizing of public amenities and deliberate damage to private houses, in addition to the gratuitous disturbance caused by drunken singing and yelling in the streets. There was nothing innocent about such behaviour. It was staged as a contemptuous display of bravado by the privileged to a community that owed at least its deference, and in many cases its unquestioning servility, to them. As such, it was the aspect most likely to provoke proscriptive legislation by the city authorities, measures that in turn lent an authentic cast to the pseudo-subversive nature of the *komos*.

Elaborated into a theatrical form, then, comedy is a cultural sublimation of a ritual of calculated social delinquency. There is nothing innocent or contingent about the entertainment it offers, which is primarily admonitory in intent. Indeed, the satirical lyric is most likely its earliest cultural form, as is suggested by Aristotle in the *Poetics*, and by his Arabic interpreters Ibn Sina (Avicenna) and Ibn Rushd (Averroes) in the eleventh and twelfth centuries. The comic work anatomized the ugly and the preposterous in society, people and their deeds, and was as such in its own way as weighty as the thematic matter of tragic drama. It may have been that the laughter of theatrical audiences was, in its earliest occurrence, furtive, the guilty demeanour of those who, while appalled at the venality on display, could not quite suppress a snigger of disdain at it. It can be amusing to see to what lengths the heartless and the pretentious will go, apparently untroubled by self-awareness, in their determination to order a recalcitrant world as they see fit. Eventually, it is the very recalcitrance that provokes the most unabashed hilarity, and a laughing audience is as vocally demonstrative of its appreciation as the groaning and crying of the spectators of tragedies once were. By the time of the classical Roman comedy, the idiom of Plautus and Terence, laughter was an integral element of the dramatic effect, produced by arch verbal jests and wit as much as by physical absurdity and the social inversion of shrewd slaves gaining the upper hand over their arbitrarily oppressive masters. Its final dilution could be measured in the tradition that has any story with a happy ending, typically one that concludes with the joining of two lovers, termed a comedy, as in Dante. Only with the revolutionary development of European theatre in the late nineteenth century did the term start to be dialectically questioned again. Chekhov calls *The Seagull* (1896) a comedy, a seemingly counter-intuitive classification for a work that depicts the disintegration of a well-to-do artistic family through existential discontent, unrequited passion and mental disturbance, all the way to the young playwright Konstantin Gavrilovich's offstage suicide at the end. Western theatre directors used to emphasizing the agonized pre-Revolutionary tension in Chekhov's scenes, the excruciated sense of their own supererogatory privilege among the Tsarist haute bourgeoisie, are hard put to it to see the criteria under which a play like *The Seagull* might fit its author's description. It is, to be sure, glancingly satirical of artistic pretension, but its themes are scarcely light-hearted and its denouement an unalloyed calamity. Penetrate deeper into the textures of the sterile confrontations among its principal characters, though, and into their objective lack of self-perception, their frustrated purposes and futile efforts, and the play's proper tonal status comes more brilliantly into focus. Its second act in particular, in which the family and friends simmer and bicker among themselves on a hot empty afternoon on Madame Arkadina's country estate, if resourcefully directed, is helplessly funny, composed as it is of sudden vituperative losses of temper, irate expressions of the famous boredom that Chekhov's characters wear like the hair-shirts of medieval penitents, and Konstantin's portentous symbolic gesture with the titular dead bird, which he has personally shot as a love-token for his repulsed beloved, Nina.

While the comic drama presented an objectified spectacle of hilarious disorder for passive audiences, nothing was quite as satisfying, as the young Greek nobles knew, as participating in anarchic behaviour oneself. Even where it was officially permitted on certain days in the religious calendar and could be indulged with impunity, so that it was not technically transgressive at all, it was a wildly popular form of recreation. Terry Castle's study of the masquerade tradition in English culture in the eighteenth century notes that, while one can be dubious as to exactly how potent the residual folk memory of medieval carnival practices such as the revels of Twelfth Night, Shrove Tuesday, May Day, Midsummer Night and Halloween continued to be in a rapidly urbanizing and industrializing society, in which the rural communities were in wholesale flight to the towns, nonetheless the comic capers of the masquerade remained an enduring form of social entertainment. Concealed behind a mask and perhaps a costume too, one could cheek one's superiors, overstep the bounds of sexual decorum and generally act the goat, as did the ancients in the guise of satyrs. In their disguises in the streets, nobody knows who anybody is, and people are free to conduct themselves against the grain of their outward personas. At a London revel of January 1724, a cardinal and a milkmaid seen strolling amorously arm in arm were in reality two cross-dressers, the former 'a pretty young Woman of good Friends', the latter 'one of the greatest Coxcombs about Town'. As Castle comments, these personal performances were not, in the spirit of Mikhail Bakhtin's Rabelaisian theory of Carnival inversion, a question of satirically pointing the way to the correct dispensation by enacting its antic *bouleversement*, but of shining an unforgiving lamp in the age of Enlightenment on the follies of the present age:

The typical masquerade epiphany is an unremitting parody of true spiritual insight. It reveals not the eternal and ineluctable rightness of things, and their perfected relation to one another, but a staggering, endlessly magnifying wrongness, the catastrophic disruption of meaningful relationship.[4]

Turning things upside down could be, and very often was, the most demonstrative means of showing that their officially prescribed order was at least an arbitrary imposition, and at worst the concretion of untruth. What has troubled cultural analysis of the phenomenon of rituals of inversion, however, down to the current epoch, is whether this is ultimately a socially affirmative or a subversive mechanism. Viewed from one angle, it was perfectly true that, as Castle argues, 'rituals of inversion can demonstrate the fictionality of classification systems',[5] and she cites the anthropologist Mary Douglas to the effect that when members of a social collective 'turn round and confront the categories on which their whole surrounding culture has been built up ... [they can] recognise them for the fictive, man-made, arbitrary creations that they are.[6] If its assailing of social hierarchy exposed the constructed nature of class divisions, then in classic Marxist terms, it pierced the veil of ideology to reveal the false consciousness that underlay such divisions and determined the social production of experience. It is at least as arguable, however, that, unlike true insurrection, such rituals acted as safety-valves by allowing the populace to express their contempt in pantomime motley before knuckling down once more after the revels were ended to the undisturbed apparatus of stratification. If a critical popular consciousness emerges from such festive exercises, nobody does anything particularly productive with it. Castle is candid enough to note this functional indeterminacy in the masquerade – 'to what extent its revelatory chaos disrupted actual social structures is ambiguous'[7] – before tending towards an advocacy of their subversive dynamics.

The question is probably best adjudicated by the historical development of inversion rituals over the centuries. Although there was frequently a mordant Swiftian wit to the English masquerades, they did not often extend to the outright delirium of the anarchic behaviour at the European Carnival of the sixteenth and seventeenth centuries or the chaotic inebriation of the late medieval English church ales or, even earlier, of the festivals of disorder in honour of Dionysus or Bacchus in the classical eras. The celebrated account by Le Roy Ladurie of the popular uprising in the French village of Romans in the Dauphiné in 1580 makes the case for the genuinely insurrectionary potential of rituals of misrule.[8] Such events as these led sometimes to measures of suppression, as at Romans, the notable example from antiquity being the Roman Senate's interdiction of the celebration of the Bacchanalia in 186 BC. The English masquerade, by contrast, was not brought to an end by official proscription, but because it passed out of fashion, which is to say that, as Castle shows, it migrated into such residual flummery as annual pageants and processions, and privatized forms of vapidly unruly, or more or less ruly, entertainment such as fancy-dress parties, Halloween trick-or-treating, firework nights, revivals of folk dancing, the snarling rivalry of opposing contingents in sports crowds, the Friday night piss-up – the variegated repertoire, in other words, of what Castle terms 'a mere holiday mood'.[9] Licensed disorder is an oxymoron either waiting to explode into the real thing, or else ready, where official sanction allows and enjoys it, to wither into the bygone, if much memorialized, aspect of cultural history that it has become.

Theories of the subversive nature of carnival have tended to be predicated on the shallow presumption that all insurrection is progressive or emancipating in its social attitudes and effects. It was not just magistrates and bishops whom revellers had in their sights, however. Outsiders who were thought to threaten the cultural balance of the community, such as Jews and suspected homosexuals, regularly found themselves the targets of much of the most vicious festive opprobrium. For the few days of the carnival period, villagers could be as openly hostile to such marginalized people as Christian decorum normally prohibited to them. As Paul Crawford notes, 'the history of post-Christian carnivalesque rituals has often been the history of anti-Semitism, played out with varying levels of aggression', invoking the tradition of pelting Jewish neighbours with stones and garbage that regularly took place at Romans.[10] Communal bonds are most effectively cemented through opposition to a perceived enemy, but the enemy need not actually represent any material threat to it to be so constituted. 'Carnival licenses transgression in the form of cross-dressing, topsy-turveydom, inversion and so on,' writes Scott Wilson; 'however, the carnivalesque suspension of social hierarchy and the law also unleashes very unpleasant forms of violence, lynchings, queer-bashing and so on, forms of transgressive "enjoyment" that bond one sort of racist or homophobic community.'[11] The difference in the two varieties of inversive practices is that some of them were directed against institutional power – the nobility, the clergy, the courts, even the strictures of familial authority – while the less prepossessing involved the targeting of those without power, but who were held in violent scorn by normative social ethics. With culpable selectivity, many polemicists and postmodernist theorists have failed to detect this distinction, instead celebrating all manifestations of disruptive popular will as liberating. Nobody flinging clods of mud and worse at passing Jews was challenging ideological hegemony, only rancorously reinforcing it, a point caught by the historian William Miller:

> For the Jews murdered during carnival, the women raped, the animals set on fire and tormented it would have been small solace

that late twentieth-century scholars would find cause for admiring such 'authentic rites', 'sites of resistance', or 'counter-hegemonic practices'.[12]

In any case, the mere fact of its being permitted, and then progressively domesticated over the centuries, particularly when it overstepped its limits, neutralizes the memory of the hostility that once energized popular revelry. If enjoyment itself, the ludic temper in the face of official solemnity, including the use of proscribed intoxicants and the refusal to work, was often the last plank of defiance of monitory authority, it was also the first point of purchase that authority had in licensing a sanitized version of the carnival mood. 'There is no slander in an allowed fool,' says Shakespeare's Olivia, 'though he do nothing but rail' (*Twelfth Night*, I:v).

The chaos in comic drama answers a need in its audiences to see the structures of society broken down, not merely the prospect of villains receiving their just deserts. When systems are stretched to the point of collapse, or at the very least to the point of contradicting themselves, in circumstances in which such rupture has a gleeful effect rather than an ominous one, the comic scenario can be as exploratory in its social hypothesizing as the blood-laced events of the tragic world. The tendency of classical comedy, as well as that of the early modern English and French theatre, was for the plots to be imbued with moral force, so that their unsavoury characters had learned ethical lessons by the end, while the sundered lovers had been reunited, or the forbidden marriage reaffirmed. To this degree, the chaos of the play's action was always resolved at the denouement. Disorder and confusion are exquisitely amusing to the audience not least because they are the wrong state of affairs, an elaboration of incongruity, the temporary defeat of logic and better judgement, and the clear implication is that they must be set right when a happy restitution is finally parcelled out. It is in this precise sense that, far from being naturally subversive, comedy is a more conservative form than tragedy. It is the events of tragedy that topple kings and overthrow tyrants, force patriarchs to realize that their time-hallowed wisdoms are nothing of the sort, destroy the ethical presumptions on which amatory and kinship relations are founded. In comedy, the fifth act sees everything returned to normal, a sigh of relief released as tears of laughter are dabbed away. As Terry Eagleton puts it:

> The audience is never in any doubt that the order so delightfully disrupted will be restored, perhaps even reinforced by this fleeting attempt to flout it, and thus can blend its anarchic pleasures with a degree of conservative self-satisfaction. As in Ben Jonson's *The Alchemist*, Jane Austen's *Mansfield Park* or Dr Seuss's *The Cat in the Hat*, we can wreak some gloriously irresponsible havoc while the parental figure is absent, but would be devastated to learn that he or she might never return.[13]

On the stage and in the cinema, the hilarity provoked by a descent into pandemonium, rendered all the more toothsome by the prospect of authority figures trying and failing to reverse or contain it, acquires a collaborative tenor through the phenomenon of shared exhilarant laughter. If the sound made by laughing is strictly anti-semantic, a wordless cackling, tittering and roaring that seems to return human emotional response to a purely animal, sublingual level, it can also sound in critically attuned ears like the bestial cruelty of rapacious crowds. It too, having been satiated by derision, needs to be stilled by the concluding restoration of order. So it sounded to Adorno, watching Charlie Chaplin's *Modern Times* (1936) at a London cinema in the year of its release, as he reported in a letter to Walter Benjamin: 'The laughter of a cinema audience ... is anything but salutary and revolutionary; it is full of the worst bourgeois sadism instead.' Stubbornly resisting the acclamation of Chaplin as one of the great subversive figures in the early cinema, he continues: 'The idea that a reactionary individual can be transformed into a member of the avant-garde through an intimate acquaintance with the films of Chaplin, strikes me as simple romanticization; for I cannot count Karacuer's favourite film director, even after *Modern Times*, as an avant-garde artist ... You need only have heard the laughter of the audience at the screening of this film to realise what is going on.'[14] When one recalls that the plot of the film involves a hapless ingenu being employed on an automated factory assembly line, which he unintentionally throws into chaos through his incompetence, this may seem a surprising verdict. Although the film clearly satirizes the degree to which humanity has become even more subservient to technology in the modern machine age than it already was in the days of the handlooms and cotton gins, however, Chaplin's Worker is no rebellious Luddite, only a puzzled innocent in a complex world of dehumanization, which everybody else prides themselves on having mastered. Every potentially defiant action of his is a mistake. He is not the communist agitator he is mistaken for on arrest after his release from hospital. He does not knowingly take cocaine in jail, only accidentally, and when, having swallowed it, he is catapulted into a slapstick state of feverish delirium, the performance plays up to the most lurid of bourgeois fears about intoxicants. When re-employed in a factory later in the film, he heroically rescues the boss from a near-fatal industrial accident, and while his fellow workers organize a strike, he only gets himself arrested when accidentally causing a brick to hit a policeman. Nothing about these events was designed to recruit the film's audience to the leftist orientation in the deeply polarized politics of the 1930s. Had Chaplin not been banned in the Nazi state on the misconceived suspicion that he was Jewish, little about the plot of *Modern Times* would have caused audiences in the Reich any ideological unease.

A deductive theoretical move, expounded with meticulous historical depth by Bakhtin, insists that because the humorous temperament, light-heartedness and merriment, came to be subdivided into gentrified and vulgar forms as between wit and ribaldry, and then banished altogether from the purview of theology, social relations and elite behaviour, its subterranean survival in carnival traditions, popular jokes and pranks, and the sardonic amusement with which misanthropes viewed the world, was constitutively subversive. Certainly, as a response to the grim asseverations of early theologians such as John Chrysostom, who preached that jesting and laughter were the devil's work, it would have seemed an obstreperous popular corrective worth cultivating, where it did not earn one the savage reprisal of ecclesiastical disfavour. 'The very contents of medieval ideology,' Bakhtin reports, '– asceticism, sombre providentialism, sin, atonement, suffering, as well as the character of the feudal regime, with its oppression and intimidation – all these elements determined this tone of icy petrified seriousness. It was supposedly the only tone fit to express the true, the good, and all that was essential and meaningful.'[15] These aspects of life can only be preserved and sanctified if subjected to the seemliness of good order, responsible self-husbandry, the discipline that hilarity destabilizes. Joie-de-vivre itself, however and wherever one managed to scrape it in an existence of drudgery, poverty and scantly rewarded toil, was the antithetical temperament to the pious urbanity enjoined on congregants, feudal tenants, domestic servants, wives and children, if not always on their social superiors. The dialectic at play, however, which is often elided by Bakhtin's broad brush, as by theorists of humour to the present day, is that between merriment as an oppositional stance towards external power and as simple disregard of it. Use of intoxicants is once again the paradigm here. Drinking during Prohibition, or taking MDMA today, may be at once an act of defiance, in that it involves breaking the law, and also a strategy pursued in itself for its power to bracket out the habitual daily routine, a mood in which the user scarcely cares what anybody else thinks of it. Too much ideological weight is loaded on to laughter, as also on to drug-taking, when it is framed as being somehow inherently dissident. In any case, the twin social theories of carnival laughter – subversion and catharsis – cannot both be true, since the one would corrode the basis of society while the other reinforced it. As Eagleton frames it, 'Carnival may be a fictionalized form of insurrection, but it also provides a safety-valve for such subversive energies. In this sense, its closest parallel today is professional sport, the abolition of which would no doubt be the shortest route to bloody revolution.'[16] If this latter point were demonstrable, however, it would only establish the analogy of sport with the safely cathartic aspect of carnival, hardly with its alleged subversion, which, as Eagleton concedes, is anyway 'fictionalized', which is to say it is both enacted as fiction and invested in itself with only fictive status as an agent of insurrection.

That laughter is not in itself the best condition for a tactical assault on power is, on the face of it, blindingly obvious. A rule-bound order can only finally be opposed by an antithetical disposition subject to its own imperatives of self-definition. Summarizing the strategic implications of the politics of humour for the possibility of a better disposition of society, Eagleton reflects:

The helpless, uncoordinated body is hardly in a state to construct that social order. In this sense, comedy represents no threat to a sovereign power. Indeed, such powers have a vested interest in the good humour of the populace. A dispirited nation may prove to be a disaffected one.[17]

Helplessness is the key attribute here. To be amused is always to be reactive, to be – willingly enough, most of the time – at the mercy of whoever, or whatever, is doing the amusing. Laughter is as psychically therapeutic as it is because it absolves the chortler for a moment of responsibility, which is precisely why it cannot also be an agent of revolutionary change, a point made by Alenka Zupančič when she states that comedy 'sustains the very oppression of the given order or situation, because it makes it bearable and induces the illusion of an effective interior freedom'.[18] There may be repressive polities intent even on policing interior freedom but, beyond the enforcement of global drug prohibition in the democratic states, most constitutional dispensations can live with it, would even indeed ideologically insist on it. Comedy, despite the self-deluding nature of many in the light entertainment industry, is one of the more useful tools to ensure it. Something like this sentiment, long before the Industrial Revolution had begun to conceive that light entertainment might be one of its staple commodities, was surely intended by Percy Shelley's reported remark to the effect that the regeneration of humanity would depend on laughter being put down.[19] Among the ancient wisdoms of the Apocrypha is the sentiment in Ecclesiasticus, 'A fool lifteth up his voice with laughter, but a wise man doth scarce smile a little' (21:20).

For comedy to be true to its own tendency of disrupting the given world, it is undoubtedly more satisfying when it deliberately fails to offer final resolution, but instead escalates the anarchic impetus of the plot until its narrative framing can no longer contain it. This procedure began to infiltrate British film comedy after the Second World War, the paragon of which is Frank Launder's *The Happiest Days of Your Life* (1950). Its plot unfolds from an administrative error in London that sees an all-girls' boarding school accidentally billeted on a boys' establishment, Nutbourne. The delicacy of having to find separate accommodation for both sets of pupils, as well as their respective teaching staffs, is soon compounded by the lack of space in which to conduct lessons, and finally by the simultaneous arrival of the parents of some of the girls and the board of male governors of another boys' school who have come to assess the boys' headmaster, Wetherby Pond (Alastair Sim), following his application for a transfer. A ramshackle rotation system is put in place to try to keep each set of visitors from seeing the other, or realizing exactly what is going on at Nutbourne. When the insistence of the girls' parents on seeing a lacrosse match runs into the provision of a rugby match for the governors, the entire deception collapses, and at that precise moment, a belated bureaucrat from the Education Ministry arrives to announce that yet another school, a co-educational one, is to be drafted in to replace the girls' school, whereupon another convoy of racketing schoolchildren draws up, a week early. In the closing dialogue, the two previously antagonistic head teachers, Pond and Muriel Whitchurch (Margaret Rutherford) are seen making discreet plans, amid the erupting bedlam, to leave the country for the good of their careers. A conventional comic ending could have had the visiting parents and governors triumphant in their condemnation of the head-teachers and the bureaucrats, as they re-establish the discipline among the rampant pupils that those nominally in charge of them had failed to instil. Common sense would prevail where hapless subterfuge and floundering improvisation had fallen short. Above all, the rioting children would be quelled by a restoration of due authority. The film, co-written by Launder with the author of the original stage play, John Dighton, refuses any such resolution. An anarchy beyond hope of any pacification has broken out by the end, putting to flight the entire framework of pedagogical protocols, bureaucratic oversight, moral delicacy and English politeness on which Nutbourne and its cognate real-life institutions rested. Zupančič makes the point that the conclusion of traditional comic plots is often disappointing, precisely in that it brings the comic business itself to an end, but in Launder and Dighton's screenplay, and in the cycle of St Trinian's films that followed it in the 1950s, the ending represents the full bloom of a raging chaotic utopia. The small boy who blows a toy trumpet into his headmaster's face in the closing cameo, as though blowing down the walls of Jericho, provoking Sim's characteristic haunted shudder, carries the hopes of all small children that, one day, the genteel regime of enforced rote learning, physical jerks, glutinous porridge, the punitive writing out of lines by the hundred, will pass. The British cinematic sub-genre of anarchic school comedy spoke to a country bankrupted and exhausted by its recent victory over fascism, portraying a world in which authoritarian rule can be defeated by mass subversion, but which yet retains the lineaments of an unmistakable decorum, and is still able to cast a backward glance at a pastoral life – beyond the slowly exploding school still lie the tranquil meadows and dusty lanes, the country railway halt bathed in eternal birdsong – that even world war has failed to shatter.

There is a functional as well as a tonal difference between the comedy of scorn that shows up the Other, the authority figure, for the risible failure that he or she is, and the more complex mechanism by which what is funny is not that failure itself but its chain of ramifying consequences, the fact that it makes funny things happen. In Zupančič's words, 'The emphasis is on the surplus, material side of the situation – it is on the level of the latter that the comedy of accidents, surprising encounters and outcomes, hilarious dialogues, productive misunderstandings, and so on, is being played out.'[20] The ne plus ultra, then, is a plot that forgoes the restoration of order in favour of the ecstatic triumph of pandemonium, in which no particular individual or couple is shown as receiving their just deserts, or overweening bully their decisive nemesis, but everybody is caught up in a force much bigger than all of them, bigger even than society itself. The implication of the school comedies' endings is that the world has comprehensively imploded and that nothing can ever be the same again. Their apocalyptic note rescues the idea of a final day of reckoning from the foreboding that surrounds it in theology and makes of it a general unshackling, a revelation or uncovering that is of a different order to the passing away of the old earth envisioned on Patmos. The chaos in these comedies is a contingent matter of a system accidentally generating its own disorder and then not being able to resolve it back into order.

By contrast, in another morphology of the chaotic comic plot, the disorder is deliberately provoked by one or more of the characters, and sustained for as long as it takes the system to accept the faultlines within its own order. A fully articulated paradigm of this narrative structure is Martin Scorsese's *The King of Comedy* (1982), which follows the desperate measures to which a sociopathic would-be celebrity, Rupert Pupkin (Robert De Niro), resorts when his attempts to break into the world of television comedy are consistently rejected. Pupkin has lived an isolated half-life in an apartment with a mother whom we never see, his only friend an apparently equally sociopathic woman called Masha (Sandra Bernhard). They are both unfathomably devoted to a middle-of-the-road chatshow host, Jerry Langford (Jerry Lewis), and after Pupkin has been treated by staff at the show's production company with polite regret, then condescension, and finally contemptuous rejection as he is physically thrown out of the building, his briefcase hurled after him, the pair hatch a plot to kidnap Langford and hold him at gunpoint for as long as it takes for the show's producers to allow Pupkin to appear on TV in his place, fronting an entire edition of the programme, complete with his own stand-up introduction. Since neither of them has ever done such a thing before, the kidnap is absurdly amateur, though minimally successful, in its implementation, until Langford manages to free himself from his bonds while Pupkin is on air and Masha is attempting an entranced ritual seduction of him. Pupkin surrenders to his arrest with the final proviso that as soon as he comes off set, he is allowed to go to the deserted bar where he normally hangs out, and tune the TV to the channel that broadcasts the show. A satisfying degree of impressed disbelief spreads through the few habitués of the bar as his lamé-jacketed figure appears on the screen. A final montage illustrates the aftermath of the episode, which has generated a proliferating literature of anxious journalism and documentary books, including Pupkin's own autobiographical memoir. He has achieved his aim of becoming a mass media celebrity, albeit by an unorthodox route.

The film is conventionally read as a parodic account of the psychic distortions to which American media culture has subjected those who wish to succeed in it, and also as a comment on the damaged personality type that is attracted to it at all costs in the first place. It is much more productively read, however, as a study in the psychology of thwarted ambition. What are the Rupert Pupkins, incandescent as they are with a sense of their own potential in an entertainment métier they believe themselves to have fully internalized and understood, supposed to do when the very system to which they ardently wish to contribute refuses to admit them? The point about ambition is that it would transgress its own principle if it accepted rejection. It expects a certain amount of rejection, but it has to persist because the end of all ambition is success, without the attainment of which its efforts are reduced to ignominious futility. The ambitious nobody must do battle with an A&R system that fails to recognize, because it has neither the resources nor the insight to recognize, his potential stardom, and the only power on earth who can insist on it is himself. Not even Masha, whom Pupkin holds in the same scarcely concealed disdain in which the system holds him, is of any use to him – except in that she proves amenable in her naïveté to helping him break the rules.

Pupkin's phosphorescent self-belief is such that he is entitled to feel that he has exhausted every possible legitimate avenue to get where he wants to be, and now the system has forced him into criminality. The end will justify the unconventional means, in which there is no serious intent to harm anybody, but the means would not have had to be so unconventional if the talent scouts had only done their job and offered him a contract in the first place. What is surprising but crucial, on a first viewing of the film, is that when Pupkin delivers his opening monologue on the hijacked show, it is not the inept fiasco we might have expected, but a passable showbiz stand-up routine of precisely the kind that Langford himself might have delivered. The disruption to the established order, an order in which talented individuals such as Rupert Pupkin are expected placidly to accept that they may well fall by the wayside because the commissioning editors cannot find time for them, or only have ears for established names, or there are just too many people wanting to do the same thing, is both a creative intervention in that order, what the Situationists might have called a *détournement* of the audition procedure, and a radical subversion of it. Pupkin emphatically does not resent the system that he needs – exasperated failure will never turn him into a mass shooter – and so his apotheosis depends on the system, as represented by Langford, recovering from his assault on it, absorbing him into its own mythology, even congratulating itself on having done so. Celebrity culture, after all, thrives on stories of people who never gave up, even to the extent of committing major felony, in their determination to make it. Nonetheless, his is a double achievement: he has been on television, becoming a media star and hot topic, and also found a way of forcing the star system into an agony of self-examination. It is the world he has broken into that has questions to resolve, not him. The chaos he reluctantly unleashed, far from being a toxin that had to be purged from the system, has been a purifying agent.

The King of Comedy reflects the second half of the ontological ambivalence of comedy outlined by Zupančič. On the one hand, as indicated in the earlier quotation, comedy is conservative in that it distracts the spectators from the misery of a faulty existence by encouraging them to titter about it. 'On the other hand, however,' she continues, 'it is precisely a surplus empty place of subjectivity that constitutes the playground of any possible change, and gets mobilized in this change.'[21] Where it watches a chaotic situation unfold, without any desire to resolve it, it has the potential to awaken a revolutionary, or at least profoundly critical, consciousness, something that goes beyond the safe territory of easy satire, which in the present day imagines itself to be the distilled essence of critical consciousness. As Peter Sloterdijk sweepingly puts it, 'In laughter, all theory is anticipated,' where 'theory' is to be read specifically as critical theory.[22]

In its purest form, comic drama exploits characteristic attributes or situations for their own comedic value, without labouring under the burden of telling us anything essential about them. In the same way, what matters first about chaos is that it has no inherent meaning in itself, but represents rather the implosion of meaning as it reigns – or reigned – supreme. A paradigmatic example of this tendency was explored in Bong Joon-ho's film *Parasite* (2019), the story of a poor Korean family, the Kims, who inveigle themselves, one by one, under false pretences, into the employ of a wealthy family, the Parks, who live in a sprawling modernist house once inhabited by its architect. When the Parks depart on a camping trip, the Kims immediately take advantage of their sudden freedom, gorging themselves on the luxurious food in the fridge and raiding the drinks cabinets. The film thus begins as a straightforward Plautean comedy of wily servants putting one over on their myopic masters. Mrs Park (Cho Yeo-jeong) is an under-occupied simpering dimwit, instantly recognizable as a comic archetype, while her husband (Lee Sun-kyun), who imagines himself to be more worldly-wise by dint of having succeeded in business, is nonetheless all too ready to be taken in by the subterfuges of Mr Kim (Song Kang-ho), who has become his chauffeur. Barely has the subversive action of the film hit its stride, however, than a much darker subplot emerges, in which the original housekeeper, whom Mrs Kim has usurped, turns out to have a husband who has been living hidden in the cellar on scraps of purloined and leftover food for the past four years. In its least satisfying sequence, which reverts to Korean cinema's comfort zone in slasher-movie cartoon horror, the oppression of the disadvantaged leads them to enact a blood-sodden retribution, but the sociopolitical point is that those who have next to nothing defeat themselves by failing to unite against the real enemy. The guilty secret in the cellar of privilege is that it is always paid for by those who gain least from it, and whose subterranean existence the well-off are comfortably able to discount, except where the evidence of it persists in the form of the noxious smell that keeps assailing Mr Park's nostrils.

By the end, the Kims have fallen short of the opportunities for disordering the world of gross inequity that their initial bravado facilitated, and a dreary return to order is effected. At the heart of the film is a dialogue between Mr Kim and his son Ki-woo (Choi Woo-shik), set in the gym where hundreds of poor families have been temporarily accommodated following catastrophic floods that have left their basement and semi-basement homes uninhabitable. Ki-woo asks his father what he plans to do to get the family out of their present fix. Mr Kim replies that the only way to ensure that plans do not fail is to have no plan at all. Who among the legions of people around them had planned to be sleeping on the floor in a gym tonight? When the world continues on its own relentless course in wholesale disregard of its victims, what does their resort to crime and immorality ultimately matter? And yet, by the long concluding sequence of the film, in which Ki-woo is writing a long letter to his now-imprisoned father, he tells him that he has a plan in life – the strikingly ordinary one of going to university, getting married and finding a lucrative job, so that one day he might have enough money to buy the house and liberate his father. An irresistible order thereby shapes the ambitions of its victims as much as those of its beneficiaries.

The countervailing truth to this heart-breaking self-delusion, the same self-delusion under which everybody in global capitalism's sprawling mansion is constrained to live, has emerged a little earlier. Regaining consciousness after brain surgery to heal the damage done by his having been smashed on the head by the housekeeper's vengeful husband, Ki-woo finds himself unable to do anything but laugh helplessly at everything he is confronted with, including the memory of his murdered sister. For a time, liberated by post-operative drugs and the psychic after-effects of brain surgery, his schoolboyish sniggering at what he knows to have been traumatic constitutes the last flicker of subversion, the last turn in 'the playground of any possible change', that events will allow him. Sloterdijk recalls the bitter laughter of the Weimar years, the spirit in which 'gaiety has to step over dead bodies, and in the end, people will laugh about the thought of corpses to come'.[23] If finding things funny can ever truly undermine them, its efficacy would look something like this – not the deliberate gag, the satirical take, the tedious bad-taste joke that reliably does the rounds in the wake of any topical catastrophe, but something more like the gratuitous psychic release provided by certain intoxicants. The problem is that it only works for the one who laughs.

Ki-woo's inappropriate laughter complicates what has been for many centuries the essential distinguishing mark of comedy and whatever its antithesis might be – tragedy, serious drama, the problem play, the naturalistic theatre of the later nineteenth century, the police procedurals and soaps of the present day. The canonical view is encapsulated by Agnes Heller in her philosophical study of the comic current in art, literature and everyday life:

> While crying, one identifies oneself with the self of a fellow creature, feeling sorrow over the world's injustice, fate, and loss; whereas in laughing, one takes the position of the world, or of some idea about it, and laughs at the foolishness of people, one's own follies included.[24]

These definitions certainly serve the thesis that comedy essentially caters to a conservative impulse, deriding the comic victims for their enmeshment in the *a priori* conditions of sociocultural and genetic existence, in the face of which they are wholly powerless. The fact that the laughter might include a candid awareness of one's own follies, as much as everybody else's, does nothing to ameliorate its fundamentally derisive force. This is a recklessly generalizing theoretical stance, though. Schopenhauer had something corrective to say about tears when he turned the lachrymose morality of the nineteenth century against itself in declaring that all crying was motivated by self-pity rather than empathy with the other, but the second half of Heller's proposition bears scrutiny too. The subversive comic currents in, say, the plays of Brecht encourage their audiences to turn their amused scorn on the mechanisms and representatives of power, whose vulnerable victims in the principal characters are the vehicles by which the audience is adjured to come to political awareness of itself. In *Mr Puntila and His Man Matti* (1948), the absurd oscillations of character that the tyrannical employer Puntila undergoes, in which the cold, class-ridden attitude of his sobriety alternates with the warm, affectionate empathy that he displays when drunk, structure the vicissitudes of a classical comic plot involving his intention to marry off his daughter, Eva, to a military attaché, in defiance of her true amorous devotion to his chauffeur and servant,

Matti. Based loosely on a Finnish original by Hella Wuolijoki in which alcoholism was mourned as a national cultural tragedy of the Finns, Brecht's play transforms the thematic of drink into a material correlative of class society. An external element, as ethereal as toxic gas and as pervasive as ideology itself, not drink but the state of drunkenness, is what keeps transmogrifying relations between master and servant between one temperamental mode and its polar opposite, in an effect that bears a metaphorical similitude with Marx's summation of religion as the heart of a heartless world. Puntila's warmth towards Matti while under the influence of drink is at once a displacement of the objective relations that prevail between them, and a brazen exposure of the fictive unreality of that displacement, much like Ki-woo's inappropriate laughter in *Parasite*.

In the English eighteenth century, comic chaos migrated from the stage into the novel, where its influence can be felt in the socially satirical currents of Defoe, Smollett and Fielding. Terry Castle expounds an argument at the conclusion of her work on the masquerade that, as the novel became more preoccupied with the fates of individuals, particularly in the nineteenth century, it departed from the collective social subversion of the masquerade tradition in poetic and dramatic literature, but the eighteenth-century novel, and not just in England, very often uses the paradigms of the *Bildungsroman* or the picaresque in order to reflect the antagonisms of a corrupt society on its central character. Tom Jones, Moll Flanders, Peregrine Pickle, Wilhelm Meister must pick their way through the great world of artifice and delusion, being moulded by it as they go, their characters partially constructed by the disorderly whirl through which they move. Only by stranding his most famous hero on a desert island, with a single archetypal colonial subject for company, can Defoe suggest that society could be renovated by being reimagined from scratch in a homosocial Eden. The ideal type of all such wayfaring individuals is

Tristram Shandy, whose story does no more than promise to unfold when its narrator can establish a firm hold on the slippery grips of narrative technique long enough to tell it. Sterne's novel of 1759 is both an extended deconstruction of the hubris of the English novel at an early stage in its development and a parodically solemn avowal that life never has a narrative shape and that, far from being malleable into the didactic structures that have supported the storytelling art since Homer, it is more likely a succession of unfortunate accidents. These began, in Tristram's case, at the moment of conception, when his mother asked his father if he had remembered to wind the clock, the distraction producing an instant humoral imbalance in the vital fluids that begot him. On the occasion of his birth, his nose was squashed by the inept manipulation of a pair of forceps by the ominously named Dr Slop, and if there is one facial feature that determines a man's fate in the world, according to Tristram's father, it is an assertive and handsome nose. The multiplication of contingent absurdities as the everyday fabric of human life would not be revisited in literary culture until the period following the First World War, but Sterne's novel had already established that misfortune is not only entirely arbitrary and, even at that, a matter of subjective definition, but also profoundly comic. 'Nothing is funnier than unhappiness,' says Beckett's Nell, acknowledging a truth more cruelly articulated against her namesake in *The Old Curiosity Shop* (1841), when Oscar Wilde said of the death of little Nell that one must have a heart of stone to read it without laughing. Castle is right, however, in suggesting that, when the nineteenth-century novel takes up the vicissitudes of individual lives, from Jane Austen's heroines through Jane Eyre and Agnes Gray to Adam Bede and Isabel Archer, it ceases to need a broad social canvas against which to throw their fates into relief. The movements of comic disorder transmute instead into the restive insurrectionary crowds of Hugo, Flaubert, Dostoevsky and Zola, where they become the grand episodes of a history in which individuals are caught up. When the rioting mineworkers assault villagers and their homes on election day in Treby Magna, George Eliot's radical hero Felix Holt finds himself prosecuted for the manslaughter of a constable who is trying to break up the affray. Convicted but pardoned, he escapes the political life in favour of marriage to the daughter of a Dissenting minister, the unrest having taught him something about himself rather than something about society.

In spite of Wilde's disdain for what posterity has been content to see as the sentimentality in Dickens' work, he is very much the exception to the brash generality that the Victorian novel is about individuals and their dehistoricized fates. There is a sense throughout his career that his characters are the thematic emblems of social tendencies that are all but opaque to most of them, either because they are too poor and deprived to take on themselves the presumption of seeing them illuminated, or because they are themselves too close to the levers of power to be aware of their insidious workings. Adorno, in an early lecture on Dickens, speaks of what he calls the 'prebourgeois' element in his fiction:

> In it the individual has not yet reached full autonomy, nor therefore complete isolation, but instead is presented as a bearer of objective factors, of a dark, obscure fate and a starlike consolation that overtake the individual and permeate his life but never follow from the law of the individual ... there is no psychology in it, or rather ... it absorbs psychological approaches into the objective meanings the novels depict.[25]

Adorno sees the illustrations by Hablot Knight Browne with which the novels were equipped as reflective of the illustrative strategy of the narratives, which mobilize their characters as figural depictions rather than deeply psychologized human beings. The interior world of the

Victorian novel was, certainly by no later than Dickens's middle period, a place where what happens to the characters is always intrinsically like them – in other words, that it flows from their own subjective dynamics. They inhabit, as Adorno puts it, 'a life space that tries of its own accord to dissolve all objectivity in subjectivity'.[26] Dickens's novels, by contrast, use an older aesthetic form to dissolve the very bourgeois world itself via their personae, which have something of the emblematic character of the comic figures in Ben Jonson. In this respect, as is sometimes observed, he is actually the last and greatest of eighteenth-century novelists. In regard to the disorder with which an unjust and poverty-stricken society invests human lives, only temporary, fragile outbreaks of genuine amity and compassion between the characters keep alive the human note that is all but drowned out in the resonant cant and hard times of their worlds.

The inversion to which comic action subjects the world is not the simple shift of focus from the highest motions of the spirit, tragedy's province, to the base and banal matter of the object world. Instead, it conjures the latter into a transformative elixir that it then applies to spirit itself. The pretensions of the lordly and the maxims of the pious are exposed in their material origins by the physical scrapes to which comic chaos condemns them. Jonson's Morose, in his misanthrope's aged yearning for quiet, is nonetheless not yet done with a coarse libidinal desire for a young wife who will conform to his behavioural requirements. The disguised boy who, in his nephew's plot, plays the perfect fiancée for him then becomes a concrete manifestation of the hypocrisy and unreasoning tyranny of his jaundiced view of humanity. Its machinations are laid bare in the three-dimensional absurdity of a conversational encounter without conversation, illustrating the entirely monopolistic nature of the old man's idea of a true union. Giorgio Agamben argues, with reference to the figure of

Pulcinella in the commedia dell'arte, that laughter – not unlike tears, in this respect – is provoked by the impossibility of communicating by saying, even when the saying takes linguistic form, a situation that Jonson has boiled down to the ineptitude of a muteness that is mistaken for meaningful.[27]

If there are movements of materiality within the zone of supposedly higher things, what comedy insists on, as Zupančič eloquently shows, is that the realm of ideals is itself a manifestation of the material. In refutation of the Platonic conception of the mind as the seat of the intellect and the soul, which during mortal life at least is tethered to the grosser purposes of the belly and the genitals, dialectical materialist philosophy has asserted that the physical being itself is the origin of the spiritual. The brain is as much a material organ as the liver and the spleen. In this sense, comedy is a less ideological discursive form than tragedy, just because it knows and acknowledges that the lofty principles of its central characters are emanations of their corporeal selves rather than objectively existing entities to which the material world in its coarseness might appeal. By contrast, the Othellos and the Antigones have persuaded themselves that they are confronting the eternal and the ineffable, while the base physical realm does its best to keep getting in the way. Devotion to a higher principle of unsullied fidelity, catalysed with an admixture of simplistic gullibility, turns the heroic Othello into a wife-murderer. Jealous possessiveness is a product of the physicality of competitive sexual longing raised to a moral principle, a delusive factor that the unillusioned Iago exploits against him, for whatever reason, in obscene imaginative detail. The extreme case of the corporealization of the spiritual is the legend of Doctor Faustus, who is prepared to let the higher part of himself go to the Devil in exchange for earthly delights and unlimited intellectual knowledge, the latter made significantly into a tradeable commodity in the hellish bargain. A deal for a temporary period of unbridled cerebral and sexual power is struck in exchange for an eternity of enslavement after death. A comical Doctor Faustus might be a boringly knowledgeable old windbag in a persistent priapic frenzy, who would gradually be made aware of the vulgarity of what had appeared to be his higher yearnings.

Not all comedy is about the reduction of high ideals to banality, but the movement from the pursuit of an abstract goal to its entanglement in the materiality of the contingent is a constant. The same mechanism can often be observed on both sides of the same comic plot. In Woody Allen's tortuously complex comedy *Manhattan Murder Mystery* (1993), two plots unravel in tandem. On the one hand is the determination of Carol (Diane Keaton), a would-be restaurateur who currently has plenty of time on her hands, to investigate what she sees as the suspect circumstances of the sudden death of the next-door neighbour's wife. The lengths to which she resorts, including obtaining the key to the neighbour's apartment under false pretences and letting herself in while he is absent so that she can hunt for clues, are a prolonged exercise in the obstacles, accidental and intentional, that are thrown in the path of a quest for justice. On the other hand, the neighbour himself, Mr House (Jerry Adler), turns out to be instrumental in a grisly plot against both his sister-in-law and his wife, for the sake of an adulterous affair he is conducting with a woman for whom he has thrown over a previous adulterous partner. The high ideal of love, as so often, is the pretext for any amount of unethical and criminal behaviour, all the way up to the murder that Carol has all along suspected, albeit in a far more byzantine conspiracy than she realizes. Much of the comic action turns on the neurotic insistence of her husband, Larry (played by Allen himself), that she is letting her imagination run riot, and his engulfing terror at the possible consequences of her increasingly reckless amateur sleuthing. The baffling chaos of the plot development, which is as intricate as a

Raymond Chandler screenplay, to the extent that it requires one of the characters to explain it all again in a simplified narrative in the film's penultimate scene, is an extended extrapolation of the principle that all principles, including both passionate love and the passion to see wrongs righted, are embroiled in the snarls of material reality, which will no more let go of them than objects themselves will obediently dissolve. One of the plot points concerns a corpse that Mr House has been seen tipping into an industrial incinerator in the dead of night, and which he is subsequently made to believe has survived the flames and may still prove his guilt. That he is, at least for a while, fooled into fearing that this outlandish claim could be true bears witness to the robustness of the physical as against the operations of abstract reason. Even a notionally existing dead body is a stronger argument than the theoretical certainty that a furnace capable of melting steel must have reduced it to ashes. Then too, 'the idea of the irreparable,' Agamben writes, 'is in itself comic'.[28]

If the comic denouement that falls short of a final and implicitly eternal eruption of chaos is bound to disappoint, as Zupančič observes, because it represents the end of the comic merriment, the resolution of the chaos and the restoration of order, it at least reflects one of the verities that prove as indestructible as the comic characters themselves – that the laughter always has to stop. Excessive laughter was one of the perversities fixed in the sights of early modern etiquette manuals as unbecoming to the life of civility. There was no dignified way of laughing that was not a genuinely unamused, facile impersonation of delight. Laughter was unseemly because it escaped rational control, it was as involuntary a somatic reaction as the bouts of hiccups to which it could often lead, but also, at the intellectual level, as much an invitation to liberty as an open cell door. It lay outside the provinces of theology and of elite behaviour, of the refined regulation of social relations more generally, and where it was deliberately provoked, it had an uncomfortably infantilizing, even bestializing, side to it. What was the point of laughter? It made the provoked buffoon look ridiculous, but it also rendered those who laughed at him into cackling hyenas, their hilarity the sound of vicious predation. Laughing was one of those activities that it would be incriminating to be caught in the middle of when the Second Coming occurred, an irresponsible self-indulgence at somebody's expense when one could be helping the helpless and attending soberly to one's own redemption. Because of these homiletic antipathies, laughter was, as we are regularly reminded by studies of the carnival and masquerade traditions, the currency of defiance, the modus operandi of satirical assaults on the hierarchies. A laughing person cannot be subjected to rational manipulation until they have stopped seeing the funny side of whatever it was, which is what earned laughter its overburdened status as a tool of emancipation in itself.

The truth of the comic only emerges in its comparative contiguity with tragic disaster. In a short essay on conflicting emotions, Montaigne states that 'we can see that not only children, who artlessly follow Nature, often weep and laugh at the same thing.'[29] That this remains a discomfiting thought is expressed by the preference in the modern dictum that you have to laugh or else you would cry, although it is never satisfactorily explained why crying would always be inappropriate. Kant points out that a good bout of hearty laughter at a banquet promotes digestion by activating the diaphragmatic muscles, but so of course does weeping. These contrasting temperaments, he also argues more tenuously, have their correlatives in the phases of life, the young preferring tragic drama while their elders are more inclined to comedy. This is because young people still possess such a store of untapped potential frivolity that they readily recover from the baleful emotional effects of tragedy, whereas the old, being prey to intimations of their own mortality and having accumulated a lifetime's bitter experience, find it harder to shake off the gloom, and are therefore much more amenable to clowning and witticisms.[30] This generalized anthropology would seem to indict both generations for their shallow evasiveness in the face of life's solemnities. If laughter is thrown into perspective by its adjacency to tears, however, the tears need no such countervailing relief. A long theological tradition of both Catholic and Orthodox variants of Christianity held that, although Jesus Christ is noted as weeping over the death of Lazarus, he never laughs, an observation extrapolable into the forbidding piety that, in the words of an early theologian writing under the pseudepigraphal guise of Ephrem the Syrian, 'laughter is the beginning of the destruction of the soul'.[31] The Encratites, a heretical second-century ascetic Christian sect, believed that anything that prompted outbreaks of joy was to be shunned like the plague, in view of which they practised celibacy, teetotalism and vegetarianism and renounced marriage as the organon of bodily corruption, an invite to licensed fornication. While St Paul abjured merely the crude raillery he heard in vulgar humour – 'Nor should there be obscenity, foolish talk or coarse joking, which are out of place' in true Christian observance (Ephesians 5:4) – thoroughgoing ascetics even found the laughter of enjoyment debilitating to the ideally suffering soul. If in doubt, best not laugh at all, especially where you feel you can't help it.

'The whole world is in a terrible state of chassis,' Sean O'Casey's 'Captain' Boyle observes repeatedly in *Juno and the Paycock* (1924), an insight compounded amid the ruination and breakup of his family when, at the play's close, as the back-breaking straw, he drops his last sixpence. Nothing does what you want it to do, an understanding that hovers in the indeterminate zone between tragic wisdom and cosmic joke. The world rattles on over the numberless bodies of its victims, who might as well not have been. Things fall into the wrong order.

Events happen all at once. A state of conflict reigns between people and within them. These tendencies contribute to history's sorrows and devastations, the conflagrating of hope. At best, they provoke a laughter that might be purgative in its bitterness. Chaos is a state that has congealed ideologically into the human condition, the Slough of Despond.

Or: things escape the brutal structures of classification, and refuse the arid temporality of the planned schedule. The arguments and dialectical disputes they trigger are the means by which the world's objectivity is denied its monumental status as a given. Throwing their enthralment into deliberate disorder is not evil, but the motive impulse of a grasp at liberty, the untethering of the creative and political imagination. Laughter, rising spontaneously from the occluded depths of interiority, as opposed to being extorted from them by comedians, is the way warmth breaks over the frost of reified experience. Chaos is a condition of possibility, a vital sign, the persistence of life, the potential conception of a dancing star.

Notes

Part 1

1   Thomas Frank (1997), *The Conquest of Cool: Business Culture, Counterculture, and the Rise of Hip Consumerism*, Chicago, IL: University of Chicago Press.

2   Eugene McCarraher (2019), *The Enchantments of Mammon: How Capitalism Became the Religion of Modernity*, Cambridge, MA: Belknap Press of Harvard University Press, p 512.

3   Sloan Wilson (1955), *The Man in the Gray Flannel Suit*, New York: Simon and Schuster, p 164.

4   McCarraher, p 512.

5   Lewis Mumford (1970), *The Myth of the Machine Vol. II: The Pentagon of Power*, New York: Harcourt Brace Jovanovich, caption to illustration 27, 'Rituals of "Counter-Culture" ', after p 340.

6   In my own case, I learned in June 2020 that a friend had been belatedly retrospectively diagnosed with coronavirus. She had had it badly, but slowly recovered from it over three weeks in late February and early March. I had spent an afternoon with her two days before she fell ill, when she was still asymptomatic but must obviously have been carrying the pathogen. Our time together included a couple of embraces and social kissing. I have no idea how I escaped it.

7   Slavoj Zizek (2020), *Pan(dem)ic! COVID-19 Shakes the World*, London: Polity Press, p 14.

8   Wallace Stevens (2015), 'The Idea of Order at Key West', in *The Collected Poems of Wallace Stevens*, New York: Vintage Books, p 136.

9   N Katherine Hayles (1990), *Chaos Bound: Orderly Disorder in Contemporary Literature and Science*, Ithaca, NY: Cornell University Press, pp 9–10.

10   Note that what this dual schema seems obviously to lack is a third
     paradigm, which would posit a state of chaos that neither resolves itself
     nor harbours concealed structures of order within it, but remains purely,
     irresolvably chaotic. This would then surely correspond at the political
     level, for all that one wishes to avoid the simple-minded equation of the
     two terms, to purist definitions of unstructured chaos as anarchism.

11   David Graeber (2016), *The Utopia of Rules: On Technology, Stupidity, and
     the Secret Joys of Bureaucracy*, New York and London: Melville House,
     p 100.

12   Lewis Mumford (1934), *Technics and Civilization*, London: Routledge and
     Kegan Paul, p 3.

13   In this summary, I rely on the account given in *Socialist Review* 173, March
     1994, by Charlie Hore, available at pubs.socialistreviewindex.org.uk/sr173/
     hore.htm, accessed 28 March 2020. Reliable recent book-length studies
     of these events are Frank Dikötter (2016), *The Cultural Revolution: A
     People's History 1962–1976*, London: Bloomsbury, and Michael Schoenhals,
     ed. (2015), *China's Cultural Revolution 1966–69: Not a Dinner Party*,
     Abingdon: Routledge.

14   Alain Badiou (2012), *The Rebirth of History: Times of Riots and Uprisings*,
     trans. Gregory Elliott, London and New York: Verso, p 92.

15   Ibid., p 81.

16   Fox Broadcasting Company (1992), *The Simpsons*, 'Kamp Krusty'.

17   The best fictive account of the Tiananmen days and their aftermath
     remains Ma Jian (2008), *Beijing Coma*, trans. Flora Drew, London: Chatto
     and Windus. Its narrative, told by a participant whose injuries at the hands
     of the authorities have left him in a mentally conscious but outwardly
     vegetative state, moves at glacial pace through hundreds of pages, the better
     to prepare the reader for the horrible enormity of the events of 4 June 1989.

18   Catherine Maxwell (2017), *Scents and Sensibility: Perfume in Victorian
     Literary Culture*, Oxford: Oxford University Press is an exhaustive
     investigation of the influence of aromatics on the aesthetic responses of the
     British fin de siècle.

19   Claude E Shannon (1948), 'A Mathematical Theory of Information', in *Bell
     System Technical Journal* 27 (July and October), pp 379–423 and 623–56.

20   McCarraher, p 272.

21   Martin Meisel (2016), *Chaos Imagined: Literature, Art, Science*, New York:
     Columbia University Press, p 290.

22   Theodor Adorno (1978), §91, 'Vandals', in *Minima Moralia: Reflections
     from Damaged Life*, trans. E F N Jephcott, London: Verso, p 139.

23   Ibid.

24   Ibid., p 140.

25 Hayles, p 100, emphasis original.

26 Thomas Carlyle (2019), *The French Revolution*, Oxford: Oxford University Press, pp 309, 560, 416, 252, all emphases original.

Part 2

1 Lawrence Kramer (1995), 'Music and Representation: In the Beginning with Haydn's *Creation*', in *Classical Music and Postmodern Knowledge*, Berkeley: University of California Press, p 75.

2 Cited in H C Robbins Landon (1977), *Haydn: Chronicles and Works Vol. IV. The Years of* The Creation, Bloomington: Indiana University Press, pp 251–2. The reference is quoted in a finely detailed analysis of Haydn's oratorio by Melanie Lowe, 'Creating Chaos in Haydn's *Creation*', *HAYDN: Online Journal of the Haydn Society of North America* 3.1 (Spring 2013), available at rit.edu/affiliate/haydn/sites/rit.edu.affiliate.haydn/files/article_pdfs/lowe_chaos_haydn_pdf04-19.pdf, accessed 29 March 2020.

3 James Joyce (2000), *Portrait of the Artist as a Young Man*, London: Penguin Books, p 110.

4 'The Creation Epic', trans. E A Speiser, in James B Pritchard, ed. (1969), *Ancient Near Eastern Texts Relating to the Old Testament*, 3rd edn, Princeton NJ: Princeton University Press, 1969, pp 60–1.

5 Rig Veda, trans. J A B Van Buitenen, in Ainslie T Embree, ed. (1988), *Sources of Indian Tradition*, 2 vols, New York: Columbia University Press, 1:21.

6 In the translation by Samuel Garth, John Dryden et al. (1717). ovid.lib.virginia.edu/garth.html.

Chapter 1

1 Michel Foucault (2002), *The Order of Things: An Archaeology of the Human Sciences*, trans. unknown, Abingdon and New York: Routledge, p 20.

2 Ibid., p 21.

3 Ibid., p 59.

4 Ibid., p 61, emphases original.

5 William James (1890), *The Principles of Psychology*, New York: Henry Holt and Company, p 633.

6   Ibid.

7   John Stuart Mill (1846), *A System of Logic*, New York: Harper and Brothers, III: vii: §1, p 216.

8   Slavoj Zizek (2019), *Sex and the Failed Absolute*, Bloomsbury Academic: London and New York, p 404.

9   James Kingsland (2019), *Am I Dreaming? The New Science of Consciousness and How Altered States Reboot the Brain*, London: Atlantic Books, pp 10–11.

10 HG Wells (1891), 'The Rediscovery of the Unique', *Fortnightly Review* 56 (July), p 109.

11 Anton Zeilinger (2005), 'The Message of the Quantum', *Nature* 438 (December), p 743.

12 Martin Meisel (2016), *Chaos Imagined: Literature, Art, Science*, New York: Columbia University Press, p 13.

13 Zizek, p 190.

14 Joseph Stefano (1960), *Psycho*, available at sfy.ru/?script=psycho, accessed 29 March 2020.

15 Henry Miller (2015), *Tropic of Cancer*, London: Penguin Classics, p 2.

16 Gottfried Leibniz, *Theodicy*, trans. E M Huggard, §12, available at gutenberg.org/files/17147

17 Ibid., §146, 147, 145.

18 Immanuel Kant, *Universal Natural History and Theory of the Heavens*, II: vii, trans. Ian Johnston, available at web.archive.org/web/20140829071546/ http://records.viu.ca/~johnstoi/kant/kant2e.htm, accessed 29 March 2020.

19 Meisel, pp 316–17.

20 Karl Marx, 'Estranged Labour', in *Economic and Philosophical Manuscripts of 1844*, trans. Martin Milligan, available at marxists.org/archive/marx/ works/1844/manuscripts/labour.htm, accessed 29 March 2020.

21 Mikhail Bahktin (1984), *Rabelais and His World*, trans. Hélène Iswolsky, Bloomington: Indiana University Press, p 6.

22 Alan Garfinkel (1983), 'Connoisseurs of Chaos', *Omni* 5 (June), p 112.

23 Michael Rothschild (2004), *Bionomics: Economy as Business Ecosystem*, Washington, DC: Beard Books, p 260.

24 Henry Miller (2015), *Tropic of Capricorn*, London: Penguin, p 147.

25 Novalis (Friedrich von Hardenberg) (1981), *Heinrich von Ofterdingen*, in *Werke in einem Band*, ed. Hans-Joachim Mähl and Richard Samuel, Munich: Hanser, p 334. Translations mine.

26 Theodor Adorno (1978), §143 'In Nuce', in *Minima Moralia: Reflections from Damaged Life*, trans. E F N Jephcott, London: Verso, p 222.

27 Theodor W Adorno (1973), *Negative Dialectics*, trans. E B Ashton, London: Routledge and Kegan Paul, 1973, p 17, translation modified.

28 Foucault, p 268.

Chapter 2

1 Jan Mieszkowski (2019), *Crises of the Sentence*, Chicago, IL: University of Chicago Press, p 7.

2 Friedrich Nietzsche (2006), *On the Genealogy of Morality*, trans. Carol Diethe, Cambridge: Cambridge University Press, p 26.

3 Peter Sloterdijk (1987), Critique of Cynical Reason, trans. Michael Eldred, Minneapolis: University of Minnesota Press, p 484.

4 Todd Kontje (2011), *The Cambridge Introduction to Thomas Mann*, Cambridge: Cambridge University Press, p 88.

5 Sloterdijk, p 504.

6 Harold James (2009), 'The Weimar Economy', in *Weimar Germany*, ed. Anthony McElligott, Oxford: Oxford University Press, pp 102–26.

7 Detlev J K Peukert (1992), *The Weimar Republic: The Crisis of Classical Modernity*, trans. Richard Deveson, New York: Hill and Wang.

8 Anthony McElligott (2009), 'Introduction', in *Weimar Germany*, ed. McElligott, pp 5–6.

9 *Frankfurter Allgemeiner Zeitung*, 4 March 1926.

10 Siegfried Kracauer (1995), 'Cult of Distraction: On Berlin's Picture Palaces', in *The Mass Ornament: Weimar Essays*, ed. and trans. Thomas Y Levin, Cambridge, MA: Harvard University Press, pp 326–7.

11 Fredric Jameson (2017), *The Ancients and the Postmoderns: On the Historicity of Forms*, London and New York: Verso, p 68.

12 Theodor W Adorno (1992), 'Commitment', in *Notes to Literature, Vol. II*, trans. Shierry Weber Nicholsen, New York: Columbia University Press, p 87.

13 Lewis Carroll (1978), *Alice's Adventures in Wonderland and through the Looking-Glass*, London: Methuen, pp 213–14.

14 Stanley Fish (2011), *How to Write a Sentence: And How to Read One*, New York: HarperCollins, p 134.

15 Mieszkowski, p 226.

16 Gertrude Stein (1995), *The Making of Americans: Being a History of a Family's Progress*, Normal: Dalkey Archive Press of Illinois State University, p 284.

Chapter 3

1 Arnold Schoenberg (1984), 'Opinion or Insight?', in *Style and Idea: Selected Writings of Arnold Schoenberg*, ed. Leonard Stein, trans. Leo Black, Berkeley: University of California Press, pp 260–1, emphasis original.

2   Arnold Schoenberg (1978), *Theory of Harmony*, trans. Roy E Carter, Berkeley: University of California Press, p 20.

3   Ibid., p 21.

4   Richard Taruskin (2010), *The Oxford History of Western Music Vol. 4: Music in the Early Twentieth Century*, Oxford: Oxford University Press, pp 320–1.

5   Ibid., p 321.

6   Ibid., p 310.

7   Theodor W Adorno (2006), *Philosophy of New Music*, trans. Robert Hullot-Kentor, Minneapolis: University of Minnesota Press, p 95.

8   Ibid., pp 95–6.

9   Ibid., p 129.

10 Peter Hill (2000), *Stravinsky: The Rite of Spring*, Cambridge: Cambridge University Press, p 81.

11 Theodor W Adorno (1999), 'Anton von Webern', in *Sound Figures*, trans. Rodney Livingstone, Stanford, CA: Stanford University Press, p 102.

12 Theodor W Adorno (2013), *Aesthetic Theory*, trans. Robert Hullot-Kentor, London: Bloomsbury Academic, p 151.

13 Fredric Jameson (2019), *Allegory and Ideology*, London: Verso, p 134.

14 Cited in Jay Winter (1998), *Sites of Memory, Sites of Mourning: The Great War in European Cultural History*, Cambridge: Cambridge University Press, p 164.

15 Martin Meisel (2016), *Chaos Imagined: Literature, Art, Science*, New York: Columbia University Press, p 182.

16 Victor Davis Hanson (2005), *A War Like No Other: How the Athenians and Spartans Fought the Peloponnesian War*, London: Methuen, p 103.

17 Walter Benjamin (1968), 'The Storyteller: Reflections on the Works of Nikolai Leskov', in *Illuminations*, trans. Harry Zohn, New York: Harcourt Brace Jovanovich, p 83, translation modified.

18 Theodor Adorno (1978), §33, 'Out of the Firing-Line', in *Minima Moralia: Reflections from Damaged Life*, London: Verso, pp 54, 55.

19 Cited in John Willett (1978), *The New Sobriety: Art and Politics in the Weimar Period 1917–33*, London: Thames and Hudson, p 117.

20 Theodor W Adorno (1973), *Negative Dialectics*, trans. E B Ashton, London: Routledge and Kegan Paul, pp 321, 323.

21 Blair Worden (2009), *The English Civil Wars: 1640–1660*, London: Weidenfeld and Nicholson, p 113.

22 *Quarterly Review* (1822), XXVIII, October, pp 197–8.

23 Available at marxists.org/archive/marx/works/1845/german-ideology/ch01a.htm, accessed 30 March 2020.

24 Cited at alphahistory.com/chineserevolution/lu-dingyi-hundred-flowers-1956, accessed 30 March 2020.

Chapter 4

1   Regina Schwarz (1985), 'Milton's Hostile Chaos: "… And the Sea Was No More"', in *ELH* 52 Summer, pp 337–74.

2   Martin Meisel (2016), *Chaos Imagined: Literature, Art, Science*, New York: Columbia University Press, p 162.

3   Aaron Santesso, 'Aesthetic Chaos in the Age of Reason', in *Disrupted Patterns: On Chaos and Order in the Enlightenment*, ed. Theodore E D Braun and John A McCarthy, Amsterdam: Rodopi, 2000, p 39.

4   Donald DeMarco, 'The Virtue of Obedience', Catholic Exchange, available at catholicexchange.com/the-virtue-of-obedience, accessed 30 March 2020.

5   Theodor Adorno (1978), §122, 'Monograms', in *Minima Moralia: Reflections from Damaged Life*, London: Verso, p 192.

6   Lynne A Isbell (2009), *The Fruit, The Tree, and the Serpent: Why We See So Well*, Cambridge, MA: Harvard University Press, pp 4–5.

7   Theodor W Adorno (1973), *Negative Dialectics*, trans. E B Ashton, London: Routledge and Kegan Paul, p 299.

8   Theodor W Adorno (1991), 'Trying to Understand *Endgame*', in *Notes to Literature, Vol. I*, trans. Shierry Weber Nicholsen, New York: Columbia University Press, pp 274–5.

9   Ibid., p 274.

10   Preston King (1974), *The Ideology of Order: A Comparative Analysis of Jean Bodin and Thomas Hobbes*, London: George Allen and Unwin, pp 277–8, emphasis original.

11   Ibid., p 279.

12   David Hume (1975), 'Of Liberty and Necessity', in *Enquiries Concerning Human Understanding and Concerning the Principles of Morals*, ed. L A Selby-Bigge and P H Nidditch, Oxford: Oxford University Press, 8.80, p 102.

13   Theodor W Adorno (1998), 'Free Time', in *Critical Models: Interventions and Catchwords*, trans. Henry W Pickford, New York: Columbia University Press, pp 167–8.

Chapter 5

1   Ingvild Sælid Gilhus (1997), *Laughing Gods, Weeping Virgins: Laughter in the History of Religion*, London: Routledge, p 44.

2   Oswyn Murray (2018), *The Symposion: Drinking Greek Style. Essays on Greek Pleasure 1983–2017*, Oxford: Oxford University Press, p 54.

3   Ibid., p 194.

4   Terry Castle (1986), *Masquerade and Civilization: The Carnivalesque in Eighteenth-Century English Culture and Fiction*, Stanford, CA: Stanford University Press, p 83.

5   Ibid., p 88.

6   Mary Douglas (1966), *Purity and Danger: Analysis of the Concepts of Pollution and Taboo*, London: Routledge and Kegan Paul, pp 169–70.

7   Castle, p 88.

8   Emmanuel Le Roy Ladurie (1980), *Carnival: A People's Uprising at Romans 1579–1580*, trans. M Feeney, London: Scolar Press.

9   Castle, p 332.

10 Paul Crawford (2002), *Politics and History in William Golding: The World Turned Upside Down*, Columbia: University of Missouri Press, p 47.

11 Scott Wilson (1995), *Cultural Materialism: Theory and Practice*, Oxford: Blackwell, p xii.

12 William Ian Miller (1997), *The Anatomy of Disgust*, Cambridge, MA: Harvard University Press, p 184.

13 Terry Eagleton (2019), *Humour*, New Haven, CT: Yale University Press, p 12.

14 Letter of 18 March 1936, in Theodor W Adorno and Walter Benjamin (1999), *The Complete Correspondence 1928–1940*, trans. Nicholas Walker, Cambridge: Polity Press, p 130.

15 Mikhail Bakhtin (1984), *Rabelais and His World*, trans. Hélène Iswolsky, Bloomington: Indiana University Press, p 73.

16 Eagleton, p 162.

17 Ibid., pp 136–7.

18 Alenka Zupančič (2008), *The Odd One In: On Comedy*, Cambridge, MA: MIT Press, p 217.

19 Cited in John Morreall (1997), *Humor Works*, Amherst, MA: HRD Press, p 3.

20 Zupančič, pp 91–2.

21 Ibid., p 217.

22 Peter Sloterdijk (1987), *Critique of Cynical Reason*, trans. Michael Eldred, Minneapolis: University of Minnesota Press, p 42.

23 Ibid., p 529. Sloterdijk also enumerates the incidences of inappropriate laughter in *The Magic Mountain* (1924), which inveigle themselves amid the rarefied sobriety of Thomas Mann's sanatorium community. The most poignant case is that of one of the Russian patients, Anton Karlowitsch Ferge, who has undergone an open pleural examination under only local anaesthetic, during which the doctor's probing instruments produced in him an unworldly sensation combining inconceivable horror and a kind

of obscene tickling. He could smell the rank odour of his innards, as well as the mortified consciousness that the internal organs do not wish to be accessed and touched in this manner. Whenever he recounts his memory of this ordeal, to do so being his principal character tic, he submits each time to that reflexive ironic laughter with which the helpless offer their last emotional resistance to a trauma they too have not been spared.

24 Agnes Heller (2005), *Immortal Comedy: The Comic Phenomenon in Art, Literature and Life*, Lanham, MD: Lexington Books, p 201.

25 Theodor W Adorno (1992), 'On Dickens' *The Old Curiosity Shop*: A Lecture', in *Notes to Literature, Vol. 2*, trans. Shierry Weber Nicholsen, New York: Columbia University Press, p 171.

26 Ibid., p 172.

27 Giorgio Agamben (2018), *Pulcinella or, Entertainment for Kids in Four Scenes*, trans. Kevin Attell, Kolkata and London: Seagull Books, p 17.

28 Ibid., p 49.

29 Michel de Montaigne (1991), 'How We Weep and Laugh at the Same Thing', in *The Complete Essays*, trans. M A Screech, London: Penguin, p 263.

30 Immanuel Kant (2006), 'On the Affects by Which Nature Promotes Health Mechanically', in *Anthropology from a Pragmatic Point of View*, trans. Robert B Louden, Cambridge: Cambridge University Press, pp 161–3.

31 Christoph Baumer (2006), *The Church of the East: An Illustrated History of Assyrian Christianity*, trans. Miranda G Henry, London and New York: I.B. Tauris, p 113.

Index

ABBA 59
  'The Day Before You Came' 59
Abbot of Unreason 87
abstract expressionism 5
Adler, Jerry 242
administered world 12, 14
Adorno, Theodor 14, 37–9, 92–5,
     122–3, 126, 142, 145–6, 148–9,
     161–2, 166–7, 190, 200–1, 208,
     223–4, 239–40
  and Max Horkheimer, *Dialectic*
    of Enlightenment 10–12, 93,
    122–3, 165
  Minima Moralia 92–3
  Negative Dialectics 94–5, 166–7
  Philosophy of New Music 145–6
Aeschylus 194
  The Oresteia 194
Aestheticism 158
Agamben, Giorgio 240–1, 243
alcohol 205
alcoholism 237
Allen, Woody 242
alphabetical order 86, 95
Altdorfer, Albrecht 153
Althusser, Louis 22
American Beauty 9
anarchism 26–7, 166, 248 n 10
anarchy 15, 40, 85, 95, 107–8, 131,
    187, 228

apocalypse 79–80, 130
Apocalypse Now 155–6
Arab Spring 25, 30
Aristophanes 211
Aristotle 86, 214
  Poetics 214, 216
Arlen, Richard 155
Art Nouveau 158
Artaud, Antonin 200
l'art pour l'art 158
Augustine of Hippo 198–9
  City of God 198–9
Auschwitz 78, 93, 152, 203
Austen, Jane 123, 238

Babel, Tower of 168
Babylonian religion 49–50, 51, 196
Bacchanalia 220
Badiou, Alain 30–34, 104
Baker, Josephine 115–16
Bakhtin, Mikhail 35, 88, 132, 218–19,
    225
Balzac, Honoré de 123
Bataille, Georges 200
Bauhaus 115, 162
Bavarian Soviet Republic 109, 114
Beckett, Samuel 77–8, 79, 80, 200–1,
    238
  Endgame 78, 201
  Happy Days 78, 80

Beckmann, Max 114, 152–3, 154
   The Grenade 152–3
   Resurrection 153
Beethoven, Ludwig van 124, 150
Beeton, Isabella 74, 86
   Book of Household Management 74
Benjamin, Walter 35, 160–1, 163
Berg, Alban 148
   Lyric Suite 148
   Violin Concerto 148
Beria, Lavrenti 178
Berlin Wall 89
Bernhard, Sandra 230
Bernhard, Thomas 200
Big Bang 53
biopower 13–14
The Birds 127–8
Black Death 78
Bonaparte, Napoleon 123
Bosch, Hieronymus 131, 153
Bow, Clara 155
Brecht, Bertolt 116, 236–7
   Mr Puntila and His Man Matti
    236–7
Breuer, Marcel 162
Brexit referendum 105–6
Browne, Hablot Knight 239
Buddhism 6
Burke, Edmund 48

The Cabinet of Doctor Caligari 116
Cage, John 48
Callot, Jacques 152
   Les Misères et Mal-heurs de la
    Guerre 152
Canetti, Elias 120
capitalism 6, 10, 15, 25, 33, 83, 84,
   171, 235
Carlyle, Thomas 40–2
   The French Revolution 40–2
   'On History' 40

Carnival 35, 88, 132, 211, 218–19,
   220–2, 225, 226, 244
Carroll, Lewis 129–33
   Through the Looking-Glass 129–33
Castle, Terry 218–20, 237, 238
Ceauşescu, Nicolae 34
Chain of Being 64–5, 69, 71
chance 3, 4, 91, 116, 135, 167, 180,
   199
Chandler, Raymond 243
chaos theory 4, 23–4, 72, 91, 135,
   167, 180, 199
Chaoskampf 196
Chaplin, Charlie 223–5
charivari 35
Chekhov, Anton 217–18
   The Seagull 217–18
Chesterton, GK 206
China 14, 17, 28–34, 105, 112, 171
Christianity 97, 245
Chrysostom, John 225
Cho Yeo-jeong 233
Choi Woo-shik 234
Cioran, Emil 200
Cleisthenes 204
cocaine 205, 224
Cold War 15, 19
Committee on Standards in Public
   Life (UK) 90
Conrad, Joseph 155
   Heart of Darkness 155
Constructivism 163
The Conversation 76
coronavirus (COVID-19) 16–19
Crawford, Paul 221
creatio ex nihilo 46–7, 52–3
Crimean War 157
Cultural Revolution 28–30, 31–2,
   33, 112
culture industry 11–12, 13, 15, 122
cyber-bullying 20

Dada 5, 138, 162, 163
Dahlhaus, Carl 150
Dante 217
Davies, Peter Maxwell 144–5
   An Orkney Wedding, with Sunrise
     144–5
Debussy, Claude 148
Decadents 158
deconstruction 22, 238
Defoe, Daniel 237
della Porta, Giambattista 64
   Magia Naturalis 64
DeLillo, Don 9
   Americana 9
Delius, Frederick 143
DeMarco, Donald 189
Democritus 167
De Niro, Robert 230
Derrida, Jacques 22
de Saussure, Ferdinand 22
Descartes, René 65–6, 67
   principle of doubt 71
   Regulae 65–6
détournement 232
Diary of a Lost Girl 116
Dickens, Charles 239–40
   The Old Curiosity Shop 238
Dighton, John 228
Dionysus 214, 215, 220
dissonance (in music) 125, 126,
   137–51
Dix, Otto 114, 153
   Cemetery between the Lines 153
Döblin, Alfred 115
   Berlin Alexanderplatz 115
Dostoevsky, Fyodor 238–9
Douglas, Mary 219
drugs 205–6
du Maurier, Daphne 127
Duvall, Robert 156

Eagleton, Terry 223, 226–7
Eisler, Hanns 116
Eliot, George 239
Elizabeth I 175, 193
Engels, Friedrich 165–6, 188
English Civil War 164, 169
Ephrem the Syrian 245
Epicurus 167
Erasmus 36
Euripides 214
   The Bacchae 214
European Union 103, 105

fascism 69, 229
Fauvism 162
Feast of Fools 87–8
Felixmüller, Conrad 114
festival of misrule 35
Fielding, Henry 237
Fish, Stanley 134
Flaubert, Gustave 238–9
Foucault, Michel 13, 63–6, 95–6
   The Order of Things 23, 63–6
France 119, 120, 152, 157, 162
Frank, Thomas 5
Frankfurt School 10–13, 14–15, 23
Freikorps 109–10
French Revolution 31, 40–2
Freud, Sigmund 139
Frye, Northrop 22
   Anatomy of Criticism 22
The Fugitive 154–5
Futurism 138, 162, 163

Garfinkel, Alan 91
gay marriage 186
George, Stefan 140
Germany 10, 14–15, 29, 89, 162
   inflation 111, 117, 119
   Weimar Republic 107–23

Gerstl, Richard 141
Gilhus, Ingvild 214–15
Gill, Eric 206
Girodet, Anne-Louis 154
Goya, Francisco 152, 154
  Los Desastres de la Guerra 152
Graeber, David 25
grammar 99–101
Great Leap Forward 28–9
Great War 108, 114, 151, 153
Greek War of Independence 157
Gropius, Walter 162
Grosz, George 114

Habermas, Jürgen 13
The Happiest Days of Your Life 227–9
Hardy, Oliver 212
Harrington, Alan 7
  Life in the Crystal Palace 7
Haydn, Joseph 47, 60, 138
  The Creation 47–8
Hayles, Katherine 24, 39
Hedren, Tippi 127
Hegel, Georg Wilhelm Friedrich 39,
    52, 68, 79, 102, 166, 168–9, 204
  Absolute Knowing 68
Heidegger, Martin 46
Heller, Agnes 236
Heraclitus 2
Herbert, George 74, 75
  Outlandish Proverbs 74, 75
Hesiod 42, 51, 77, 179, 184
  Theogony 51
Hill, Peter 147
Hinduism 6, 196
Hiroshima 152
Hitchcock, Alfred 127–8
Hitler, Adolf 119, 121
Hobbes, Thomas 59, 121
Homer 238

homosexuality 186
Hong Kong democracy movement
    103, 104–5
Hubbard, Al 6
Hugo, Victor 238–9
Hume, David 203–4
  Treatise of Human Nature 203–4
Hundred Flowers Campaign 171
Hussein, Saddam 164

Ibn Rushd (Averroes) 216
Ibn Sina (Avicenna) 216
Industrial Revolution 36–7, 227
Institute for Social Research 10
instrumental reason 11
intoxicants 5, 8, 42–3, 205–6, 222,
    224, 225–6, 235
Isbell, Lynne 197–8
Ives, Charles 142–4
  Three Places in New England
    142–4

Jakobson, Roman 22
James, Harold 119–20
James, William 66–7, 69, 70, 71
Jameson, Fredric 123–4, 150
jazz 115–16
Johnson, BS 135
  The Unfortunates 135
Jonson, Ben 213, 240–1
  Epicoene 213
Jörmungandr 196–7
Joyce, James 48, 134–5
  Finnegans Wake 134–5
  A Portrait of the Artist as a Young Man 48, 135
  Ulysses 135
Joyless Street 116
Judaism 102
Jugendstil 158

Kafka, Franz 95
Kaiser, Georg 116
Kant, Immanuel 31, 71, 82–3, 84,
    199–200, 243–4
    Critique of Practical Reason
        199–200
    Critique of Pure Reason 71
    Kantian block 73
Kapp, Wolfgang 109
Keaton, Diane 242
Khrushchev, Nikita 171
King, Preston 203
The King of Comedy 230–3
Kingdom of Heaven 43
Kipling, Rudyard 195
    The Jungle Book 195
koan 97
komos 100, 131, 215–16
Kontje, Todd 115
Kracauer, Siegfried 121–3, 128
Kramer, Lawrence 47

Lacan, Jacques 22
League of Nations 163–4
Leary, Timothy 6
Lee Sun-kyun 233
Léger, Fernand 154
Leibniz, Gottfried 80–2
    Theodicy 80–2
Lenin, Vladimir 32
Leviathan 195–6
Leviné, Eugen 114
Lévi-Strauss, Claude 22
Lewis, Jerry 230
Lisbon earthquake 78, 82
Locke, John 184
Lord of Misrule 87
Lotan 196
Lucretius 167
    De Rerum Natura 167
Lu Dingyi 171

McCarraher, Eugene 6, 8, 36
MacDonagh, John 155
McElligott, Anthony 120–1
Magnificat 75, 87
Mahler, Gustav 42, 123–6, 128, 135,
    137, 143
    death-shrieks 42, 124–6
    Symphony No 2 ('Resurrection')
        124–6, 143
Mammen, Jeanne 114
Manhattan Murder Mystery 242–3
Mann, Thomas 115
    Disorder and Early Sorrow 115
    The Magic Mountain 115, 254–5
        n 23
Mao Zedong 28–30, 31–2, 33,
    112, 171
Marcos, Ferdinand 34–5
Marcuse, Herbert 10
Marinetti, Filippo 163
Marryat, Frederick 73
    Masterman Ready 73
Marx, Karl 84–5, 102, 165–6, 188, 237
    (and Friedrich Engels) *The
        German Ideology* 170–1
    Marxism 10, 12, 22, 102, 166, 168,
        219
masquerade 35, 218–20, 237
MDMA 226
Meisel, Martin 37, 73, 83, 132, 158–9,
    182
Metropolis 116
Mieszkowski, Jan 100–1, 134
Milhaud, Darius 147–8
    Five Studies for Piano and
        Orchestra 147–8
Mill, John Stuart 67, 71
    System of Logic 67
Miller, Henry 77, 91
    Tropic of Cancer 77
Miller, William 221–2

Milton, John 20, 42, 174–83, 185
  Pandaemonium 20, 42, 177–83
  Paradise Lost 42, 174–83
Modern Times 223–5
Moholy-Nagy, László 153–4
  Dying Soldier 153–4
Montaigne, Michel de 243
Mozart, Wolfgang Amadeus 138
Mumford, Lewis 8, 27–8
  Technics and Civilization 27–8
Murray, Oswyn 215–16

Nabokov, Vladimir 4
Nansen Fugan 97
Nazism 4, 10, 29, 112, 118, 120–1,
  159–60, 224
Neue Sachlichkeit 114, 162
Newtonian science 72, 81, 83
Nietzsche, Friedrich 1, 36, 89, 100–1,
  112, 133, 134
  Zarathustra 1, 36
1917 155
Nobbs, David 9
Norton, Thomas 193
  Gorboduc 193–4
Nosferatu 116
Novalis (Georg von Hardenberg) 92
  Heinrich von Ofterdingen 92
NSDAP (Nazi Party) 117–18

O'Casey, Sean 245
  Juno and the Paycock 245
Occupy movement 25–26, 104
October Revolution 113
Our Wife 212
ouroboros 196–7
Ovid 54–56, 60, 168
  Metamorphoses 54–6, 131

Pandora's Box 116
parables (wedding feast) 74–5

Parasite 233–5, 237
Paris peace conference 118
Paul of Tarsus (St Paul) 173–4, 185,
  186, 245
Peloponnesian Wars 159–60
Perkins, Anthony 127
Petronius 192
  Satyricon 192
Peukert, Detlev 120–1
Picasso, Pablo 154
  Guernica 154
Piscator, Erwin 162, 163
Plato 86, 95, 100
Plautus 217
Pope, Alexander 183–5
  The Dunciad 183–5
Pre-Raphaelite Brotherhood 158
Prigogine, Ilya and Isabelle Stengers
  24, 39
  Order out of Chaos 24, 39
primal communism 166
Prince des Sots 87
Psycho 76, 127

quantum physics 53, 73
Quarterly Review 170

rappel à l'ordre 5, 162
Rathenau, Walter 111
rationality 10, 11, 23
Red Army Faction (Baader-Meinhof
  Group) 15
Red Guards 29–30
Religious Tract Society 73
Remarque, Erich Maria 115
  All Quiet on the Western Front 115
Rig Veda 50, 52
riots 30–4
Roh, Franz 114
Romantic movement 3, 92, 137,
  141, 188

Rothschild, Michael 91
Russia 30, 157, 163, 164
Rutherford, Margaret 228

Sackville, Thomas 193
   Gorboduc 193–4
Sadler, William 154
Santesso, Aaron 183
Sartre, Jean-Paul 46
Saturnalia 87–8
Schlemmer, Oskar 162
Schlichter, Rudolf 114
Schönberg, Arnold 138–42, 147,
   148, 150
   'Opinion or Insight?' 138
   Moses und Aron 148
   Piano Concerto 148
   Second String Quartet 140
   Six Little Pieces for Piano 141
   String Trio 148
   A Survivor from Warsaw 148
   Theory of Harmony 139–40
   Violin Concerto 148
Schopenhauer, Arthur 37, 200,
   236
Schubert, Franz 138
Schwartz, Regina 182
   'Milton's Hostile Chaos' 182
Second World War 4, 12, 37, 105,
   159, 164, 227
Seneca 192, 193
   Thyestes 192
Shakespeare, William 56–60, 151–2,
   189–93
   3 Henry VI 56–7
   King Lear 80
   Othello 59–60, 192, 212, 241
   The Rape of Lucrece 57
   Romeo and Juliet 58
   Titus Andronicus 189–93
   Troilus and Cressida 58–9

   Twelfth Night 222
   Venus and Adonis 57
Shannon, Claude 36
Sheen, Martin 155
Shelley, Percy 227
Sim, Alastair 228, 229
The Simpsons 32
slave trade 78
Sloterdijk, Peter 114–15, 117, 118,
   233, 235
Smith, Adam 83–84
   The Wealth of Nations 83–4
Smollett, Tobias 237
Snakes on a Plane 198
social media 19–20
Socratic dialogue 100, 115
Song Kang-ho 234
Soviet Union 110, 171
Spain 152, 154
SPD (Social Democratic Party) 108–9
Spengler, Oswald 200
Spenser, Edmund 57
   The Faerie Queene 57
Stalin, Joseph 171
State Law and Order Restoration
   Council (Myanmar) 90
Stefano, Joseph 76
Stein, Gertrude 134
   The Making of Americans 134
Sterne, Laurence 238
   Tristram Shandy 238
Stevens, Wallace 20–1
   'The Idea of Order at Key West'
   20–1
Strangers on a Train 127
Stravinsky, Igor 143
   The Rite of Spring 145–7
structuralism 21–2
Sun Tzu 158
Symbolism 158
symposium 100, 131, 215

Taruskin, Richard 140–1
Terence 217
Tiananmen Square protests 32–4, 105
Tolstoy, Leo 37
Toscanini, Arturo 13
Toynbee, Arnold 101
Treaty of Rapallo 110
Treaty of Versailles 89, 110–11, 118
twelve-tone system 148–9
28 Days Later 79
Twitter 20
Typhon 197

Ubermensch 206–7
United Nations 163–4
United States 4, 10, 14, 37, 103, 164
Updike, John 8
   Rabbit, Run 8

Vietnam War 155
void 45–6, 47, 50, 51, 54, 56, 68, 181, 182, 183, 198
Vritra 196

Wagner, Richard 125, 137, 156
   Die Walküre 156
Walker, Robert 127
Walton, Isaak 169
   The Compleat Angler 169
Webern, Anton 142
   Five Movements for String Quartet 142
   String Trio 148

   String Quartet 148
   Symphony 148
   Variations for Piano 148
Weill, Kurt 116
Weimar Republic 107–23
Wells, HG 71–2, 128
   'The Rediscovery of the Unique' 71–2
Whyte, William 7
   The Organization Man 7
Wilde, Oscar 238, 239
Wilson, Scott 221
Wilson, Sloan 7
   The Man in the Gray Flannel Suit 7
Wings 155
Woodstock festival 8
Wuolijoki, Hella 237
Wyndham, John 79
   The Day of the Triffids 79

Yates, Richard 8
   Revolutionary Road 8
Yeats, WB 107–8
   'The Second Coming' 107–8

Zeilinger, Anton 73
Zemlinsky, Mathilde 141
Zen Buddhism 97
Zhou Enlai 171
Zizek, Slavoj 17, 69–70, 75–7
Zola, Emile 238–9
Zupančič, Alenka 227, 228–9, 233, 241, 243